VERGIL

Aeneid Book 4

The Focus Vergil Aeneid Commentaries

For intermediate students

Aeneid 1 • *Randall Ganiban, editor* • *Available now*

Aeneid 2 • *Randall Ganiban, editor* • *Available now*

Aeneid 3 • *Christine Perkell, editor* • *Available now*

Aeneid 4 • *James O'Hara, editor* • *Available now*

Aeneid 5 • *Joseph Farrell, editor* • *Available 2012*

Aeneid 6 • *Patricia Johnston, editor* • *Available 2012*

For advanced students

Aeneid 1–6 • *Available 2012 (Single volume. Contributers as listed above)*

Aeneid 7–12 • *Available 2013 (Available only as a single volume)*

Contributors:

Randall Ganiban, editor • *Aeneid 7*

James O'Hara, editor • *Aeneid 8*

Joseph Farrell, editor • *Aeneid 9*

Andreola Rossi, editor • *Aeneid 10*

Charles McNelis, editor • *Aeneid 11*

Christine Perkell, editor • *Aeneid 12*

VERGIL

Aeneid Book 4

James J. O'Hara
University of North Carolina, Chapel Hill

Focus Publishing
R. Pullins Company
Newburyport, MA
www.pullins.com

Vergil
Aeneid Book 4
© 2011 James J. O'Hara

Focus Publishing/R. Pullins Company
PO Box 369
Newburyport, MA 01950
www.pullins.com

Interior illustration by Sam Kimball.

ISBN 13: 978-1-58510-228-0

Printed in the United States of America

12 11 10 9 8 7 6 5 4 3

1112H

Table of Contents

Preface

Aeneid 4 tells the story of Dido's love for Aeneas, and her death at her own hands after Aeneas heeds Jupiter's command that he leave her and continue on to play his destined role in Italy. This volume is an introductory commentary on *Aeneid* 4 for use at the intermediate level or higher. It provides a generous amount of basic information about grammar and syntax, as well as a complete vocabulary at the back of the book, so that students of varying experience will have what they need to understand Vergil's Latin. At the same time, it addresses issues of interpretation and style so that students of all levels will have a richer experience of the poem. Finally it includes extensive bibliographical references that will help readers pursue areas of special interest.

Like the other volumes in this series, the commentary takes as its starting point the notes in the valuable school edition of T.E. Page's *Vergil: Aeneid 1-6* (1894); briefer and differently focused versions of the new commentaries will also appear together in volumes on *Aeneid* 1-6 and 7-12 aimed at more advanced students. When still useful for today's student, Page's comments have been retained, but on nearly every line consideration has been given to the differing needs of today's student, and to the opinions of a century of scholarship that post-dates Page, both on Vergil's Latin and on literary and interpretive questions. The general introduction is by Randall Ganiban, general editor of the commentaries on *Aeneid* 1-6, and my appendices on meter and on stylistic terms are adapted from those in his 2008 *Aeneid* 2 commentary, and in fact this Preface draws upon his as a model and even repeats some of his sentences. The vocabulary for *Aeneid* 4 is adapted from that of the MacMillan/St. Martin's Press school edition by Rev. H. M. Stephenson, originally published in 1888.

The Latin text of *Aeneid* 4 used here is based on that of F.A. Hirtzel (Oxford, 1900), with several changes in punctuation and with the following differences in readings: at 4.269 I print *ac* where he has *et*, at 4.559 *iuventa* where he has *iuventae*, at 4.427 *cinerem* where he and Conte have *cineres* (see n.), at 4.593 *diripientque* where he and Conte print the emendation *deripientque*, and at 4.646 *rogos* where Hirtzel has *gradus* (Mynors, Geymonat and Conte print *rogos*). This edition places the Latin text and commentary on the same page. Often references are given to sections of Allen and Greenough's *New Latin Grammar* (1903; cf. Mahoney 2001), or to my appendix on stylistic terms and appendix on meter: the end of the Introduction to Book 4 will describe these references further.

Thanks are due to a number of friends and colleagues for their assistance in my work on this project, though none can be held responsible for any errors that remain. My former colleague Maura Lafferty read a draft of an early section and gave useful comments based on her experience teaching Vergil in fifth-semester Latin. Four Chapel Hill graduate students did excellent work as research assistants: Dennis McKay, who made crucial contributions at the start of the project, John Henkel, who gave learned comments based on his close reading of a draft and on his experience teaching *Aeneid* 4 with a version of the commentary, and then later in the process Erika Damer and Zack Rider were dependable and precise. Zoe Stamatopoulou at the University of Georgia and Adam Gitner at Princeton also taught with a draft of the commentary and made useful comments both on content and on clarity and effectiveness. I was fortunate enough to have a draft of the whole commentary read by my colleague Cecil Wooten, whose help makes me feel more optimistic that I may have gotten Vergil's Latin right, by Vergilian Matthew Carter, who made a number of precise and helpful points especially on meter and style, and by my teacher David Ross, who made suggestions on Latin and on style and also tried to make sure I wasn't missing the poetic forest for the philological trees. I thank my Focus-*Aeneid* teammates Joe Farrell, Christine Perkell and Pat Johnston for discussions in person and by email. Warmest thanks go to Randall Ganiban for his invitation to work on *Aeneid* 4 for Focus, and for the patience, learning, and insight into Vergil's Latin that have characterized his excellent comments on my shaggy drafts and his responses to my endless questions.

I dedicate this volume to the memory of the Rev. Thomas Tighe, S.J., and the Rev. Robert Healey, S.J., the Jesuits with whom I first read Vergil at Boston College High School and the College of the Holy Cross.

J.O'H.
Chapel Hill

Introduction to Vergil's *Aeneid*

Vergil's lifetime and poetry

Publius Vergilius Maro (i.e. Vergil)[1] was born on October 15, 70 BCE near the town of Mantua (modern Mantova) in what was then still Cisalpine Gaul.[2] Little else about his life can be stated with certainty, because our main source, the ancient biography by the grammarian Donatus (fourth century CE),[3] is of questionable value.[4] The historical and political background to Vergil's life, by contrast, is amply documented and provides a useful framework for understanding his career. Indeed, his poetic development displays an increasing engagement with the politics of contemporary Rome, an engagement that culminates in the *Aeneid*.

Vergil lived and wrote in a time of political strife and uncertainty. In his early twenties the Roman Republic was torn apart by the civil wars of 49-45 BCE, when Julius Caesar fought and defeated Pompey and his supporters. Caesar was declared *dictator perpetuo* ("Dictator for Life") early in 44 BCE but was assassinated on the Ides of March by a group of senators led by Brutus[5]

---

1 The spelling "Virgil" (*Virgilius*) is also used by convention. It developed early and has been explained by its similarity to two words: *virgo* ("maiden") and *virga* ("wand"). For discussion of the origins and potential meanings of these connections, see Jackson Knight 1944, 36-7 and Putnam 1993, 127-8 with notes.

2 Cisalpine Gaul, the northern part of what we now think of as Italy, was incorporated into Roman Italy in 42 BCE. Mantua is located ca. 520 kilometers north of Rome.

3 This biography drew heavily from the *De poetis* of Suetonius (born ca. 70 CE).

4 Horsfall 1995, 1-25; 2006, xxii-xxiv argues that nearly every detail is unreliable.

5 Kingship was hateful to the Romans ever since Brutus' own ancestor, Lucius Junius Brutus, led the expulsion of Rome's last king, Tarquin the Proud, in ca. 509 BCE, an act that ended the regal period of Rome and initiated the Republic (cf. *Aeneid* 6.817-18). In killing Caesar, Brutus claimed that he was following the example of his great ancestor—an important concept for the Romans.

and Cassius. They sought to restore the Republic, which, they believed, was being destroyed by Caesar's domination and intimations of kingship.[6]

The assassination initiated a new round of turmoil that profoundly shaped the course of Roman history. In his will, Caesar adopted and named as his primary heir his great-nephew Octavian (63 BCE-14 CE), the man who would later be called "Augustus."[7] Though only eighteen years old, Octavian boldly accepted and used this inheritance. Through a combination of shrewd calculation and luck, he managed to attain the consulship in 43 BCE, though he was merely nineteen years of age.[8] He then joined forces with two of Caesar's lieutenants, Marc Antony (initially Octavian's rival) and Lepidus. Together they demanded recognition as a Board of Three (*triumviri* or "triumvirs") to reconstitute the state as they saw fit, and were granted extraordinary powers to do so by the Roman senate and people. In 42 BCE they avenged Caesar's murder by defeating his assassins commanded by Brutus and Cassius at the battle of Philippi in Macedonia, but their alliance gradually began to deteriorate as a result of further civil strife and interpersonal rivalries.

Vergil composed the *Eclogues*, his first major work, during this tumultuous period.[9] Published ca. 39 BCE,[10] the *Eclogues* comprise a sophisticated collection of ten pastoral poems that treat the experiences of shepherds.[11] The poems were modeled on the *Idylls* of Theocritus, a Hellenistic Greek poet of the third century BCE (see below). But whereas

---

6   For the reasons behind Caesar's assassination and the fall of the Republic, see the brief accounts in Scullard 1982, 126-53 and Shotter 2005, 4-19.

7   See below.

8   By the *lex Villia annalis* of 180 BCE, a consul had to be at least forty-two years of age.

9   Other works have been attributed to Vergil: *Aetna, Catalepton, Ciris, Copa, Culex, Dirae, Elegiae in Maecenatem, Moretum*, and *Priapea*. They are collected in what is called the *Appendix Vergiliana* and are generally believed to be spurious.

10   This traditional dating, however, has been called into question through re-evaluation of *Eclogue* 8, which may very well refer to events in 35 BCE. See Clausen 1994, 232-7.

11   Coleman 1977 and Clausen 1994 are excellent commentaries on the *Eclogues*. For a discussion of the pastoral genre at Rome, see Heyworth 2005. For general interpretation of the *Eclogues*, see Hardie 1998, 5-27 with extensive bibliography in the notes, and Volk 2008a.

Theocritus' poetry created a world that was largely timeless, Vergil sets his pastoral world against the backdrop of contemporary Rome and the disruption caused by the civil wars. *Eclogues* 1 and 9, for example, deal with the differing fortunes of shepherds during a time of land confiscations that resonate with historical events in 41-40 BCE.[12] *Eclogue* 4 describes the birth of a child during the consulship of Asinius Pollio (40 BCE) who will bring a new golden age to Rome.[13] By interjecting the Roman world into his poetic landscape,[14] Vergil allows readers to sense how political developments both threaten and give promise to the very possibility of pastoral existence.

The *Eclogues* established Vergil as a new and important poetic voice, and led him to the cultural circle of the great literary patron Maecenas, an influential supporter and confidant of Octavian. Their association grew throughout the 30s.[15] The political situation, however, remained precarious. Lepidus was ousted from the triumvirate in 36 BCE because of his treacherous behavior. Tensions between Octavian and Antony that were simmering over Antony's collaboration and affair with the Egyptian queen Cleopatra eventually exploded.[16] In 32 BCE, Octavian had Antony's powers revoked,

12   Octavian rewarded veterans with land that was already occupied.

13   This is sometimes called the "Messianic Eclogue" because later ages read it as foreseeing the birth of Christ, which occurred nearly four decades later. The identity of the child is debated, but the poem may celebrate the marriage between Marc Antony and Octavian's sister Octavia that resulted from the treaty of Brundisium in 40 BCE; this union helped stave off the immediate outbreak of war between the two triumvirs. For more on this poem, see Van Sickle 1992 and Petrini 1997, 111-21, as well as the commentaries by Coleman 1977 and Clausen 1994.

14   In addition to the contemporary themes that Vergil treats, he also mentions or dedicates individual poems to a number of his contemporaries, including Asinius Pollio, Alfenus Varus, Cornelius Gallus, and probably Octavian, who is likely the *iuvenis* ("young man") mentioned at 1.42 and perhaps also the patron addressed at 8.6-13.

15   For the relationship between Augustus and the poets, see White 2005. White 1993 is a book-length study of this topic. For an overview of literature of the Augustan period from 40 BCE-14 CE, see Farrell 2005.

16   In addition to the political conflicts, there were also familial tensions: Antony conducted a decade-long affair with Cleopatra, even though he had married Octavia, Octavian's (Augustus') sister, as a result of the treaty of Brundisium in 40 BCE (see n. 13 above). Antony divorced Octavia in 32 BCE.

and war was declared against Cleopatra (and thus in effect against Antony as well). During a naval confrontation off Actium on the coast of western Greece in September of 31 BCE, Octavian's fleet decisively routed the forces of Marc Antony and Cleopatra, who both fled to Egypt and committed suicide in the following year to avoid capture.[17] This momentous victory solidified Octavian's claim of being the protector of traditional Roman values against the detrimental influence of Antony, Cleopatra, and the East.[18]

Vergil began his next work, the *Georgics*, sometime in the 30s, completed it ca. 29 BCE in the aftermath of Actium, and dedicated it to Maecenas. Like the *Eclogues*, the *Georgics* was heavily influenced by Greek models—particularly the work of Hesiod (eighth century BCE) and of Hellenistic poets[19] such as Callimachus, Aratus, and Nicander (third–second centuries BCE). On the surface, it purports to be a poetic farming guide.[20] Each of its four books examines a different aspect or sphere of agricultural life: crops and weather signs (book 1), trees and vines (book 2), livestock (book 3), and bees (book 4). Its actual scope, however, is much more ambitious. The poem explores the nature of humankind's struggle with the beauty and difficulties of the agricultural world, but it does so within the context of contemporary war-torn Italy. It bears witness to the strife following Caesar's assassination, and sets the chaos and disorder inherent in nature against the upheaval caused by civil war (1.461-514). Moreover, Octavian's success and victories are commemorated both in the introduction (1.24-42) and conclusion (4.559-62) of the poem, as well as in the beginning of the third book (3.1-39). Thus once

---

17   For the history of the triumviral period, see the brief accounts in Scullard 1982, 154-71 and Shotter 2005, 20-7; for more detailed treatments, see Syme 1939, 187-312, Pelling 1996 and Osgood 2006. For discussion of the contemporary artistic representations of Actium, see Gurval 1995.

18   This ideological interpretation is suggested in Vergil's depiction of the battle on Aeneas' shield (8.671-713).

19   See discussion below.

20   Recent commentaries on the *Georgics* include Thomas 1988 and Mynors 1990. For interpretation, see the introduction to the *Georgics* in Hardie 1998, 28-52 with extensive bibliography in the notes, and Volk 2008b. Individual studies include Wilkinson 1969, Putnam 1979, Johnston 1980, Ross 1987, Perkell 1989, and Nappa 2005. For allusion in the *Georgics*, see Thomas 1986, Farrell 1991, and Gale 2000.

again, the political world is juxtaposed against Vergil's poetic landscape, but the relationship between the two is not fully addressed.[21]

Octavian's victory represented a turning point for Rome's development. Over the next decade, he centralized political and military control in his hands. He claimed to have returned the state (*res publica*) to the senate and Roman people in 27 BCE.[22] His powers were redefined, and he was granted the name "Augustus' ("Revered One") by the senate. It is true that he maintained many traditional Republican institutions, but in reality he was transforming the state into a monarchy. So effective was his stabilization and control of Rome after decades of civil war that he reigned as *Princeps* ("First Citizen") from 27 BCE to 14 CE, creating a political framework (the Principate) that served the Roman state for centuries.[23]

Vergil wrote his final poem, the *Aeneid*, largely in the 20s, during the first years of Augustus' reign, when the Roman people presumably hoped that the civil wars were behind them but feared that the Augustan peace would not last. The *Aeneid* tells the story of the Trojan hero Aeneas. He fought the Greeks at Troy and saw his city destroyed, but with the guidance of the gods and fate he led his surviving people across the Mediterranean to a new homeland in Italy.[24] As in the *Eclogues* and *Georgics*, Vergil interjects his contemporary world into his poetic world. In the *Aeneid*, however, the

---

21   The overall meaning of the *Georgics* is contested. Interpretation of the *Georgics*, like that of the *Aeneid* (see below), has optimistic and pessimistic poles. Otis 1964 is an example of the former; Ross 1987 the latter. Other scholars, such as Perkell 1989, fall in between by discerning inherent ambivalence. For discussion of these interpretive trends, see Hardie 1998, 50-2.

22   Augustus, *Res Gestae* 34.

23   For general political and historical narratives of Augustus' reign, see the relatively brief account in Shotter 2005; longer, more detailed treatments can be found in A. H. M. Jones 1970, Crook 1996, and Southern 1998. A classic and influential book by Syme 1939 paints Augustus in extremely dark colors. For broader considerations of the Augustan age, see the short but interesting volume by Wallace-Hadrill 1993 and the more comprehensive treatments by Galinsky 1996, 2005. For the interaction of art and ideology in the Augustan Age, see Zanker 1988.

24   For general interpretation of the *Aeneid*, see the recent overviews provided by Hardie 1998, 53-101, Perkell 1999, Anderson 2005, Johnson 2005, Fratantuono 2007, and Ross 2007. For the literary and cultural backgrounds, see Martindale 1997, Farrell 2005, and Galinsky 2005.

thematic connections between these two realms are developed still more explicitly, with Aeneas' actions shown to be necessary for and to lead ultimately to the reign of Augustus. (See below for further discussion.)

Vergil was still finishing the *Aeneid* when he was stricken by a fatal illness in 19 BCE. The ancient biographical tradition claims that he traveled to Greece, intending to spend three years editing his epic there and in Asia, but that early on he encountered Augustus, who was returning to Rome from the East, and decided to accompany him. Vergil, however, fell ill during the journey and died in Brundisium (in southern Italy) in September of 19 BCE. The *Aeneid* was largely complete but had not yet received its final revision. We are told that Vergil asked that it be burned, but that Augustus ultimately had it published. While such details regarding Vergil's death are doubted, the poem clearly needed final editing.[25] However, its present shape, including its sudden ending, is generally accepted to be as Vergil had planned.

Vergil and his predecessors

By writing an epic about the Trojan war, Vergil was rivaling Homer, the greatest of all the Greek poets. The *Aeneid* was therefore a bold undertaking, but its success makes it arguably the quintessential Roman work because it accomplishes what Latin poetry had always striven to do: to appropriate the Greek tradition and transform it into something that was both equally impressive and distinctly "Roman."

Homer's *Iliad* tells the story of the Trojan war by focusing on Achilles' strife with the Greek leader Agamemnon and consequent rage in the tenth and final year of the conflict, while the *Odyssey* treats the war's aftermath by relating Odysseus' struggle to return home. These were the earliest and most revered works of Greek literature,[26] and they exerted a defining influence on both the overall framework of the *Aeneid* and the close details of its poetry. In general terms, *Aeneid* 1-6, like the *Odyssey*, describes a hero's return (to a new) home after the Trojan war, while *Aeneid* 7-12, like the *Iliad*, tells the story of a war. But throughout the *Aeneid*, Vergil reworks ideas, language, characters, and scenes from both poems. Some ancient critics faulted Vergil for his use

---

25   We can be sure that the poem had not received its final revision for a number of reasons, including the presence of roughly fifty-eight incomplete or "half" lines. See commentary note on 4.42-4.

26   These poems were culminations of a centuries-old oral tradition and were written down probably in the eighth century BCE.

of Homer, calling his appropriations "thefts." Vergil, however, is said to have responded that it is "easier to steal his club from Hercules than a line from Homer."[27] Indeed, Vergil does much more than simply quote material from Homer. His creative use and transformation of Homeric language and theme are central not only to his artistry but also to the meaning of the *Aeneid*.

Though Homer is the primary model, Vergil was also influenced significantly by the Hellenistic Greek tradition of poetry that originated in Alexandria, Egypt in the third century BCE. There scholar-poets such as Apollonius, Callimachus, and Theocritus reacted against the earlier literary tradition (particularly epic which by their time had become largely derivative). They developed a poetic aesthetic that valued small-scale poems, esoteric subjects, and highly polished style. Hellenistic poetry was introduced into the mainstream of Latin poetry a generation before Vergil by the so-called "neoterics" or "new poets," of whom Catullus (ca. 84-ca. 54 BCE) was the most influential for Vergil and for the later literary tradition.[28]

Vergil's earlier works, the *Eclogues* and *Georgics*, had been modeled to a significant extent on Hellenistic poems,[29] so it was perhaps a surprise that Vergil would then have turned to a large-scale epic concerning the Trojan war.[30] However, one of his great feats was the incorporation of the Hellenistic and neoteric sensibilities into the *Aeneid*. Two models were particularly important in this regard: the *Argonautica* by Apollonius of Rhodes, an epic retelling the hero Jason's quest for the Golden Fleece, and Catullus 64, a poem on the wedding of Peleus and Thetis.[31] Both works brought the great and elevated heroes of the past down to the human level, thereby offering

---

27 *...facilius esse Herculi clavam quam Homeri versum subripere* (Donatus/ Suetonius, *Life of Vergil* 46).

28 Clausen 1987, 2002, George 1974, Briggs 1981, Thomas 1988, 1999, and Hunter 2006 display these influences, while O'Hara 1996 provides a thorough examination of wordplay (important to the Alexandrian poets) in Vergil.

29 The *Eclogues* were modeled on Theocritus' *Idylls*; the *Georgics* had numerous models, though the Hellenistic poets Callimachus, Nicander, and Aratus were particularly important influences. See above.

30 For example, at *Eclogue* 6.3-5, Vergil explains in highly programmatic language his decision to compose poetry in the refined Callimachean or Hellenistic manner rather than traditional epic. See Clausen 1994, 174-5.

31 On the influence of Apollonius on Vergil, see the important book by Nelis 2001.

new insights into their strengths, passions and flaws, and both greatly influenced Vergil's presentation of Aeneas.

Of Vergil's other predecessors in Latin literature, the most important was Ennius (239-169 BCE), often called the father of Roman poetry.[32] His *Annales*, which survives only in fragments, was an historical epic about Rome that traced the city's origins back to Aeneas and Troy. It remained the most influential Latin poem until the *Aeneid* was composed, and provided a model not only for Vergil's poetic language and themes, but also for his integration of Homer and Roman history. In addition, the *De Rerum Natura* of Lucretius (ca. 94-55/51 BCE), a hexameter poem on Epicurean philosophy, profoundly influenced Vergil with its forceful language and philosophical ideas.[33]

Finally, Vergil drew much from Greek and Roman[34] tragedy. Many episodes in the *Aeneid* share tragedy's well-known dramatic patterns (such as reversal of fortune), and explore the suffering that befalls mortals often as a result of the immense and incomprehensible power of the gods and

---

32   Ennius introduced the dactylic hexameter as the meter of Latin epic. Two earlier epic writers were Livius Andronicus who composed a translation of Homer's *Odyssey* into Latin, and Naevius who composed the *Bellum Punicum*, an epic on the First Punic War. Both Naevius and Livius wrote their epics in a meter called Saturnian that is not fully understood. For the influence of the early Latin poets on the *Aeneid*, see Wigodsky 1972.

33   See Hardie 1986, 157-240 and Adler 2003. The influence of the Epicurean Philodemus on Vergil (and the Augustans more generally) is explored in the collection edited by Armstrong, Fish, Johnston, and Skinner 2004. For Lucretius' influence on Vergil's *Georgics*, see especially Farrell 1991 and Gale 2000.

34   The earliest epic writers (Livius, Naevius and Ennius; see above) also wrote tragedy, and so it is not surprising that epic and tragedy would influence one another. Latin tragic writing continued into the first century through the work of, e.g., Pacuvius (220-ca. 130 BCE) and Accius (170-ca. 86 BCE). Their tragedies, which included Homeric and Trojan War themes, were important for Vergil. However, since only meager fragments of them have survived, their precise influence is difficult to gauge.

fate.[35] As a recent critic has written, "The influence of tragedy on the *Aeneid* is pervasive, and arguably the single most important factor in Virgil's successful revitalization of the genre of epic."[36]

The *Aeneid* is thus indebted to these and many other sources, the study of which can enrich our appreciation of Vergil's artistry and our interpretation of his epic.[37] However, no source study can fully account for the creative, aesthetic, and moral achievement of the *Aeneid*, which is a work unto itself.

The *Aeneid*, Rome, and Augustus

While Aeneas' story takes place in the distant, mythological past of the Trojan war era, it had a special relevance for Vergil's contemporaries. Not only did the Romans draw their descent from the Trojans, but the emperor

---

35   Cf., e.g., Heinze 1915, trans. 1993, 251-8. Wlosok 1999 offers a reading of the Dido episode as tragedy, and Pavlock 1985 examines Euripidean influence in the Nisus and Euryalus episode. Hardie 1991, 1997, Panoussi 2002, 2009 and Galinsky 2003 examine the influence of tragedy, particularly in light of French theories of Greek tragedy (e.g. Vernant and Vidal-Naquet 1988), and draw important parallels between the political and cultural milieus of fifth-century Athens and Augustan Rome. On tragedy and conflicting viewpoints, see Conte 1999 and Galinsky 2003.

36   Hardie 1998, 62. See also Hardie 1997.

37   See Farrell 1997 for a full and insightful introduction to the interpretive possibilities that the study of intertextuality in Vergil can offer readers. For a general introduction to intertextuality, see Allen 2000. For the study of intertextuality in Latin literature, see Conte 1986, Farrell 1991, 1-25, Hardie 1993, Fowler 1997, Hinds 1998, and Edmunds 2001. For Vergil's use of Homer, see Knauer 1964b, Barchiesi 1984, in Italian, Gransden 1984, and Cairns 1989, 177-248. Knauer 1964a, written in German, is a standard work on this topic; those without German can still benefit from its detailed citations and lists of parallels. For Vergil's use of Homer and Apollonius, see Nelis 2001.

Augustus believed that Aeneas was his own ancestor.[38] Vergil makes these national and familial connections major thematic concerns of his epic.

As a result, the *Aeneid* is about more than the Trojan war and its aftermath. It is also about the foundation of Rome and its flourishing under Augustus. To incorporate these themes into his epic, Vergil connects mythological and historical time by associating three leaders and city foundations: the founding of Lavinium by Aeneas, the actual founding of Rome by Romulus, and the "re-founding" of Rome by Augustus. These events are prominent in the most important prophecies of the epic: Jupiter's speech to Venus (1.257-96) and Anchises' revelation to his son Aeneas (6.756-853). Together these passages provide what may be called an Augustan reading of Roman history, one that is shaped by the deeds of these three men and that views Augustus as the culmination of the processes of fate and history.[39]

This is not to say that the associations among Aeneas, Romulus, and Augustus are always positive or unproblematic, particularly given the ways that Aeneas is portrayed and can be interpreted.[40] To some, Vergil's Aeneas represents an idealized Roman hero, who thus reflects positively on Augustus by association.[41] In general this type of reading sees a positive imperial ideology in the epic and is referred to as "optimistic" or "Augustan." Others are more troubled by Vergil's Aeneas, and advocate interpretations that challenge the moral and spiritual value of his actions, as well as of the role

---

38   Augustus' clan, the Julian *gens*, claimed its descent from Iulus (another name for Aeneas' son Ascanius) and thus also from Aeneas and Venus. Julius Caesar in particular emphasized this ancestry; Augustus made these connections central to his political self-presentation as well. See, e.g., Zanker 1988, 193-210 and Galinsky 1996, 141-224.

39   See O'Hara 1990, however, for the deceptiveness of prophecies in the *Aeneid*.

40   For general interpretation of the *Aeneid*, see n. 24 (above).

41   This type of reading is represented especially by Heinze 1915, trans. 1993, Pöschl 1950, trans. 1962, and Otis 1964. More recent and complex Augustan interpretations can be found in Hardie 1986 and Cairns 1989.

of the gods and fate. Such readings perceive a much darker poetic world[42] and have been called "pessimistic" or "ambivalent."[43] Vergil's portrayal of Aeneas is thus a major element in debates over the epic's meaning.[44]

Randall Ganiban, *Series Editor*

---

42   See, e.g., Putnam 1965, Johnson 1976, Lyne 1987, and Thomas 2001. Putnam's reading of the *Aeneid* has been particularly influential. Of the ending of the poem he writes: "By giving himself over with such suddenness to the private wrath which the sight of the belt of Pallas arouses, Aeneas becomes himself *impius Furor*, as rage wins the day over moderation, disintegration defeats order, and the achievements of history through heroism fall victim to the human frailty of one man" 1965, 193-4. For a different understanding of Aeneas' wrath, see Galinsky 1988.

43   For a general treatment of the optimism/pessimism debate, see Kennedy 1992. For a critique of the "pessimistic" view, see Martindale 1993; for critique of the "optimistic" stance and its rejection of "pessimism," see Thomas 2001, and for brief historical perspective on both sides, see Schmidt 2001. For the continuing debate over the politics of the *Aeneid* and over the Augustan age more generally, see the collections of Powell 1992 and Stahl 1998.

44   Indeed some readers also question whether it is even possible to resolve this interpretive debate because of Vergil's inherent ambiguity. See Johnson 1976, Perkell 1994, and O'Hara 2007, 77-103. Martindale 1993 offers a critique of ambiguous readings.

Introduction to Book 4:
Its Role in the *Aeneid*

Book 4 depicts the tragedy of Dido, Vergil's most memorable character, in the most celebrated, influential, moving and powerful part of the *Aeneid*. The reader approaching Book 4 should be familiar with the events of Books 1-3. In Book 1 Dido and Aeneas met after Aeneas and his men were shipwrecked on Dido's shores by the storm sent by Juno to divert him from Italy, and Venus sent Cupid in disguise to make Dido fall in love with him. In Books 2 and 3 we are to imagine Dido listening to Aeneas' narration of the fall of Troy and of his wanderings; at the end of 2 the *imago* of his wife Creusa tells him a "royal wife" awaits him in "Hesperia," and Book 3 ends with the death of his father Anchises. In Book 4, Dido resists but then yields to her love for Aeneas (after further interference from the gods), and a relationship that she thinks is marriage, but which must end with Aeneas' departure, after Jupiter sends Mercury to remind him that his mission requires him to continue on to Italy, where a kingdom awaits him and his son Ascanius. The speeches of Dido and Aeneas after she discovers that he is leaving are brilliantly crafted masterpieces showing doomed lovers in an impossible position, as Dido rages passionately and Aeneas suppresses his emotions. More than half of the book—which is the shortest book in the poem—describes Dido's reaction to Aeneas' imminent departure: she deceives her sister by feigning an elaborate magical ritual, curses Aeneas in a way that has a lasting impact both on the rest of the poem and on Roman history, and then kills herself.

The book is a marvel of effective adaptations from earlier poems and genres; the reader should both admire the skill with which Vergil recasts and combines earlier material, and ponder the effects of our recollections of these models on our reactions to scenes and characters. Book 4 offers us, in Wendell Clausen's words, "a love story told in Hellenistic style," which is to say in the style of post-classical Greek literature, and "an epyllion or miniature epic, so far as the larger decorum of epic permitted, concentrating on the woman's emotion and ending unhappily" (Clausen 1987: 40). Romans of Vergil's time knew a Dido story in which she never met Aeneas (cf. references in 198 n.): either Vergil or the third-century BCE Roman poet Naevius invented the story of their love. Dido's role echoes many models, each of which casts interesting light on her character and actions. From Homer she recalls the females and males who threaten to delay Odysseus: not only the marriageable young Nausicaa, the goddess Calypso and the witch Circe, but also the Cyclops Polyphemus who curses Odysseus as Dido will Aeneas, and Alcinoos who is both Odysseus' host and the audience for his tales, which are the model for Aeneas' narrative in Books 2 and 3. Dido also resembles the young Medea of Apollonius' third-century BCE *Argonautica*, worried about being betrayed by Jason, the older Medea of Euripides's fifth-century tragedy, furious that she has been betrayed, and the Ariadne abandoned by Theseus in Catullus 64, written just a generation before Vergil. The importance of tragedy extends beyond the borrowings from the *Medea*, as the several other allusions to tragic models and even an overt reference to a tragic character (cf. 471 n.) show. In her death scenes Dido resembles Euripides' Alcestis, Deianeira the wife of Heracles in Sophocles' *Women of Trachis*, and above all the Ajax of Sophocles' play and perhaps Roman versions, whose proud suicide prefigures Dido's.

Like many tragic characters, Dido can be seen as ruined either by the gods or by her own actions and choices—or by both. We can see Aeneas in the role of Odysseus fleeing a female who delays his return, but also as Jason not only with Medea, but also with Apollonius' Queen Hypsipyle, from whom Jason departs on cordial terms in *Argonautica* Book 1. If Dido is like Ariadne then Aeneas is like Catullus' Theseus, except that we know more of why he leaves. Besides the borrowings from Catullus, there are links to recent love poetry, including elegies written in the previous decade about male speakers who neglect traditional Roman values when overcome or even "enslaved" by love of a woman; the vivid depiction of Dido's feigned magic in particular suggests the use of magic in love poetry. Love gone wrong was featured also in the mythical stories of "Sorrows of Love" summarized by the Greek scholar-poet Parthenius for Vergil's friend the Latin elegiac poet Cornelius Gallus (both Parthenius and Gallus are key figures in the history of Latin literature whose work is mostly lost). There are echoes too of Lucretius' Epicurean poem *De Rerum Natura*, from the generation before Vergil, both on the subject of love (which Lucretius advised not being troubled about) and on the gods' lack of interest in human affairs.

Book 4 suggests recent and more distant Roman history as well. Dido's deathbed curse of Aeneas is presented as the "aetion" or origin story of the enmity between Rome and Carthage, the city in North Africa directly across from Sicily, which led to three memorable and perilous wars from the mid-third to mid-second century BCE. In telling this origin story Vergil pursues themes from Roman history, but also writes aetiological poetry of the type popular with the third-century Alexandrian poets like Callimachus and Apollonius who were so influential on him: there are times when Vergil is most Roman by being most Alexandrian. Within the poem itself, Aeneas' disastrous encounter with Dido also explains why he faces trouble in Italy in Books 7-12, because some of his troubles match Dido's curse. The North African queen Dido is also linked to Cleopatra Queen of Egypt, and so Aeneas' affair with her suggests those of both Julius Caesar and especially Mark Antony with Cleopatra: in leaving Dido Aeneas does what Antony would not (cf. above pp. 3-4). But although numerous details mark Dido as a foreigner, other features of the text make her share Roman values, including how she rules her people, consults the gods, and proudly reviews her life as she faces her death. Besides shifting and incomplete allegorical correspondences with particular figures, there is a more general allegorical point about the necessity and cost of choosing duty over personal concerns, in contrast to the self-serving actions of the powerful military figures whose quest for personal preeminence helped destroy the Roman Republic in the century leading up to the Battle of Actium in 31 BCE.

How should readers interpret these links to literary models and historical figures? And how should the actions of Aeneas and Dido in Book 4 affect our views of Aeneas' mission, and of the poem's attitude toward Augustan or Roman values? These are complex and challenging questions. The book follows tragedy's practice of presenting irresolvable conflict that can be looked at from different viewpoints. Dido's furious anger against Aeneas is given full expression, and the feelings of Aeneas relatively little attention, yet his mission has been explained earlier, and is affirmed here. Many have found Aeneas cold and unsympathetic, while others admire his willingness to sacrifice personal happiness for his duty. Certainly he is an imperfect hero, even though critics of some eras have tried to explain away any perceived flaws; readers of Book 4 should remember that at the end of Book 3 he lost the guidance of his father Anchises. Dido can be seen as a victim of the gods or of Aeneas' carelessness, or as a dangerous representative of unrestrained passion or *furor*. As the latter she would be associated with

Juno and Allecto and other female characters in the poem, and gender will also influence how we read the book: Juvenal 6.435 complains about a woman who "pardons Dido." Both Dido and Aeneas live in a world in which confusion and misunderstanding seem inevitable: questions of right, wrong, duty, loyalty, piety, guilt and innocence in the story of Dido and Aeneas are blurred and ambiguous beyond any simple resolution.

Juvenal's line about the woman favoring Dido makes him part of a long series of authors and artists from antiquity to the present who contribute to the "reception" of the Dido story (see esp. Lord 1969, Desmond 1994, and the essays in Burden 1998). Ovid deals briefly with the story in *Metamorphoses* 14.78-81, and his *Heroides* 7 is a letter from Dido to Aeneas; from exile Ovid writes in a poetic letter to Augustus that no part of the *Aeneid* is read more than the story of Dido and Aeneas (*Tristia* 2.533-6). The story is discussed or imitated by Petronius, Silius Italicus, Apuleius, and Augustine who in *Confessions* 1.13 talks with regret of how he wept for Dido but not for his own sinfulness. In the fifth century CE Macrobius says that no book of the *Aeneid* was more popular with painters, sculptors and designers of tapestries (*Saturnalia* 5.17.; cf. Anderson 2006). Later allusions or versions come in Fulgentius' allegorical treatment, medieval courtly romance, Chaucer's *Legend of Good Women*, Marlowe's *Dido, Queen of Carthage*, Dante both when he mentions Dido and when he is describing Beatrice, Purcell in his seventeenth-century opera *Dido and Aeneas*, and even the songs of the contemporary pop-star "Dido" (on whom see Smith 2003).

The bibliography on Book 4 is vast. In general see the commentaries of Pease 1935 and Austin 1954 (and a "Green and Yellow" Cambridge Commentary by Sergio Casali is forthcoming), and also the work of Heinze 1993, Newton 1957, Pöschl 1962, Monti 1981, Commager 1981, Clausen 2002 and 1987, Perkell 1981, Horsfall 1990 and 1995, Nuttal 1998, Spence 1999, Schiesaro 2008. On models and intertextuality see Pease 1935, Clausen 2002 and 1987, Cairns 1989 on Dido and elegy, Nelis 2001 and Krevans 2002-3 on Apollonius, Schiesaro 2008, and Panoussi 2009. On reception see Desmond 1994, Burden 1998, Starr 1991, Thomas 2001, Schiesaro 2008. The section of Servius's late-fourth-century commentary dealing with *Aeneid* 4 has now been translated by McDonough et al. 2004. Further references are given below for many passages.

Please note: the following commentaries on Book 4 will be cited by the author's last name without date: Page 1894, Pease 1935, Austin 1954, Conington 1963 and R. D. Williams 1971-2. The fundamental debt of the volumes in this series to the commentary of Page 1894 has been described in the Preface. References to *Allen and Greenough's New Latin Grammar* ("AG;" see Mahoney 2001) are provided by section number (e.g. "AG §333"), which will be the same in the 1903 edition, Mahoney's revision, or the version online at the Perseus Project (www.perseus.tufts.edu). *OLD* refers to the *Oxford Latin Dictionary* (2nd edition 1996). References to Ennius are made to the editions of Skutsch (Sk.), Jocelyn (J), and Warmington (W). Terms marked with an asterisk (e.g. "alliterative*") are defined in my appendix on stylistic terms; for metrical features there are references (e.g. 64 n.) to the appendix on meter.

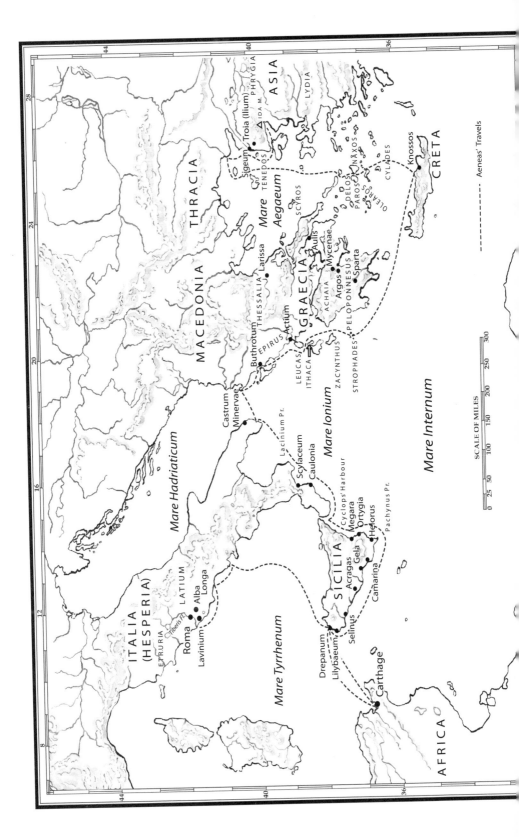

- - - - - Aeneas' Travels

SCALE OF MILES

0   25 50   100   150   200   250   300

ITALIA (HESPERIA)

LATIUM

ETRURIA

Tiberis Fl.

Roma

Alba Longa

Lavinium

Mare Tyrrhenum

Drepanum

Lilybaeum

Selinus

SICILIA

Acragas

Gela

Camarina

Helorus

Ortygia

Megara

Cyclops' Harbour

Pachynus Pr.

Caulonia

Scylaceum

Lacinium Pr.

Castrum Minervae

Mare Ionium

Carthage

AFRICA

Mare Internum

Mare Hadriaticum

MACEDONIA

THRACIA

Larissa

THESSALIA

Buthrotum

EPIRUS

Actium

LEUCAS

ITHACA

ZACYNTHUS

STROPHADES

GRAECIA

ACHAIA

Aulis

Mycenae

Argos

PELOPONNESUS

Sparta

Mare Aegaeum

SCYROS

Sigeum

Troia (Ilium)

IDA M.

PHRYGIA

ASIA

LYDIA

TENEDOS

DELOS

PAROS

NAXOS

OLEAROS

CYLADES

Knossos

CRETA

LIBER QUARTUS

At regina gravi iamdudum saucia cura

1-172: Dido resists and then yields to her passion for Aeneas.
The book begins with Dido's growing love for Aeneas, described in alliterative* lines of vivid imagery of fire and wound, much of it suggestive of treatments of love in Greek drama and epigram, Catullus, and Lucretius (1-5). Dido cannot sleep (as lovesick heroines often cannot). She tells her sister Anna of her attraction to Aeneas but determination to remain loyal to her dead husband Sychaeus, saying that to yield to Aeneas would be a violation of *pudor*, in a way that probably suggested to Roman readers the old notion that a woman should have only one husband throughout her lifetime (6-30; see 27 n.). Anna, playing the advisor role familiar from Greek drama and epic (see 8 n.), argues for the advantages both to Dido and to Carthage of yielding to her feelings for Aeneas, and persuades Dido to consult the gods (31-55). Dido sacrifices, but (as the poet laments) consulting the omens cannot help her, though Vergil does not tell us exactly why, and to some extent the reader's ignorance matches Dido's (56-66). As she burns with love and wanders the city Vergil compares her to a deer fatally wounded by an unknowing shepherd (66-73). More symptoms of love follow, and construction on the new city of Carthage stops (74-89). Juno and Venus, each thinking to deceive the other, conspire to have Aeneas and Dido meet in a cave during a storm that interrupts a hunt (90-128); hunting imagery will also be prominent throughout the book. The plan is carried out: the hunt (depicted on the well-known Low Ham mosaic from a Roman villa in England; see Anderson 2006, who also discusses more recent discoveries) begins with a simile (141-50) comparing Aeneas to Apollo, which corresponds with the simile that linked Dido to Diana in 1.498-502. The encounter in the cave is marked by supernatural signs that mimic or mock a real wedding ceremony (165-8); from now on Dido considers herself married to Aeneas (see 160-72 n.), but the narrator says that with the name "marriage" she covers over a *culpa* (169-72).

1. **AT regina**: these words begin three sections of Book 4, here, at 296 and at 504; at 12.54 they are used of the Latin queen Amata, in one of many echoes of the Dido story in Books 7-12. **saucia cura:** "wounded by care/love," as though the adjective were a passive verb. The phrase recalls Ennius *Medea* 216 J = 261 W *amore saevo saucia*, Lucretius, *DRN* 4.1048 *saucia amore* (see the extensive note of Brown 1987 ad loc.), and Catullus 64.250, where Ariadne *multiplices animo volvebat saucia curas*. We are in the world of Greek and Roman poetry about love. Wound imagery and wounds will recur, as Vergil breathes life into old erotic clichés: Dido is metaphorically* wounded by love here and in the next line, is compared to a wounded deer in the simile at 68-73, and will literally die by sword in 659-92; in the last passage the image becomes reality, as often in Vergil. Cf. Newton 1957, Hardie 1986, 232-3 (on "figure to reality"), Lyne 1989, 179-81, Nelis 2001, 130, Clausen 1997, 40-1 = 2002, 75-6, Ross 2007, 33-4. On love supposedly being foreign to Roman epic but often featured in it, see Hinds 2000.

vulnus alit venis et caeco carpitur igni.
multa viri virtus animo multusque recursat
gentis honos: haerent infixi pectore vultus
verbaque, nec placidam membris dat cura quietem.   5
postera Phoebea lustrabat lampade terras
umentemque Aurora polo dimoverat umbram,

2. **venis:** probably instrumental ("feeds *with* her veins/blood"), but could also describe place ("*in* her veins"), with the preposition omitted as often in poetry. **caeco...igni:** "hidden," "unseen"; in 1.688 Venus told Cupid to breathe unseen fire (*occultum inspires ignem*) into Dido. *Igni* is an i-stem ablative, though *igne* occurs in other writers, and at *Aen.* 8.255. Fire imagery will also be crucial throughout the book, and as with the wound imagery, metaphor* will become reality with the real fire of Dido's pyre: cf. 23, 67, 281, 360, 640, 670, as well as Aeneas' men's view of the fire at 5.1-6. Here in 2 the fire imagery includes the word *cura*, derived etymologically* by Vergil's older contemporary Varro and by the fourth-century Vergilian commentator Servius from *cor urit* ("burns the heart"; see O'Hara 1996, 150 for etymologizing in 1-5). **carpitur:** "is wasted," "consumed bit by bit." Note the alliteration* in 2-3 of "v," "c," and "m."

3. **multa...multus:** recalls *multum...multa* in 1.3-5 in the description of Aeneas' struggles; applied to *virtus* and *honos* here, the words suggest both Aeneas' abundant supply of these heroic qualities, and that thoughts of them recur to Dido frequently. **viri virtus:** Cicero and others comment on the derivation *virtus < vir*, stressing that the word means "manly courage and virtue," and Vergil's juxtaposition here seems to point to that etymology*.

4. **gentis honos:** suggests both Aeneas' own ancestry, and the Trojans more generally; Dido associates birth and quality, as would a Roman aristocrat (cf. her words in 12). **infixi:** the word is used metaphorically* here, then literally of a wound in 689 when Dido is dying; *haerent* here is also echoed by *haeret* in the simile of the wounded deer at 69-73. **vultus:** either poetic plural for "face," or a plural suggesting that repeated images of Aeneas occur to Dido; the latter would suggest the images of the absent lover as described at Lucretius, *DRN* 4.1061-2: *nam si abest quod ames, praesto simulacra tamen sunt / illius et nomen dulce obversatur ad auris*; cf. too below 83 *absens absentem*.

5. **nec...dat:** "and does not allow." **nec...quietem:** cf. the similar phrase used of Aeneas' anxiety at 10.217: *neque enim membris dat cura quietem*; for *placida quies* in earlier descriptions of distressed heroines cf. Reed 2007, 61.

6-7. **postera...umbram:** Vergil has many ways to describe dawn (there is a full list in Sparrow 1931, 85-7); these two lines examine it from slightly differing perspectives (theme and variation*). **Phoebea:** < *Phoebeus*, "of Phoebus Apollo the sungod"; modifies *lampade*. **lustrabat:** probably "move over," "traverse," but the word can also suggest illumination and purification (cf. Horsfall on 7.148). **Aurora:** goddess of dawn, modified by *postera* in 6. **polo:** ablative of separation < *polus*, "the end of an axis," "a pole"; = "the heavens."

cum sic unanimam adloquitur male sana sororem:
"Anna soror, quae me suspensam insomnia terrent!
quis novus hic nostris successit sedibus hospes,   10
quem sese ore ferens, quam forti pectore et armis!
credo equidem, nec vana fides, genus esse deorum.
degeneres animos timor arguit. heu, quibus ille
iactatus fatis! quae bella exhausta canebat!

8. **unanimam:** "of one mind," "like-minded"— but Anna will dismiss the concerns that Dido enumerates in 15-29. Does this suggest that Dido was not sincerely committed to the lofty standards she sets for herself? Anna plays the advisor role like that of the nurse in Euripides' *Hippolytus*, and, from Apollonius Rhodius' *Argonautica*, both the sister of Medea (3.645-743) and the nurse of Queen Hypsipyle (1.668-97); see Nelis 2001, 136-9, Krevans 2002-3, and on her speech Highet 1972, 80-1. **male sana:** "not sane," "disturbed," with the adverb modifying the adjective; *male* + adjective is a feature of colloquial Latin (see Austin's note).

9. **insomnia:** neuter plural = "dreams"; Vergil adapts Medea's words at Apoll. Rhod. *Arg.* 3.636, and more generally the literary motif of the dreaming woman in love; cf. Monti 1981, 53. The alternate manuscript reading *terret* would make *insomnia* a feminine singular (= "sleeplessness").

9-14: The interrogatives *quae...quis...quem...quam...quibus...quae* are used in exclamation: *quae...insomnia* (n. plural) = "what dreams...!" (AG [=Allen & Greenough] §333); the repetition of a word in different cases like this is called polyptoton*.

10. **hospes:** guest-friendship and the conventions for the treatment of guests in ancient epic provide one vantage point for viewing the relationship of Dido and Aeneas; cf. 323-4 and n., and Gibson 1999.

11. **quem sese ore ferens:** "'bearing himself with what an aspect," though that is not a very literal translation of this difficult Latin, which would be "bearing what a self...!" The interrogative/exclamatory adjective *quem* matches the case of the reflexive pronoun *sese* which it modifies. *os* = "'mouth'" < *os, oris*, n., and by synecdoche* "face, appearance," though it could also refer to speech. **quam:** not the pronoun but the adverb: "how ...." **forti pectore et armis:** ablatives of quality or description (AG §415); *armis* is taken by some as < *arma*, "weapons," by others as < *armus*, "shoulder"; it may suggest both, as at 12.433, where Aeneas puts his arms (and weapons) around his son Ascanius.

12. **credo...genus esse deorum:** indirect statement, interrupted by the interjection *nec vana fides* (supply *est* and cf. ellipsis*; forms of *esse* will often be omitted). Dido has heard that Aeneas is of divine stock (cf. 1.615-18), and his story and the qualities she mentions here make her believe it; contrast 365 below.

14. **iactatus:** used by the main narrator of Aeneas' toils at 1.3 (cf. above 3 n. on *multa...multus*) and by the shade of his father Anchises in the underworld, also with an exclamatory pronoun, at 6.693. **exhausta:** from *exhaurio*, "go through," "endure," or more literally "drink to the last dregs." **canebat:** the poet's word for his own activity (cf. 1.1 *cano*), it suggests Aeneas as "singer" of Books 2-3, as Odysseus is of *Odyssey* 9-12 (cf. esp. *Od.* 11.368 where Alcinoos likens him to a singer), but it literally must mean "narrate," since we cannot imagine that Dido hears Aeneas speak in hexameters, although Vergil might be playing with the idea of the overlap between himself and Aeneas as narrator in Books 2-3.

si mihi non animo fixum immotumque sederet   15
ne cui me vinclo vellem sociare iugali,
postquam primus amor deceptam morte fefellit,]
si non pertaesum thalami taedaeque fuisset,
—huic uni forsan potui succumbere culpae. Classy
Anna, fatebor enim, miseri post fata Sychaei   20
coniugis et sparsos fraterna caede penatis

15-16. si...non...sederet: *sederet* is imperfect subjunctive in a present contrary-to-fact condition; its subject is the whole noun clause *ne...iugali* ("not to be willing" or "that I not be willing"), with *vellem* an imperfect subjunctive in a substantive clause. **fixum immotumque:** neuter in agreement (as a predicate after *sederet*) with the substantive clause *ne...iugali* (AG §289d). **cui:** "anyone" = *alicui*, which is not used after *nisi, si, num* or *ne*; here it is the indirect object of *sociare*.

17. amor: here either Sychaeus (see below n. on 20-1) or the love Dido felt for him. **deceptam...fefellit:** Latin often uses a participle (*deceptam*, supply *me*) and a verb (*fefellit* < *fallo*) where English would have two verbs. Both verbs mean "deceive"; that love frustrated and deceived her because it ended with Sychaeus' death. Aeneas uses *fefellit* at 2.744 to describe his wife Creusa's disappearance.

18. si non pertaesum...fuisset: Dido adds a second protasis, this one past contrary-to-fact: "If I had not been...." *Pertaesum...fuisset* is pluperfect subjunctive of an impersonal semi-deponent; *pertaedit* (*mihi*) + genitive means "I am extremely weary of, disgusted at" (the prefix *per-* is intensifying). The impersonal construction accounts for the neuter *pertaesum*. **thalami taedaeque:** "marriage-bed" and "torch," hendiadys* for "marriage," since torches were used at weddings. Is Dido weary of or disgusted with marriage because her first husband died, or (as we soon learn) because she has rejected local African suitors?

19. huic: construe with *culpae*, but a temporary ambiguity allows a reader, before coming to *culpae*, to think *huic* refers to Aeneas (Clausen 1987, 42 = 2002, 77). **potui:** expresses possibility and so the indicative can stand in the apodosis of a condition where we might expect the subjunctive (AG §517c; for *potui* with present infinitive, see AG §486a). **culpae:** Dido refers to the idea of yielding to Aeneas as a *culpa*, which can mean "fault," "offence," "wrongdoing" or "weakness"; cf. 172 n.

20-1. fata Sychaei: Sychaeus was Dido's husband, treacherously murdered at the hearth (*penates*) by her brother Pygmalion (see 1.343-59), from whom she fled, moving from Tyre in Phoenicia to the site of Carthage in North Africa. *Fata Sychaei* could mean "the death of Sychaeus" or simply "what happened to Sychaeus." Line 21 is more specific, as often with clauses in Vergil introduced by *et*, and points to the former. **fraterna caede:** "the murder carried out by my brother." The phrase appears at Catullus 64.181 (a poem influential on *Aen.* 4) in words Ariadne uses to describe Theseus' killing of her half-brother the Minotaur. **penatis:** V. uses both *-is* and *-es* for 3rd decl. accus. pl. (Aulus Gellius, *Noctes Atticae* 13.21 says he chose whichever sounded best; cf. Conte 2009, xxvi); the manuscripts often offer both forms, and modern editors must chose. Cf. *pallentis* 26, *manis* 34, etc.

solus hic inflexit sensus animumque labantem
impulit. agnosco veteris vestigia flammae.]
 ⌐sed mihi vel tellus optem prius ima dehiscat
vel pater omnipotens abigat me fulmine ad umbras,   25
pallentis umbras Erebo noctemque profundam,
⌐ante, pudor, quam te violo, aut tua iura resolvo.   *Class*

22. **hic:** i.e. Aeneas. The meter shows that the "i" is short, so that this can only be the nominative singular masculine of the demonstrative, in which the vowel was short in early Latin (as it is in most Latin textbooks today) but long later; Vergil uses the short vowel here as an archaism suggestive of earlier Latin poetry. **sensus:** accusative plural, fourth declension. **labantem:** < *labo, labare*, "totter, be ready to fall"; either proleptic* after *impulit* ("drives it so that it begins to fall"), or Dido describes herself as turned, tottering, and driven without quite knowing what came first, what next; for imagery of collapse see also 391 n. Cupid in 1.719-22, following Venus' instructions, began to wipe out Dido's memory of Sychaeus and tempt her with a new love.

23. **agnosco veteris vestigia flammae:** Aeneas makes Dido feel the fire of erotic passion just as Sychaeus did; Dido uses the same fire imagery as the narrator (cf. 2 n.).

24-6. **sed mihi...:** Dido would rather have the earth swallow her up, or Jupiter (*pater omnipotens*) blast her with lightning, than allow herself to violate *pudor* and its laws. Is this the typically overstated and easy claim of a lover (Pease) or is Dido more seriously calling destruction upon herself, with a "solemn and awful prayer" (Austin; cf. also Hardie 1986, 269)? Different readers' answer to this question will do much to determine how they react to the events of Book 4. **optem:** "potential subjunctive of assertion, like *velim*, but a much stronger word, for *optare* marks an ambition or an ideal. *Dehiscat* (like *abigat* below) is a jussive dependent on *optem*" (Austin; cf. AG §447). **prius:** seems unnecessary to us with *ante* in 27, but follows Homeric usage, and *tellus ... dehiscat* is a Homeric phrase (e.g. *Iliad* 4.182). **umbras, / pallentis umbras:** Vergil often uses epanalepsis* or the syntactically unnecessary repetition in one line of a word from the previous line in order to create pathos or suggest strong emotion (see Wills 1997). **Erebo:** the underworld (personified when invoked by Dido below in 510). **noctemque profundam:** does the adjective suggest the depth of the night, or the darkness of the underworld deep below the earth?

27. **pudor:** addressed by Dido in an apostrophe* that also involves personification*. *Pudor* is a key but elusive term. Kaster 1997, 4-5: "*pudor* primarily denotes a displeasure with oneself caused by vulnerability to just criticism of a socially diminishing sort.... People feel *pudor* not only because they are seen, or fear being seen, by someone else, but also because they see themselves and know that their present behavior falls short of their past or ideal selves." Dido may feel *pudor* because she had wished to remain loyal to Sychaeus; note her fear in 534 of the derision of the suitors mentioned in 35-8. But Kaster also notes that for women, *pudor* "was largely limited to a single frame of reference—the sexual: the *pudor* of women is, in effect, congruent with their *pudicitia*, or sexual respectability." Is Dido to be judged more as a public figure, or as a (Roman) woman? What laws or restraints of *pudor* would Dido violate by pursuing Aeneas, especially if she sought to marry him? Dido's feelings also involve the Roman concept of *univiratus*, or a woman's having only one husband for life, which in Vergil's time was partly revered, partly ignored as old-fashioned. Only *univirae* could sacrifice to the goddess Pudicitia, but around the time of the posthumous publication of the *Aeneid* widows were strongly encouraged to remarry by the Augustan marriage laws of 18 BCE. Cf. Treggiari 1991, 233-7, Rudd 1990, 154-9.

ille meos, primus qui me sibi iunxit, amores
abstulit; ille habeat secum servetque sepulcro."
sic effata sinum lacrimis implevit obortis.⏋   30
Anna refert: "o luce magis dilecta sorori,
solane perpetua maerens carpere iuventa
nec dulcis natos Veneris nec praemia noris?
id cinerem aut manis credis curare sepultos?⏌
esto: aegram nulli quondam flexere mariti,   35

28-9. **ille meos, primus qui:** = *ille, qui primus me sibi iunxit, meos amores abstulit*; the convoluted word order (cf. hyperbaton*) reflects Dido's confusion and agitation, and adds emphasis to the first three words. For *primus* as an adjective with adverbial force cf. AG §290. **meos...amores:** "my love," perhaps even "my ability to love"; the plural is common. Sychaeus will in fact have and keep Dido's love in the underworld: see 6.473-4. **sepulcro:** ablative of place. Note the nine "s" sounds in 28-9; the triple alliteration* at the end of 29 may suggest archaic Latin verse like that of Ennius, whose epic *Annals* date to the early second century BCE, and others.

31. **luce:** ablative of comparison, "light (of life)," "life." **sorori:** dative of agent common in poetry after perfect passive participles (here *dilecta*), where in prose we would expect *a/ab* + ablative (AG §375).

32. **perpetua...iuventa:** ablative of time or duration of time, probably "for your whole youth," rather than "endless youth." Since Dido has been married, the logic may seem strained to us, thinking that marriage ends a girl's "youth," but the point is probably that Dido has not yet had a child, which for a Roman reader is what an adult woman should do. Dido should probably be thought of as having married and lost Sychaeus while quite young, and so as still fairly young (so Clausen 1987, 106-7 = 2002, 211-12). **carpere:** 2nd person singular future indicative passive, alternate form of *carperis*; meter shows that the first "e" is long; for the meaning, cf. *carpitur* in 2.

33. **Veneris nec:** in prose would be *nec Veneris*; the postponement of connective particles is a stylistic device providing metrical flexibility that the neoteric poets of the mid-first century BCE (e.g. Catullus) took over from the Hellenistic poets (e.g. Callimachus and Theocritus, 3rd century BCE). See Ross 1969, 67-9. **noris:** syncopated form of *noveris*, future perfect of *nosco*, but to be translated as a simple future, just as the perfect form *novi* means "I have learned, I know."

34. **cinerem aut manis:** *cinis* is the "ash" of a corpse; the *manes* are the spirit(s) of the dead. Anna suggests that both Sychaeus' body (*cinis*) and spirit (*manes*) have been buried, and asks whether they care about "this" (*id*), i.e. Dido's denying herself the pleasures of love. Several times in Book 4 Dido's attitude, like Anna's here, will resemble that of the Epicureans (including the poet Lucretius from the generation before Vergil), who all taught that humans have no sensation after death (cf. nn. on 209, 379, 550-1, and also Dyson 1996 and Gordon 1998). Petronius *Satyr.* 111 has a seducer use this line on the "Widow of Ephesus."

35-8. **esto:** future imperative, "so be it," "granted..."; looks forward to what Anna says next. **aegram:** in what way does Anna think Dido is "sick" (cf. *male sana* in 8)? With sorrow for Sychaeus? With disgust at her suitors (cf. above 18)? **flexere:** = *flexerunt*; this alternate form of the 3rd plural perfect is extremely useful in the hexameter. **mariti:** (potential) husbands.

non Libyae, non ante Tyro; despectus Iarbas,
ductoresque alii, quos Africa terra triumphis
dives alit: placitone etiam pugnabis amori?
nec venit in mentem quorum consederis arvis?⟧
hinc Gaetulae urbes, genus insuperabile bello,   40
et Numidae infreni cingunt et inhospita Syrtis;
hinc deserta siti regio lateque furentes
Barcaei. quid bella Tyro surgentia dicam
germanique minas?

Libyae...Tyro: probably locatives, though for *Tyro* we would expect *Tyri*; it may be a "local ablative or an ablative of origin" (Austin). **Iarbas**: an African king whose complaints to his father Jupiter will soon play a crucial role in the story (cf. 196-221); his name is trisyllabic. **triumphis / dives**: Africa is "rich in victories" (ablative of specification, AG §418), but the phrase may also suggest the later triumphal processions of Roman generals victorious over Carthaginian foes in the Punic wars. **amori**: dative, not ablative; dative with verbs of contending is a poetic construction (AG §368a); prose would have *cum* + ablative (cf. 108 *tecum...contendere*).

39. **quorum**: possessive genitive with *arvis* introducing the indirect question that is the subject of *venit*: "does it not occur to you in whose fields...?" **consederis**: perfect subjunctive in indirect question, in primary sequence after *venit*, which meter shows to be present tense, not perfect.

40-1. **genus**: in loose apposition to *Gaetulae urbes*, as though Vergil had said *Gaetuli*. The Gaetuli live to the south of Carthage. **bello**: ablative of specification. **infreni**: "without bridles," which is how the Numidians (who live southwest of Carthage) ride, but also with the suggestion that they are themselves "unbridled" or uncontrollable. **inhospita Syrtis:** the dangerous sandbanks off the coast between Carthage and Cyrene; cf. 1.111.

42-4. **siti**: ablative of cause (AG §404), explaining why the area is deserted. **Barcaei**: the people of Barce, a city of Cyrenaica actually founded much later; the word may also suggest Hannibal, who belonged to the Barca family. **quid...dicam**: deliberative subjunctive (AG §444). Anna uses the figure of *praeteritio**, in which a speaker pretends or claims to "pass over" a topic, but nevertheless discusses it in whole or in part. **Tyro**: ablative of place from which or place where. **germanique minas?**: for the danger from Dido's brother, cf. 20-1 n.

Line 44 is the first example in Book 4 of a "half-line," a line left unfinished at the time of Vergil's death. In his *Life of Vergil*, Donatus claims that on his deathbed Vergil wanted the *Aeneid* burned but ultimately left it in the hands of Varius and Tucca to edit *ea conditione ..., ne quid adderent quod a se editum non esset, et versus etiam imperfectos, si qui erant, relinquerent.* There are roughly 58 incomplete verses in the entire *Aeneid* (the number is disputed because some half-lines may have been completed by later readers and thus now seem complete). There are five half-lines in Book 4 (44, 361, 400, 503, 516). Some half-lines have seemed to modern readers to work so well that some think Vergil meant to leave them incomplete (cf. 361 and n.), but this seems extremely unlikely. On half-lines see Sparrow 1931, Pease on 4.44, Gould 1990, 109-12 (who says "The conclusion is inescapable: Virgil had no intention of leaving half-lines in the *Aeneid*"), Austin on 6.94, Harrison on 10.16, Horsfall on 7.702.

dis equidem auspicibus reor et Iunone secunda   45
hunc cursum Iliacas vento tenuisse carinas.
quam tu urbem, soror, hanc cernes, quae surgere regna
coniugio tali! Teucrum comitantibus armis
Punica se quantis attollet gloria rebus!
tu modo posce deos veniam, sacrisque litatis   50
indulge hospitio,|causasque innecte morandi,
dum pelago desaevit hiems et aquosus Orion,
quassataeque rates, dum non tractabile caelum."
    His dictis impenso animum flammavit amore
spemque dedit dubiae menti solvitque pudorem.| 55

45-6. dis...auspicibus...et Iunone secunda: double ablative absolute construction, modifying the indirect statement whose verb is *tenuisse*. Anna mentions Juno as patron of both marriage and Carthage (her special concern for Carthage is a major theme in *Aeneid* 1 and 4; see 1.12-22 and below 106), and goes on to suggest that she is "favorable," in ironic ignorance of her role in sending the storm that brought Aeneas to Carthage (see 1.50-75). **carinas:** literally "keels," but a frequent synecdoche* for "ship."

47-9. **quam...quae...quantis:** cf. above on 9 for interrogatives used in exclamations; here as there we have the repeated *qu-* words. **Teucrum:** genitive plural; the archaic –*um* form (rather than –*orum*) suggests epic style. **Punica...gloria:** would sound chilling for Romans, given how close Carthage came to defeating them in the Punic wars; in one sense the phrase indicates what is at stake in the Dido-Aeneas episode, which provides a mythological "aetion" or origin-story for the enmity between Rome and Carthage (see 615-29 n., and the passages collected in Horsfall 1990, 128-31).

50. **modo:** adverb. **posce deos veniam:** double accusative after a verb of asking (AG §396). *Venia* can mean "leave" or "permission" to do something, with no connotation of wrong, or it can mean "forgiveness" for a wrong done; Anna must mean the former. **sacrisque litatis:** *litare* is "to obtain favor by sacrificing." Pease: "the ablative absolute here expresses a condition; if the sacrifices have turned out favorably Dido may assume that the gods favor her course of action."

51. **hospitio:** dative after *indulge*. **morandi:** gerund after *causas*, almost = *morae*.

52-3. **aquosus Orion:** probably a second subject for *desaevit*, although *sunt or est* must be supplied for each noun in 53. The constellation's November setting is usually accompanied by storms; at 309-13 and 430 weather will figure in Dido's pleas to Aeneas not to depart. Orion's name begins with a long "o" in Greek and at *Aen.* 3.517, 7.719, a short "o" here, 1.535 (where Austin has a good note), 10.763, and a few other times in Latin verse. **quassataeque rates:** Aeneas' ships were "shattered" in the storm in Book 1 (1.551 *quassatam...classem*).

54-89. *Dido sacrifices to see if the gods will approve of her love for Aeneas. Her passion grows, and a simile compares her to a deer wounded by an unknowing shepherd.*

54. **impenso:** our oldest manuscripts and commentators disagree as to whether to read *impenso* or *incensum* here; Austin suggests, *his dictis incensum animum inflammavit amore*; see his n.

55. **solvitque pudorem:** "and broke down her sense of shame" or "and unshackled shame," i.e. set it free from all restraints. Cf. Medea's farewell to shame at *Arg.* 3.785-6, and above 27 n.

principio delubra adeunt pacemque per aras
exquirunt; mactant lectas de more bidentis
legiferae Cereri Phoeboque patrique Lyaeo,
Iunoni ante omnes, cui vincla iugalia curae.
ipsa tenens dextra pateram pulcherrima Dido   60
candentis vaccae media inter cornua fundit,
aut ante ora deum pinguis spatiatur ad aras,
instauratque diem donis, pecudumque reclusis
pectoribus inhians spirantia consulit exta.

56. **pacem:** i.e. *pax deorum*, suggesting "freedom from divine anger, approval of current activities" (*OLD*). Dido seeks to learn the will of the gods through extispicy, a type of divination that involved reading the internal organs (cf. *exta* in *64*) of sacrificial animals.

57. **de more:** "in accordance with custom," which dictates that the victims should be without blemish or fault, and perhaps of a certain age and appearance. **bidentis:** "sheep" that are one to two years old; at this age sheep have two prominent teeth, which appear to be their only ones.

58. **legiferae Cereri Phoeboque patrique Lyaeo:** Dido sacrifices to Ceres the lawgiver, Phoebus Apollo, Dionysus Lyaeus, and Juno the goddess of marriage, probably for their association with the founding of cities and with marriage.

59. **vincla iugalia:** "bonds of marriage"; Juno was sometimes called *Iuno Iuga*; cf. Feeney 1991, 133, and also Hersch 2010, 118-22 who sees Dido's sacrifices as like those before a Roman wedding. **curae:** dative of purpose in double dative construction (AG §382), with *sunt* understood.

60. **dextra:** supply *manu* (ellipsis*).

61. **candentis:** = *candidae*; Vergil often uses a participle where he might have used an adjective. The animal may be white because it is offered to a deity in heaven (Pease). **fundit:** may have *pateram* in 60 as its object, or may be used with no object, with *tenens* alone governing *pateram*.

62. **pinguis:** "rich," "greasy," because of the blood and fat of the victims slaughtered there.

63. **instaurat:** a technical term from Roman religious practice which denoted the repetition of acts and sacrifices if there had been a problem with the performance of them. Dido "renews" or "inaugurates" the day with her sacrifices (*donis* are lit. "gifts").

64. **pectoribus:** the final syllable is lengthened in arsis (see appendix on meter, 146 with Pease's n., and Austin on 1.308). **inhians:** "gaping over," "poring over" (with dative). **spirantia:** "living," "palpitating," since the entrails were consulted the moment they were laid bare; Vergil in a sense "zooms in" to give us a vividly realistic close-up of the sacrifice, yet we cannot see exactly what Dido sees.

heu, vatum ignarae mentes! quid vota furentem,   65
quid delubra iuvant? est mollis flamma medullas
interea et tacitum vivit sub pectore vulnus.
uritur infelix Dido totaque vagatur
urbe furens, qualis coniecta cerva sagitta,
quam procul incautam nemora inter Cresia fixit   70
pastor agens telis liquitque volatile ferrum
nescius: illa fuga silvas saltusque peragrat
Dictaeos; haeret lateri letalis harundo.

65. **heu…**: the narrator turns aside in apostrophe*, but with interestingly ambiguous syntax. If *vatum* here is possessive genitive with *mentes*, then the phrase means "alas, ignorant minds of prophets," since prophets know nothing about the future. If objective genitive with *ignarae*, then it means "minds ignorant of prophets," suggesting that the rites have been performed incorrectly, or that Dido and Anna misunderstood the haruspices. The reader's difficulty in handling the syntax of the genitive *vatum* parallels the difficulty both Dido and the reader have in interpreting the entrails. Dido does not learn from the sacrifices that her love for Aeneas is going to lead to a bad end; the reader does not learn exactly why this happens. See O'Hara 1993. **quid:** (along with *quid* in the next line) an adverbial accusative or accusative of respect, best translated as "how?" or "in what way?" **furentem:** the problem of *furor* or the passionate madness that overcomes human beings in love and war is a major theme in the *Aeneid*, as it was in Vergil's earlier *Eclogues* and *Georgics. Furor* is associated with Juno, Dido (cf. 69, 91, 101, 283, 298, 376, 433, 465, 501, 548, 646, 697), Turnus, and at times Aeneas; in Book 1 Jupiter predicts that under the future Caesar *furor impius* (the adjective specifically suggests the madness of civil war) will be locked up in chains (1.295), and at the end of the poem Aeneas as he kills Turnus will be described as *furiis accensus et ira / terribilis* (12.946-7).

66-7. **est:** 3rd sing. of *edo*. **mollis:** probably accusative plural with *medullas*, but could be a nominative with *flamma*. **medullas:** the marrow within the bones is often the site of erotic passion in love poetry; cf. Rosenmeyer 1999. The imagery of fire and hidden wound recalls lines 1-2.

68-9. **infelix:** Dido's characteristic epithet; cf. 1.712, 1.749, 4.450, 4.529, 4.596, 6.456. As applied to Dido, it primarily means "unlucky," "ill-starred," and always foreshadows her ultimate doom, but it may also carry the original agricultural connotation of "infertile" or "barren," for Dido will never have children, as she notes in 327-30; see Anna's argument about *dulcis natos* in 32-3, Pease here and Gutting 2006, 265-7. **furens:** see on 65 *furentem*.

69-73. **qualis…:** like Homer, Vergil often uses extended similes* to comment on the narrative; in this book see 143-50, 301-3, 402-7, 441-8, 669-71. Here Vergil builds upon the imagery of 4.1-5 by comparing Dido to a deer wounded by an unwitting shepherd, just as Medea flees like a frightened young deer at Apoll. Rhod., *Arg.* 4.12-13. The simile interacts with both literal and metaphorical* "wounding" and "hunting" elsewhere in the book, and elsewhere in the poem; see Johnson 1976, 78-82, Lyne 1989, 179-81, Keith 2000, 113-14, Nelis 2001, 131-5, Clausen 1987, 43-5, 2002, 79-81. On Vergilian similes generally, see West 1990, Lyne 1989, Williams 1983. **nescius:** suggests that

nunc media Aenean secum per moenia ducit
Sidoniasque ostentat opes urbemque paratam,   75
incipit effari mediaque in voce resistit;
nunc eadem labente die convivia quaerit,
Iliacosque iterum demens audire labores
exposcit pendetque iterum narrantis ab ore.
post ubi digressi, lumenque obscura vicissim   80
luna premit suadentque cadentia sidera somnos,
sola domo maeret vacua stratisque relictis

Aeneas is unaware of what is happening to Dido (the word is stressed by being delayed in enjambment*), while *letalis harundo* foreshadows Dido's death. **Dictaeos:** adjective; Dicte is a mountain in Crete. The Cretan setting may suggest the deer is searching for an herbal cure for wounds mentioned by Servius here and on 12.413; see references at O'Hara 1996, 235-6, Nelis 2001, 133. **lateri:** dative, as if with the compound verb *inhaeret*.

74. **media:** modifies *moenia*, so that the phrase means "within the walls." **Aenean:** Greek accusative singular: nominative *Aeneas*, genitive and dative *Aeneae*, accusative *Aenean* (*Aeneam* occurs in other authors), ablative *Aenea* (AG §44).

75. **Sidonias:** "Phoenician"; Sidon was a Phoenician city. **urbemque paratam:** "the building of the city"; Latin tends to avoid verbal nouns and, where English would use such nouns followed by a genitive, Latin often employs a noun and past participle in agreement.

76. **incipit effari...:** the inability to speak is a commonplace symptom of the lover; cf. Catullus 51.7-9 (although the text of Catullus is faulty at that point) and its model in Sappho 31.7-9 and the passages in Pease.

77. **eadem:** probably not Dido but the *convivia*; Dido seeks to repeat the festive dinner that began in Book 1 and featured Aeneas' narrative of Books 2 and 3.

78. **labores:** "struggles," "toils"; *labor* is a characteristic of Aeneas' mission throughout the whole poem (cf. 1.10 *tot adire labores*, 12.435 *disce, puer, virtutem ex me verumque laborem*).

79. **pendetque...:** at Lucretius, *DRN* 1.37 *eque tuo pendet resupini spiritus ore*, the breath of Mars, as he lies in Venus' lap gazing up at her, "hangs from her lips"; the graphic phrase describes the listener with head upturned towards the speaker's lips, so near that he seems literally to hang from them. Cf. too Catullus 64.70 *tota pendebat perdita mente*, of Ariadne in love with Theseus. **narrantis:** supply *Aeneae* (genitive singular).

80. **digressi:** supply *sunt*.

81. **suadentque cadentia sidera somnos:** repeated from 2.9, with the beautiful and sleepy alliteration* of "s" with coincidence of ictus and accent (see appendix on meter).

82. **stratis...relictis:** the coverings (< *sterno*) of the couch "abandoned" after the feast; dative with *incubat*.

incubat. illum absens absentem auditque videtque,
aut gremio Ascanium genitoris imagine capta
detinet, infandum si fallere possit amorem.   85
non coeptae adsurgunt turres, non arma iuventus
exercet portusve aut propugnacula bello
tuta parant: pendent opera interrupta, minaeque
murorum ingentes aequataque machina caelo.

83. **absens absentem:** "absent she sees and hears the absent one"; the repetition in a different case (polyptoton*) stresses the contrast between Aeneas' physical absence and his constant presence in her mind. Dido feels the classic symptoms of love in Greek and Roman poetry, explained scientifically at Lucretius, *DRN* 4.1061-2 (quoted above, 4 n.). **auditque videtque:** the first –*que* is logically unnecessary. Austin: "this use of double –*que* is a mannerism of high epic style, very common in Virgil, Lucan and Statius; it is never found in classical prose. It goes back to Ennius, who took it over from Homer's use of τε … τε."

84-5. **aut…:** "or charmed by the resemblance to his father she holds Ascanius in her lap, (to see) if she can (i.e. in the hope that she may) trick her unspeakable passion." Here *si* introduces an indirect question, with the question word, which implies effort or trying, omitted as often: see AG §576.d, which quotes Caesar, *BG* 6.37 *circumfunduntur hostes si quem aditum reperire possent*, "the enemy pour round (to see) if they can find entrance." Dido tries to cheat her love by displaying affection for his son Ascanius as a substitute for Aeneas (on substitution in Book 4, esp. of bodies, see Bowie 1998).

86. **non coeptae adsurgunt turres…:** love makes Dido neglect the building of her city, which was in progress when Aeneas arrived in Book 1; cf. 1.437 *o fortunati, quorum iam moenia surgunt*. Literary and historical models for Dido like Circe, Calypso, and Cleopatra can be seen as deterring a male hero from his fate or duty, but it is Dido herself who is turned from her duty by her encounter with Aeneas.

87-8. **portusve aut:** here –*ve* probably connects the two statements whose verbs are *exercet* and *parant*, while *aut* connects *portus* and *propugnacula*, although when –*ve aut* occurs at 530 (see n.) it is *aut* that connects the verbs. The combination –*ve aut* is rare, and appears in a different construction at 2.7 *Myrmidonum Dolopumve aut duri miles Vlixi*. **bello tuta:** "for defence in war"; literally "safe (i.e. affording security) in war."

89. **machina:** probably a "crane" used in construction, and possibly suggestive of the device which brought gods in at the end of some tragedies (*deus ex machina*; cf. Nuttal 1998, 46-7 on Vergil here); cf. 2.46, of the wooden horse. Some think it refers to the "structure" of the walls themselves.

Quam simul ac tali persensit peste teneri~   90
cara Iovis coniunx nec famam obstare furori,
talibus adgreditur Venerem Saturnia dictis:
"egregiam vero laudem et spolia ampla refertis
tuque puerque tuus (magnum et memorabile numen),
una dolo divum si femina victa duorum est. ~   95
nec me adeo fallit veritam te moenia nostra]

90-128. Juno and Venus, each thinking to deceive the other, agree to work together to arrange a marriage between Aeneas and Dido. Juno explains that at a hunting party she will create a storm to drive Aeneas and Dido to take refuge alone together in a cave, where they will celebrate their "nuptials."

Vergil imitates scenes in both Homer and Apollonius. In *Iliad* 14, Hera (the Greek equivalent of Juno) seeks the help of Aphrodite (=Venus) in seducing Zeus, so that she may interfere in the war without his knowledge during his post-coital sleep. In a scene near the start of *Arg.* 3, itself modeled on *Iliad* 14, Hera and Athena visit Aphrodite to get her to make Medea fall in love with Jason; Vergil has already imitated in *Aen.* 1.657-722 the part of that scene in which Aphrodite sends Eros on that mission. The interference of the gods here follows that of *Aen.* 1, and to some extent parallels Juno's interference with Turnus in Books 7-12. On the gods here, see Feeney 1991, Konstan 1986, and on Juno more generally both Feeney 1991 and Johnson 1976; on the gods generally, see also Horsfall 1995, 138-43, with further references, Ross 2007, 61-76, and Hejduk 2009 on Jupiter.

90. **Quam:** Dido, subject of the infinitive *teneri* in indirect statement. **peste:** suggests both "disease" and "disaster"; cf. Catullus 76.20 of his love for Lesbia, *Aen.* 1.712 where Dido is *pesti devota futurae,* and in a different but not unrelated sense 7.505, as the Italians, under the influence of Allecto, move towards war.

91-2. **nec famam obstare furori:** "and that (concern for her) reputation does not stand in the way of Dido's mad passion." **Saturnia:** = Juno, daughter of Saturn (cf. 372 n.).

93-4. **egregiam…:** the position of *egregiam* marks the sarcasm and irony*, cf. 6.523. *Refero* is regular for *bringing home* spoils in triumph, cf. 10.862-3 *spolia…referes; Geo.* 3.12 *referam…palmas.* In Tibullus 1.6.3-4 a lover asks Amor whether trapping him is a source of *gloria magna* for the god. **vero:** adverb. **tuque puerque:** as in 83 (see n.), the first *−que* is logically unnecessary, and need not be translated.

96. **nec me adeo fallit:** "nor indeed does it escape me" or "I know full well." *Adeo* usually emphasizes a single word, but here marks the whole phrase *nec me fallit,* which by itself by litotes* is "I know well." In the indirect statement which is the subject of *fallit,* the pronoun *te* is the subject of *habuisse* and is modified by *veritam,* and *moenia* is direct object of *veritam.*

suspectas habuisse domos Karthaginis altae.
sed quis erit modus, aut quo nunc certamine tanto?
quin potius pacem aeternam pactosque hymenaeos
exercemus? habes tota quod mente petisti: 100
ardet amans Dido traxitque per ossa furorem.
communem hunc ergo populum paribusque regamus
auspiciis; liceat Phrygio servire marito
dotalesque tuae Tyrios permittere dextrae."
        Olli (sensit enim simulata mente locutam,   105
quo regnum Italiae Libycas averteret oras)

---

98. sed quis erit modus: "but what end/limit will there be?" Cf. *Ecl.* 10.28 *ecquis erit modus?* and especially *Aen.* 12.793 *quae iam finis erit, coniunx?*, Jupiter's words to Juno. **aut quo nunc certamine tanto?:** "or where do we (go) now in such a contest/battle?" *Quo* = "to what place" and is not connected with the ablatives *certamine tanto*.

99-100. quin…exercemus?: "instead, why do we not pursue?" cf. *Ecl.* 2.71-2 *quin tu…paras?* The word *quin* is used "in questions equivalent to commands or exhortations" (*OLD* s.v. *quin* A.1; cf. too AG §449b). **pacem aeternam:** the reader knows that it is not eternal peace, but the never-ending enmity called for in Dido's curse (see 615-29) that will mark the history of the Trojan-Italian-Romans and the Carthaginians; Book 4 tells an origin-story for that hatred. In Vergil's question at 12.503-4, *tanton placuit concurrere motu, / Iuppiter, aeterna gentis in pace futuras?*, it is the Trojans and Italians who are fated to be allied for all time (although that arrangement is imperiled both in that part of Book 12 and often in Roman history). **pactos:** < *paciscor*, "arrange, agree upon," often used of marriage.

101. traxitque…: for the bones as the seat of inmost feeling, cf. 66-7 and n. on *medullas*; the image here could be of flame, or of poison.

102. communem: predicative, and emphatic by position. Juno suggests, "In common therefore let us rule (one) people …and with equal authority." Only the *imperator* in a Roman army could take the *auspicia*, so *auspicia* and *imperium* often bear almost the same meaning. Cf. *auspiciis* in 341 and in 7.256, *paribusque in regna… / auspiciis*, suggesting a parallel between the situations here and in Book 7.

103. liceat…: "let her serve a Phrygian husband and yield her Tyrians to your hand(s) as a dowry." The bitterness is marked. *Liceat* = "she may for all I care"; "Phrygian" is contemptuous for "Trojan" (cf. 215 n.); so too *servire* for *nubere*.

105. olli: archaic dative form of the pronoun, used also at 1.254, where Jupiter is speaking to Venus. We are reminded of that conversation about the Roman future, as Venus conceals from Juno the knowledge that she has learned from it. **enim:** explains that Venus gave a crafty reply because she knew that Juno was not being honest. **simulata mente:** "with feigned feeling"; in the Latin *mente* one can see the origin of adverbs of manner in Romance languages like French *sincèrement* or Italian *sinceramente* ("sincerely").

106. quo: introduces a purpose clause. **regnum Italiae:** the kingdom that Aeneas was destined to found in Italy. Juno wanted Carthage, not Rome, to rule the world (cf. 1.12-22). **oras:** accusative of place to which, with the preposition omitted as often in poetry (AG §427g).

sic contra est ingressa Venus: "quis talia demens
abnuat aut tecum malit contendere bello?
si modo quod memoras factum fortuna sequatur.
sed fatis incerta feror, si Iuppiter unam   110
esse velit Tyriis urbem Troiaque profectis,
miscerive probet populos aut foedera iungi.
tu coniunx, tibi fas animum temptare precando.
perge, sequar." tum sic excepit regia Iuno:
"mecum erit iste labor. nunc qua ratione quod instat   115
confieri possit, paucis (adverte) docebo.
venatum Aeneas unaque miserrima Dido
in nemus ire parant, ubi primos crastinus ortus
extulerit Titan radiisque retexerit orbem.
his ego nigrantem commixta grandine nimbum,   120
dum trepidant alae saltusque indagine cingunt,

---

108. **tecum:** goes with *contendere* but is placed earlier in the line to gain ironical emphasis.

109. **si modo…:** "if only (as I hope) fortune brings this about in the way you say." The Latin is dense, as language often is in tough diplomatic negotiations. *Quod memoras factum* is "this deed, which you mention" and *fortuna sequatur* (which recurs at 8.15) is literally "fortune follows" but with the sense of "favorable fortune" as in the phrase *fortuna secunda*.

110. **sed fatis incerta feror…:** more dense and ambiguous phrasing, which Austin calls "an experiment in language." Does *fatis* modify *incerta*, or *feror*, or the whole concept *incerta feror*? Venus' feigned uncertainty conceals what she learned from Jupiter at 1.257-96. **si:** "whether" (AG §576d).

113. **tu coniunx:** supply *Iovis es* (ellipsis*). **tibi fas…:** supply *est*; "for you it is right to explore Jupiter's intentions with entreaty."

115-16. **nunc qua…:** "now by what means our present (immediate) purpose (*quod instat*, lit. 'that which presses upon us') may be fulfilled, briefly, pay attention, (and) I will explain to you." *Confieri* for *confici* is common. **paucis:** supply *verbis*. **adverte:** supply *animum*, "pay attention."

117. **venatum:** accusative supine with verb of motion (*ire*) expressing purpose (AG §509).

119. **Titan:** the sun, a child of the Titan Hyperion. **radiisque…:** "and with his rays will have revealed the world," which was previously covered in darkness; cf. 9.461 *rebus luce retectis;* Ovid, *Met.* 8.1-2 *retegente diem /…Lucifero; Met.* 9.795 *postera lux radiis latum patefecerat orbem.*

121. **alae:** "the beaters on horseback." Roman cavalry fought on the "wings," so a troop on horseback was called an *ala*. Here the beaters act like cavalry wings, driving the game up on either side to Aeneas and Dido. **indagine:** "with a net" set up to drive the prey in the desired direction.

desuper infundam et tonitru caelum omne ciebo.
diffugient comites et nocte tegentur opaca:
speluncam Dido dux et Troianus eandem
devenient. adero et, tua si mihi certa voluntas,   125
conubio iungam stabili propriamque dicabo.
hic hymenaeus erit." non adversata petenti
adnuit, atque dolis risit Cytherea repertis.
        Oceanum interea surgens Aurora reliquit.
it portis iubare exorto delecta iuventus,   130
retia rara, plagae, lato venabula ferro,

---

124. **Dido dux et Troianus:** temporary syntactic ambiguity makes it appear for a moment as
if Dido is the *dux* (so Clausen 1987, 24 = 2002, 43); Dido is memorably called *dux femina
facti* at 1.364.

125. **adero:** "I will be present," i.e. as the goddess of marriage (cf. 59 and 166).

126. **conubio...:** virtually repeated from 1.73, where Juno offers a bride to Aeolus as a bribe
to get him to send a storm to wreck Aeneas' fleet. With the forms *conubiis* and *conubio*
(three times each in the poem), it is not clear whether the "u" and the "i" following the "b"
are short vowels, or whether the "u" is long and the "i" consonantal. Cf. Horsfall on 7.253,
and below 213 n.

127. **hic hymenaeus erit:** probably "this will be their marriage"; *hae erunt nuptiae* (Servius),
but in this sense the word usually appears in the plural (cf. 99) and the singular often
means "wedding song" (cf. Hersch 2010, 239-42, Caldwell 2008); that we are not quite
sure what Juno is saying here is probably appropriate. If *hic*, which must have a long "i,"
is nominative singular masculine of the demonstrative, Vergil is using a different prosody
than he did in 22 (see n.); it could be the adverb.

128. **dolis risit...repertis:** "and smiled at the discovery of her (Juno's) trickery"; *dolis repertis*
is probably ablative absolute. Venus or Aphrodite is "laughter-loving" in many texts,
including *Iliad* 14.211, one of Vergil's models here, but there Hera also smiles at the way
she deceives Aphrodite. **Cytherea:** a cult title of Venus derived from her association with
Cythera, an island in the Aegean; see 1.257, 1.680, and also *Arg.* 3.108, one of Vergil's
models here.

*129-59. At dawn the hunting party assembles; Dido appears dressed in regal splendor, and as
Aeneas joins her a simile compares him to Apollo. The hunt begins, and Ascanius longs for more
dangerous prey than deer.*

131. **rara:** "meshed"; probably a general epithet of all nets (*retia*); some distinguish between
wide-meshed nets and the *plagae* used for smaller game. With the nominatives in 131 some
verb such as "are brought" must be supplied (by zeugma*) from *ruunt* in 132 or *it* in 130.

Massylique ruunt equites et odora canum vis.
reginam thalamo cunctantem ad limina primi
Poenorum exspectant, ostroque insignis et auro
stat sonipes ac frena ferox spumantia mandit.   135
tandem progreditur magna stipante caterva
Sidoniam picto chlamydem circumdata limbo;
cui pharetra ex auro, crines nodantur in aurum,
aurea purpuream subnectit fibula vestem.

---

132. **Massyli:** adjective referring to a people who live west of Carthage. **odora canum vis:** "the keen-scented strength of hounds," though *odorus* elsewhere means "giving forth scent." For the phrase cf. Lucretius, *DRN* 4.681 *promissa canum vis* and 6.1222 *fida canum vis,* themselves based on models in Homer that speak of the strength of force of a hero (*Il.* 11.690, 14.418, 23.720; more references in Pease) and perhaps the early Roman poet Ennius, who has *virum vis* (fr. 229 Sk. = Sp. fr. 5 W). The final monosyllable in a hexameter, which produces clash of ictus and accent (see appendix on meter), makes the rhythm sound Ennian or at least archaic.

133. **cunctantem:** "lingering." The word works to heighten the reader's sense of expectation: there is a pause before the central figure of Dido appears; cf. Segal 1990, and Caldwell 2008, who compares the hesitation of brides in wedding songs.

134. **Poenorum:** "Phoenicians" = "Carthaginians." **ostroque...et auro:** signs of Carthage's great wealth; dye from a shell found near Dido's home city of Tyre was the source of most purple dye in the ancient world.

135. **sonipes:** both this compound adjective and the marked alliteration* of the whole line suggest epic, Ennius in particular.

136. **progreditur:** Dido is the subject, even though the horse was subject of the last sentence.

137. **circumdata:** passive participle with "middle" sense (in imitation of the Greek middle voice, which often acts like a reflexive) and a direct object (*chlamydem*), "wearing (lit. 'having thrown round herself') a Sidonian robe with broidered border" (cf. AG §397a and b). Looked at from a different perspective, *chlamydem* can be called a "retained accusative," with the case "retained" from an imagined active construction; see Thomas 1992, 136-7, Harrison 1991, 290-1, and Austin on this line.

138-9. **auro...aurum, / aurea:** for the repetition in different forms (polyptoton*) with gold, see 8.659-61 and 11.774 (with Reed 2007, 56, Wills 1996, 286, Hardie 2006, 28-9); cf. 1.448-9 for bronze. **nodantur in aurum:** "are knotted onto gold," i.e. onto golden hairpins or the like. Line 139 is a golden line,* with two adjectives and the two nouns they modify surrounding a central verb; cf. Conrad 1965, 234-41. The term was not used in antiquity (it is used by John Dryden, in the 1685 Preface to Sylvae), so it is just a coincidence that Vergil uses a golden line to describe gold. The richly stylized line adds to the stately and elegant feel of Dido's entrance, and again (see 134 n.) purple and gold suggest the wealth of Carthage.

nec non et Phrygii comites et laetus Iulus   140
incedunt. ipse ante alios pulcherrimus omnis
infert se socium Aeneas atque agmina iungit.
qualis ubi hibernam Lyciam Xanthique fluenta
deserit ac Delum maternam invisit Apollo
instauratque choros, mixtique altaria circum   145
Cretesque Dryopesque fremunt pictique Agathyrsi:
ipse iugis Cynthi graditur mollique fluentem
fronde premit crinem fingens atque implicat auro,

---

140. **Phrygii:** adjective form of a post-Homeric name for the Trojans; cf. 215 n. **Iulus:** alternate name for Aeneas' son Ascanius, which stresses his connection both with Troy and with the *gens Iulia* of Julius and Augustus Caesar (cf. esp. 1.267-8). The name scans as trisyllabic, since the initial "i" is a vowel, not a consonant as in Iulus.

141. **ante alios pulcherrimus omnis:** for this strong superlative, cf. 1.347 *scelere ante alios immanior omnis*; the whole phrase will be applied to Turnus at 7.55-6 (both here and there the context suggests attractiveness as a potential husband). Servius Auctus notes that the adjective tells us how Aeneas appeared to Dido: in modern terms we might say that it is focalized (cf. Fowler 2000, Laird 1997, 286) through her.

142. **infert se socium:** "moves to meet her"; *socium* modifies *se* in the reflexive expression *infert se* (lit. "brings himself as companion").

143. **hibernam Lyciam:** "his winter dwelling in Lycia" (although *hibernam* here is the adj., *Lyciam* the noun) where he had a shrine at Patara near the mouth of the river Xanthus. The comparison in 143-50 of Aeneas to Apollo recalls that of Dido to Diana in 1.498-502, just as the comparison of Jason to Apollo in Apoll. Rhod. *Arg.* 1.307-10 is linked to that of Medea to Artemis (=Diana) in *Arg.* 3.876-84. On the simile*, which likens Aeneas to a particularly foreign and exotic Apollo, see Pöschl 1962, 60-8, Nelis 2001, 133, Weber 2002 (who argues that many details of the simile, esp. in 146, are suggestive of Dionysus), Hardie 2006, Caldwell 2008, and Miller 2009, 7, 159.

144. **Delum maternam:** the island on which Apollo was born.

146. **Cretesque Dryopesque...Agathyrsi:** note the polysyndeton*; the first –*que* is lengthened in arsis (see appendix on meter, and 64 n.), in imitation of Greek practice with the similar construction τε ... τε (cf. 83 n., and see Pease here, Clausen on *Ecl.* 4.51, Weber 2002, 328). This "foreign" meter adds to the oddly exotic quality of the god to whom Aeneas is compared (cf. 215 with n.). Crete is far south of Delos, the Dryopes come from the northern part of Greece, and the Agathyrsi from Scythia further to the North.

147-8. **Cynthi:** mountain on Delos; on the programmatic significance of Apollo's epithet *Cynthius* and its suggestion of Callimachus, see Clausen on *Ecl.* 6.3. The epithet is also the source of the elegist Propertius' name for his beloved, Cynthia. **fluentem...crinem:** the eternally youthful Apollo is always represented with "flowing locks"; at 216 Iarbas will deride Aeneas for having hair wet presumably with unguent (see 216-17 n.).

tela sonant umeris: haud illo segnior ibat
Aeneas, tantum egregio decus enitet ore.   150
postquam altos ventum in montis atque invia lustra,
ecce ferae saxi deiectae vertice caprae
decurrere iugis; alia de parte patentis
transmittunt cursu campos atque agmina cervi
pulverulenta fuga glomerant montisque relinquunt.   155
at puer Ascanius mediis in vallibus acri
gaudet equo iamque hos cursu, iam praeterit illos,
spumantemque dari pecora inter inertia votis
optat aprum, aut fulvum descendere monte leonem.

---

149. **tela...umeris:** i.e. the arrows in the quiver on his shoulder. The allusion to Hom. *Il.* 1.46, where Apollo's weapons clang as he arrives to bring plague to the Greeks, may suggest (as did the deer simile in 68-73) that Aeneas brings destruction to Dido (Otis 1964, 73-4, Miller 2009, 159). For suggestions of the *Iliad* in Book 4, cf. nn. on 169, 173-97, 227-9, 238-78, 285-6, 365-6, 443, 554-83, 607, 669, 672, and also Hughes 2002.

151. **ventum:** supply *est;* "they came." The passive of intransitive verbs is often used impersonally (AG §208d).

152. **deiectae:** "dislodged" by the beaters whose job it is to drive the animals towards the hunters.

153. **decurrere:** = *decurrerunt.*

154-5. **agmina...:** the deer "group together their dusty columns" as if they were in military formation. **pulverulenta...:** the three dactyls that start the line make its meter imitate the running of the deer. **montisque relinquunt:** the clause is appended in parataxis*, but actually introduces an explanatory clause, "as they leave..."; cf. 6.361.

156-9. **at puer Ascanius...:** the youthful enthusiasm of Aeneas' son Ascanius and his desire for more dangerous prey provide a light note before the dark storm and its aftermath; in 7.496-9 Ascanius' zeal for hunting leads to the start of the war in Italy. On hunting in the *Aeneid*, especially by young men, see the index to Hardie on *Aen.* 9.

Interea magno misceri murmure caelum
incipit, insequitur commixta grandine nimbus,
et Tyrii comites passim et Troiana iuventus
Dardaniusque nepos Veneris diversa per agros

160-72. A storm descends; Aeneas and Dido take refuge in a cave, and their fatal union is accomplished according to Juno's plan, amid thunder, lightning and other signs.
The encounter in the cave is modeled on the marriage of Medea and Jason in a cave (*Arg.* 4.1128-69), with less obvious suggestions also of their first meeting in *Arg.* 3.936-1145; cf. Nelis 2001, 148-9. Vergil's passage suggests either a wedding or a parody of a wedding, and the event is described in such a way that it is hard to known what is really happening; cf. Johnson 1976, 163 n. 42, Desmond 1994, 29, and on the Roman wedding in general Hersh 2010. From now on Dido considers Aeneas her husband; we are not told Aeneas' thoughts.

Are Dido and Aeneas to be thought of as married? The Roman notion of marriage did not depend on paperwork, or (most scholars have thought) on a ceremony, but required "simply the consent of both parties that it was marriage" (G. Williams 1968, 382, but Hersh 2010, 51-5 argues that public declaration of consent may have been necessary). The only marriages to which Roman law paid full attention were those between two free Roman citizens, but claims by some scholars that Aeneas as a proto-Roman cannot marry Dido are highly suspect. The narrator uses terms suggestive of marriage in 166-8 (see n.), and every detail suggests that Dido thinks of marriage, from the stress on children in 33 and 327-9, to her every reference to the relationship (cf. 316, 324, 431). Aeneas will claim in a crucially important passage (338-9) that he never thought they were married, and for many readers this will be enough; others may think that in helping to build Dido's city he was publicly acting like a husband (cf. Mercury's insult *uxorius*, 266). Later authors such as Ovid (*Phrygius maritus*, *Met.* 14.79), Silius Italicus (*profugus maritus, Punica* 8.53), and Dante (Dido is Aeneas' second *coniunx* in *De Monarchia* 2.3.2) refer to them as husband and/or wife, though this need not determine how we read Vergil. In fact the scenes most crucial to a determination of what was said or understood by Dido and Aeneas are never put before our eyes; it can hardly be an accident that in the second half of the poem the same is true of the question of whether Turnus and Lavinia were engaged; both issues are also marked by ambiguous uses of the term *data dextera* (307 and n.). On marriage, see Williams 1968, Monti 1981, 30-6 and 44-8, Lyne 1989, 46-8, Wiltshire 1989, 90-3, Rudd 1990, Feeney 1990, Horsfall 1995, 128-30, Gibson 1999, Caldwell 2008, and Hersch 2010.

160. **magno misceri murmure:** "to be troubled with mighty murmurings." The same onomatopoetic* alliteration* occurs in 1.124; cf. *magno…murmure* at Lucretius, *DRN* 6.101 and 197; both he and Vergil probably recall the archaic alliteration of Ennius.

163. **Dardaniusque nepos Veneris:** Ascanius, since Venus is his father's mother. *Dardanius* = "Trojan," after Dardanus, the son of Jupiter who was the ancestor of the Trojans; cf. 3.167 and below 365, where Dido in her anger denies that Dardanus is the founder of Aeneas' line.

tecta metu petiere; ruunt de montibus amnes.⌋
speluncam Dido dux et Troianus eandem 165
deveniunt. prima et Tellus et pronuba Iuno
dant signum; fulsere ignes et conscius aether
conubiis, summoque ulularunt vertice Nymphae.⌋ 168
ille dies primus leti primusque malorum 169
causa fuit; neque enim specie famave movetur 170
nec iam furtivum Dido meditatur amorem:
coniugium vocat, hoc praetexit nomine culpam.

---

165. **speluncam...**: repeated from 124 (see n.), so that Juno's plan is carried out in the same words in which it was announced, with present tenses replacing her futures. What looks like a simple accident is thus strongly marked as the result of divine will, and the words acquire a certain ominous character that fits well with what follows.

166-8. **prima...**: much of the description suits both celestial phenomena, and aspects of a Roman wedding. **Tellus...aether:** suggests the mythical *Hieros Gamos* or "Sacred Marriage" of Earth and Sky, with Earth as the primal mother and Sky (*Aether*) as the universal father descending into her lap in fertilizing showers (cf. Lucretius, *DRN* 1.250-64 with Fowler 2000, 141-8, and Verg. *Geo.* 2.325-35 with Thomas' n.). **pronuba:** usually the matron who assists the bride (cf. 7.319 *Bellona manet te pronuba*); at a wedding she might give the "sign" for the ceremony to start, but what sign Earth and Juno give here is not clear. **fulsere ignes:** lightning flashes take the place of the usual nuptial torches. **conscius aether:** provides a fleeting suggestion of a universal conspiracy. **conubiis:** for scansion, cf. 126 n. **ulularunt:** the shriek of the Nymphs is the bridal hymn (for *hymenaeus*, cf. 127 n.). The onomatopoetic* verb is more often used of mourning (as at 2.488, 4.667) or of animals (*Geo.* 1.486, wolves, in a series of bad omens); cf. too *Aen.* 4.609 *Hecate...ululata*.

169. **ille dies primus leti primusque malorum:** a clear foreshadowing of the doom awaiting Dido, perhaps recalling *Il.* 11.604, of Patroclus, κακοῦ δ' ἄρα οἱ πέλεν ἀρχή, a line that also marks a crucial step towards disaster. Cf. too *Aen.* 7.481-2, also in the context of a hunt, *quae prima laborum / causa fuit*.

171. **furtivum...amorem:** the phrase suggests the clandestine affairs of Latin love poetry (which Dido thinks she is not pursuing); cf. Catullus 7.8, Tibullus 1.5.75, Ovid, *Fasti* 6.573.

172. **coniugium...culpam:** "she calls it marriage: with that name she covers over her fault." For *culpa*, cf. 19 n. Does the narrator condemn what she is doing, or is the line "focalized" through Dido (or looked at from her perspective or point of view; cf. Fowler 2000), so that she is overcoming her previous sense that marriage to Aeneas would have involved *culpa*? Does Dido "call" (*vocat*) the relationship a marriage openly, or only in her mind? Does she "cover over" a fault, or her previous sense that marriage to Aeneas would have involved *culpa*? Cf. below on *dolos* in 296, where the word may represent only Dido's view of the situation.

Extemplo Libyae magnas it Fama per urbes,
Fama, malum qua non aliud velocius ullum:
mobilitate viget virisque adquirit eundo,   175
parva metu primo, mox sese attollit in auras
ingrediturque solo et caput inter nubila condit.
illam Terra parens ira inritata deorum

173-295: Jupiter intervenes to tell Aeneas to leave Carthage.
Rumor, vividly personified as a winged creature, spreads tales of Dido and Aeneas' love
throughout Libya (173-97), and Iarbas, a rejected suitor, complains to his father Jupiter that
the woman who rejected him has taken up with an effeminate Easterner (198-218). In a
passage modeled on Zeus' sending of Hermes to tell Calypso to release Odysseus in *Odyssey*
5, Jupiter tells Mercury to remind Aeneas of his mission, and Mercury flies to earth by
way of a vividly described and semi-personified Mt. Atlas (219-58). Mercury finds Aeneas
splendidly dressed in gifts from Dido, and helping to build Carthage. He calls Aeneas
uxorius, and delivers Jupiter's message that he should leave Carthage (259-78). Aeneas is
stunned, but immediately tells his men to prepare to depart, while he looks for the best
opportunity to tell *optima Dido* (279-95).

The description of personified* Rumor in 173-97 has not been admired in every age,
but recent critics have been more appreciative. It recalls the Homeric depiction of Rumor
in *Il.* 2.93 and *Od.* 24.413 (which Vergil closely follows in 173), as well as that of Rumor
in Hesiod, *Works* 760-4, and of Strife in *Il.* 4.442-3. There are also borrowings from
Apollonius and from Lucretius' discussion of lightning, and links to passages on giants
both in other poets and elsewhere in the poem. The passage was imitated by Ovid and
Statius, who both carried personification* to greater lengths than Vergil. Rumor will play
an important role later in the book (298, 666) and in the poem. Cf. Feeney 1991, 241-8,
364-91, Nelis 2001, 154, Hardie 1986, 373-81, with forthcoming work on rumor expected
from Hardie.

174. **Fama:** epanalepsis*. **qua:** ablative of comparison; the relative pronoun is postponed,
or we could say that *malum* which is modified by *non aliud...ullum* is drawn ahead to an
earlier position in the phrase.

175. **mobilitate...:** "thrives by moving and takes on strength as she goes" (*eundo* is ablative
gerund of *ire*). Similar language at Lucretius, *DRN* 6.340 describes the momentum of
lightning as it falls.

176-7. **parva...:** "small at first in fear...." The description is from that of Strife in *Il.* 4.442.
Line 177 is repeated at 10.767, of the giant Orion to whom Mezentius is compared. For
giants, see 179 n., and for their thematic role on the poem, Hardie 1986, 85-156, and
O'Hara 2007, 96-101.

178. **ira...deorum:** "provoked by (her) anger against the gods," with *deorum* as objective gen.
Earth was angry at how her sons the Titans were treated.

extremam, ut perhibent, Coeo Enceladoque sororem
progenuit pedibus celerem et pernicibus alis,   180
monstrum horrendum, ingens, cui quot sunt corpore plumae,
tot vigiles oculi subter (mirabile dictu),
tot linguae, totidem ora sonant, tot subrigit auris.
nocte volat caeli medio terraeque per umbram
stridens, nec dulci declinat lumina somno;   185
luce sedet custos aut summi culmine tecti
turribus aut altis, et magnas territat urbes,
tam ficti pravique tenax quam nuntia veri.
haec tum multiplici populos sermone replebat
gaudens, et pariter facta atque infecta canebat: 190
venisse Aenean Troiano sanguine cretum,
cui se pulchra viro dignetur iungere Dido;

---

179. **extremam…sororem:** "last…as their sister." Coeus was a Titan, but Vergil joins him with Enceladus and the Giants. The Titans and Giants, both offspring of Earth who warred against heaven, are often confused. Lines 178-80 recall descriptions of Typhoeus in Hes. *Theog.* 820-22 and Apoll. Rhod. *Arg.* 2.38-40. **ut perhibent:** cf. Thomas on *Geo.* 1.247 for the usual use of such phrases to mark allusion to a source text, or to suggest disbelief by attributing a claim to a source other than the poet.

181. **monstrum…:** cf. 3.658, of the Cyclops, as here with harsh elisions. The eyes as numerous as the feathers suggest the plumage of a peacock. Vergil may allude to the myth of Io's watcher Argus (cf. 7.791), whose many eyes when he was slain became the ornament of the peacock; see Ovid, *Met.* 1.722-3, perhaps inspired by the lost poem *Io* by Catullus' friend Calvus.

183. **subrigit:** "pricks." So *arrigere, erigere aures* commonly; cf. 2.303 *arrectis auribus.*

184 **caeli medio terraeque:** the noun *medium* in the ablative = "(in the area) between"; cf. 9.230 *castrorum et campi medio,* with Hardie's n.

185. **stridens:** "hissing"; perhaps of the sound of Rumor's flight (cf. 1.397 *stridentibus alis*) but probably of its cry. *Stridere* is used of any hard grating sound.

186. **sedet custos:** "sits sentinel," on the watch for anything that may happen.

188-90. **tam…:** "clutching what is false and foul (lit. 'crooked') no less than reporting truth" (cf. 193 n.) So Numanus in 9.595 reports things *digna atque indigna relatu.* **ficti…tenax:** an objective genitive is common after adjectives in -*ax*, e.g. *capax, edax, rapax.* **ficti pravi… veri:** neuter adjectives used as substantives to express abstract ideas. **facta atque infecta:** Statius, *Thebaid* 3.430, of Fame, has *facta infecta loqui.* See also 193 n.

191. **venisse Aenean:** indirect statement after *canebat.*

192. **cui…viro:** "to whom as a husband"; Rumor describes the union as a marriage. **dignetur:** subjunctive in a dependent clause in indirect statement (AG §580).

nunc hiemem inter se luxu, quam longa, fovere
regnorum immemores turpique cupidine captos.
haec passim dea foeda virum diffundit in ora.   195
protinus ad regem cursus detorquet Iarban
incenditque animum dictis atque aggerat iras.
    Hic Hammone satus rapta Garamantide nympha
templa Iovi centum latis immania regnis,
centum aras posuit vigilemque sacraverat ignem,   200
excubias divum aeternas, pecudumque cruore
pingue solum et variis florentia limina sertis.

---

193. **hiemem...fovere:** lit. "keep the winter warm" (as the indirect statement continues) but
with a suggestion too of embracing and fondling one another. After *quam longa* supply *sit,*
as in 8.86 *ea,...quam longa est, nocte,* "on that night throughout its length," lit. "as long
as it is." **luxu:** suggests both self-indulgence and the opulence of Dido's palace, which for
Roman readers may have suggested that of Cleopatra (cf. 215 and 663-4 and nn.)
    What in Rumor's report is not true? That Dido considers Aeneas her husband? That she
neglects her kingdom (but see 261-4 for Aeneas supervising construction)? That they are
captives of foul desire?

195. **foeda:** probably to be construed with *dea,* but the syntax may be ambiguous, and
nothing prevents it from coloring both *haec* and *ora.*

198-218. *Iarbas, son of Jupiter Ammon, angrily taunts his father as a powerless deity, who allows
his son to be scorned by a foreign woman for an eastern adventurer.*

198. **Hic...:** "he the son of (lit. 'born from') Ammon and a Garamantian nymph raped by
him." In the pre-Vergilian myth, Dido kills herself rather than agree to marry Iarbas; cf.
Justinus *Epit.* 18.6, and see Lord 1969, Horsfall 1990, 138-9, Hexter 1992, 340, Starks
1999, 262-4, and on this passage Hejduk 2009, 292-4. Hammon or Ammon was a Libyan
deity usually, as here, identified with Jupiter. The Garamantes are "tribesmen of the eastern
Sahara" (Clausen on *Ecl.* 8.44). For those raped or "carried off" by Jupiter, cf. Ganymede
(1.28, a cause of Juno's anger, and 5.252-7) and Juturna the sister of Turnus (12.878).

200-2. **posuit...sacraverat:** the tenses suggest that he built the temples after first dedicating
the "sleepless fire" (which resembles Vesta's eternal fire at Rome). It is then better to take
solum and *limina* as nominatives—"and the ground (in the temples) (was—supply *erat*) fat
with blood...," for if *sacraverat* is allowed to govern *solum* and *limina,* it is hard to explain
why we have *posuit templa* but *sacraverat limina.* Williams suggests that it is "possible to
regard the nouns as accusative after some verbal notion taken by zeugma from *sacraverat.*"
Gould and Fairclough's Loeb text removes the problem by putting a semi-colon after
aeternas.

isque amens animi et rumore accensus amaro
dicitur ante aras media inter numina divum
multa Iovem manibus supplex orasse supinis: 205
"Iuppiter omnipotens, cui nunc Maurusia pictis
gens epulata toris Lenaeum libat honorem,
aspicis haec? an te, genitor, cum fulmina torques
nequiquam horremus, caecique in nubibus ignes
terrificant animos et inania murmura miscent?   210
femina, quae nostris errans in finibus urbem
exiguam pretio posuit, cui litus arandum
cuique loci leges dedimus, conubia nostra

---

203. **amens animi:** "mad in mind." Cf. 300 *inops animi;* 529 *infelix animi;* 2.61 *fidens animi;* 5.202 *furens animi.* Some call *animi* in these phrases a locative (cf. AG §358), but Williams here, with references to his and to Austin's notes elsewhere, calls it a genitive of "sphere in which" (cf. AG §349d on genitive of specification).

204. **dicitur:** a curious use of this word, which often distances the speaker from a story, or alludes to a source; see 179 n.

206-7. **nunc:** "now," emphatic, i.e. since my piety has so taught them. **Maurusia:** adjective; Mauretania is on the African coast west of Carthage. **pictis...toris:** couches covered with decorative embroidery; the phrase is used also at 1.708 in the description of Dido's banquet. **Lenaeum...honorem:** "Lenaean offering," i.e. offering of wine; *Lenaeus* is a cult-title of Dionysus.

209-10. **nequiquam...caeci...inania:** emphatic repetition of the same idea—are our terrors "vain," your lightning "aimless" (literally "blind") and your thunderings "empty mutterings"? Iarbas, who introduced the worship of Ammon to his country, here questions it using the language of the Epicureans (see 34 n.; *terrificant* in 210 is Lucretian, used at *DRN* 4.34 in an explanation of false fear of ghosts) and others who criticized traditional religious practice.

211. **femina...:** scornful. "A woman," and she "a wanderer," has "bought the right to build" a "tiny" city; I granted her "the shore to plough" (*arandum* is a gerundive — AG §500.4) and fixed "the terms of holding the land," and yet rather than be my bride she seeks to be Aeneas' slave. Dido will in 373 refer with similar anger to her generous treatment of the shipwrecked Aeneas. For the buying of the site of Carthage, cf. 1.367. *Litus* here means land by the sea, as in 7.797-8 *sacrumque Numici / litus arant,* but *litus arare* is also proverbial for doing something useless (*OLD* 1b). **errans:** some ancient sources say that the Punic name Dido means "wandering" or "wanderer," and Vergil may allude to that derivation here; see Pease here, O'Hara 1996, 152-3, Reed 2007, 93-5.

213. **loci leges:** the conditions under which she is to hold the land. **conubia:** the second syllable must scan long here, as in the five other times this form appears in the poem, and is perhaps lengthened in arsis (see appendix on meter and cf. 146 n.); cf. 126 n.

reppulit ac dominum Aenean in regna recepit.
et nunc ille Paris cum semiviro comitatu,   215
Maeonia mentum mitra crinemque madentem
subnexus, rapto potitur: nos munera templis
quippe tuis ferimus famamque fovemus inanem."

---

214. **dominum:** emphatic, "a master" (cf. 103 *servire*), not a husband.

215. **Paris:** the Trojan prince, both distant cousin and brother-in-law to Aeneas, and the man with whom Helen ran off, leading to the Trojan War. Iarbas both alludes to Trojan guilt in the war, and claims that Aeneas is the type of a warrior whose conquests are only over women. For Aeneas as another Paris, cf. 7.321, 363, 9.138-9. **semiviro comitatu:** the rhythm produced by the four-syllable line-end *comitatu*, with clash of ictus and accent in the fifth foot (see appendix on meter), adds to the "foreign" sound of the line (cf. 146 and n.). In the *Aeneid* Trojans are several times associated, mainly by their enemies, with the effeminacy that became associated with the Phrygians in post-Homeric times, in part because of the worship of the goddess Cybele by eunuch priests; cf. 103, 9.598-620 (the taunts of Numanus), 12.99 *semiviri Phrygis* (Turnus of Aeneas; see 216-17 n. on *crinemque madentem*). Vergil may also suggest Antony and Cleopatra in Egypt (cf. Hor. *Carm.* 1.37.9-10 *contaminato cum grege turpium / morbo virorum*). Which qualities of the Trojans and Italians will survive in the amalgam produced by the agreement of Jupiter and Juno in 12.791-840 is a difficult but important question. Cf. O'Hara 1990, 140-50 with earlier references, and 2007, 96-101, Hardie on 9.138-9, Starks 1999, 273-4, Syed 2004, and Reed 2007, 85 (on this passage) and *passim*. C. Williams 1999, 145-7 discusses Vergil's use here and elsewhere of the motif of the "womanish womanizer."

216-17. **mitra:** Eastern head-gear fastened with strings, associated often with women (like Ariadne in Catullus 64.63), but also with Paris; Pease cites many passages. Maeonian = Lydian, from the land bordering Phrygia. **crinemque madentem:** Highet 1972, 118 says the alliteration of "m" (seven in one line) suggests effeminacy. Turnus adds more details in describing Aeneas at 12.99-100: "hair curled with hot iron and dripping with myrrh." The description of hair with unguent both fits the stereotype of the Trojans in the previous note (Hector mentions Paris' hair at *Il.* 3.55), and resonates with descriptions of hard-partying males of Vergil's day. Cf. Cic. *In Pisonem* 25 *erant illi compti capilli et madentes cincinnorum fimbriae, Post Red. in Sen.* 13 *vini somni stupri plenus, madenti coma, composito capillo*; Suet. *Aug.* 86.3 (the emperor teases his — and Vergil's — friend Maecenas for his "unguent-dripping curls," *myrobrechis ... cincinnos*); Dio Cassius 46.18.3 (another orator accuses Cicero of scenting his hair). Often hair-unguent is associated with partying or with love; cf. Hor. *Carm.* 1.5.1-2 *puer... perfusus liquidis... odoribus;* Prop. 2.4.5 *nequiquam perfusa meis unguenta capillis,* Ovid, *Ars* 3.443 *nec coma vos fallat liquido nitidissima nardo.* **subnexus:** a middle form (cf. 137 n.), "having tied"; some scholars prefer the form in most manuscripts, *subnixus,* "having rested." **rapto:** "prey," "booty." **nos:** in strong contrast with *ille,* "(yet) we."

218. **quippe:** suggesting irony*, and followed by fiercely alliterative* f's.

Talibus orantem dictis arasque tenentem
audiit Omnipotens, oculosque ad moenia torsit   220
regia et oblitos famae melioris amantis.
tum sic Mercurium adloquitur ac talia mandat:
"vade age, nate, voca Zephyros et labere pinnis,
Dardaniumque ducem, Tyria Karthagine qui nunc
exspectat fatisque datas non respicit urbes,   225
adloquere et celeris defer mea dicta per auras.
non illum nobis genetrix pulcherrima talem
promisit Graiumque ideo bis vindicat armis;

219-37. In answer to Iarbas' prayer Jupiter summons Mercury and orders him to remind Aeneas of his mission, and to say that if Aeneas has no ambition himself, he has no right to ruin his son's hopes.

Jupiter sends Mercury (often used as the messenger of the gods), just as Zeus sends Hermes to Calypso to free Odysseus in *Od.* 5.28-42. Jupiter's brief prophecy of the fated Roman rule (229-31) is to be compared with the major prophecies in 1.257-96, 6.756-853, 7.96-101, 8.630-728, 12.834-40. On this first scene, cf. Estevez 1982 and Hejduk 2009, 292-5, and on Jupiter's sending of Mercury, cf. Harrison 1985, Hardie 1986, 276-9, Feeney 1991, 173-5 and 1998, Ross 2007, 15-17.

220. **Omnipotens:** Jupiter, as in 25 and 206; cf. 693 and n., where the epithet is used of Juno. **oculos...torsit:** "turned his eyes" but with a suggestion of sudden, violent movement.

222. **adloquitur ac:** the last syllable of the verb is lengthened in arsis (see appendix on meter and cf. 146 n.).

223. **voca Zephyros:** he is to summon the West Wind to aid his flight. **labere:** impv. of a deponent. **pinnis:** those on his winged sandals (*talaria,* 239; cf. *alatis ... plantis,* 259).

225. **exspectat...:** "waits and has no regard for the cities granted him by fate." *Exspecto* usually has a noun or a clause as an object, but here is used absolutely: he is simply "waiting" without object or aim.

226. **adloquere:** impv. of a deponent. **celeris:** a transferred epithet (it is Mercury and not the breezes that will be swift) and so an instance of enallage,* on which see Conte 2007, 98-100, who says on another passage (p. 91) that such a Vergilian syntactical inversion may "charge [a] phrase with expressive force," and also "compresses a complex thought by leaping over the intermediate articulations through a daring condensation"; cf. nn. to 303, 385, 477, 506, 623, 683.

227-8. **non illum...talem:** when Venus rescued Aeneas at Troy, she did not promise that he would be *this* kind of man. The clauses with *promisit* and *vindicat,* however, are presented in parataxis rather than with the second subordinate to the first. The present tense *vindicat* suggests that the effect of his rescue is regarded as still continuing. **Graium:** genitive plural; cf. 47-9 n. **bis:** i.e. once when she rescued him from Diomedes, *Il.* 5.311-18, the second time at the fall of Troy; cf. too how Paris (see 215 n.) is saved by Venus in *Il.* 3.380-2. For Diomedes in the *Aeneid* cf. 1.97, 11.282-4 and the reversal at 12.896-906 where Turnus before his defeat is linked by allusion to Diomedes (Lyne 1987, 132-9, Quint 1993, 69-83, Fletcher 2006).

sed fore qui gravidam imperiis belloque frementem
Italiam regeret, genus alto a sanguine Teucri   230
proderet, ac totum sub leges mitteret orbem.
si nulla accendit tantarum gloria rerum
nec super ipse sua molitur laude laborem,
Ascanione pater Romanas invidet arces?
quid struit? aut qua spe inimica in gente moratur   235
nec prolem Ausoniam et Lavinia respicit arva?
naviget! haec summa est; hic nostri nuntius esto."
Dixerat. ille patris magni parere parabat

229-30. **fore:** = *futurum esse* (AG §170a), in an indirect statement after *promisit*; the relative clause of purpose (AG §531) introduced by *qui* is the predicate. **gravidam imperiis:** probably in connection with *bello frementem* (and compared with 10.87 *gravidam bellis urbem*) means "teeming with military commands," i.e. opportunities for a great *imperator*. The implication is that Italy needs leaders, not lovers.

231. **totum…:** Aeneas was never himself "to make the whole earth pass beneath his laws," but he was to do so by "handing down a race from Teucer's lofty line" (230).

233. **nec super…:** "nor for the sake of his own fame …." *Ipse* is put between *super* and the ablative that this preposition governs because *ipse* and *suus* have such strong attraction for one another, and both emphasize Aeneas.

234. **Ascanione pater:** *pater* is added to emphasize the argument— "does *the father* grudge his son?"

235. **spe inimica:** no elision here, but instead hiatus (see appendix on meter); Austin's long note here suggests that Vergil often uses hiatus when a speaker pauses as if unsure what to say next. **inimica in gente:** Mercury in 271 omits the description of the Carthaginian race as *inimica*, so that Aeneas will not hear Jupiter's reference to the Punic Wars.

236. **prolem Ausoniam:** the adjective *Ausonius* = "Italian" and *Lavinia … arva* refers to the fields around the city Aeneas will found and name after his Italian wife Lavinia (cf. 1.2-3 *Lavinia … litora*). Conington suggests that this line "is the same as *genus alto a sanguine Teucri* regarded from another side. There we were to think of Rome as derived from Troy: here we are to think of it as the representative of Italian greatness." But the line points also to the conflict in the tradition over whether Alba Longa and then Rome will be ruled by the descendants of Ascanius or by those of Aeneas and Lavinia's Italian son Silvius (see 6.763 *tua postuma proles*, and cf. O'Hara 2007, 88-90).

238-78. *Mercury flies down to Carthage by way of Mt Atlas, and finds Aeneas supervising the building of Carthage, wearing a luxurious Tyrian cloak and a jeweled sword. Mercury insults Aeneas for being tamed by a woman, delivers his message from Jupiter, and disappears.*

The start of the passage is closely modeled on *Od.* 5.43-8, the description of Hermes (= Mercury) preparing to deliver to Calypso the message from Zeus that she must let Odysseus go. There are also suggestions of the similar scene at *Il.* 24.339-48 (Hermes coming to Priam), and of Hermes' role as bringer of souls to Hades as in *Od.* 24.1-10; cf. 242-4 n.

imperio: et primum pedibus talaria nectit
aurea, quae sublimem alis sive aequora supra   240
seu terram rapido pariter cum flamine portant.
tum virgam capit: hac animas ille evocat Orco
pallentis, alias sub Tartara tristia mittit,
dat somnos adimitque, et lumina morte resignat.
illa fretus agit ventos et turbida tranat   245
nubila. iamque volans apicem et latera ardua cernit
Atlantis duri caelum qui vertice fulcit,

239. **talaria:** the winged sandals or anklets (cf. 259) of Mercury.

240. **sublimem alis:** "soaring on wings," i.e. the wings of the *talaria*, cf. 223 n.

241. **pariter...:** "along with the swift breeze," which he calls to his aid (226), and which helps to bear him along.

242-4. **hac...resignat:** a parenthetical description of his wand. Mercury was conductor of the dead or *pyschopompos* (a Greek term glossed by *animas ... mittit*). The phrase *animas... mittit* suggests either shades sent to visit mortals in dreams, or shades restored to life as in "Orphic-Pythagorean beliefs in reincarnation" (see Austin, and 6.724-51). **Orco:** "from the underworld"; Orcus = Dis, lord of the underworld, and by metonymy* his name is used for the underworld itself. **Tartara:** n. accusative plural, "the underworld," the land bound by the River Tartarus. **dat somnos adimitque:** from *Od.* 5.47-8, 24.3-4 and *Il.* 24.343-4; in *Il.* 24 Hermes will literally put some to sleep (445-7) and wake others (677-89); it is not clear whether in this passage Vergil refers to sleep or figuratively to the sleep of death. **lumina morte resignat:** "unseals eyes in death" or "from death." The former would allude to a Roman custom of opening the closed lids of the dead on the pyre (*illos* [sc. *oculos*] ... *in rogo patefacere, Quiritium magno ritu sacrum est,* Pliny, *Nat. Hist.* 11.150), perhaps so that the dead may see their way as he leads them down to Orcus (cf. Pease and Austin here). The rendering "unseals from death" would return to the idea of 242 *animas ille evocat Orco*, or refer mysteriously to some aspect of existence in the underworld. Servius suggests that *resignat = claudit*, "closes."

245. **illa:** resuming the narrative after the parenthesis— "relying on it (i.e. the wand)." **agit ventos:** the god is said to "drive" the winds, as previously (223, 241) he has been said to "fly" or "be carried along with" them; the poet presents the same idea in different ways which are not strictly consistent. **tranat:** literally "swims across," i.e. "flies through"; 6.16 has *enavit* of Daedalus' flight.

247. **Atlantis duri:** Vergil describes this mountain in Northwestern Africa in terms and with an epithet equally suited to Atlas the "rocky" mountain and Atlas the "patient" Titan who holds up the heavens on his shoulders (cf. Dido's words at 481), and whose name could be derived from a Greek word for "enduring," an etymology* to which the adjective *durus* points (cf. O'Hara 1996). Strabo 17.3.2 and Pliny *NH* 5.13 mention a local or Roman soldiers' name for Mt. Atlas that sounds like Durus. The enduring patience of Atlas may be a model for what Aeneas must do (at 8.134-42 Aeneas will note that both he and Evander are descended from Atlas); others note that Atlas was punished for rebelling against Jupiter, like many of the "giants" mentioned or alluded to in this poem (see 176 n.).

Atlantis, cinctum adsidue cui nubibus atris
piniferum caput et vento pulsatur et imbri,
nix umeros infusa tegit, tum flumina mento   250
praecipitant senis, et glacie riget horrida barba.
hic primum paribus nitens Cyllenius alis
constitit: hinc toto praeceps se corpore ad undas
misit avi similis, quae circum litora, circum
piscosos scopulos humilis volat aequora iuxta.   255
haud aliter terras inter caelumque volabat
litus harenosum ad Libyae, ventosque secabat
materno veniens ab avo Cyllenia proles.
ut primum alatis tetigit magalia plantis,
Aenean fundantem arces ac tecta novantem   260
conspicit: atque illi stellatus iaspide fulva

---

248. **Atlantis:** epanalepsis* of the name Atlas, calling attention to the significance of the name (see preceding n.).

249-51. **caput…umeros…mento…barba:** the mountain is personified* as an old man with "pine-wreathed head," "snowy mantle," "streaming cheeks," and "frozen beard."

252. **paribus nitens…alis:** "balancing on even wings," i.e. just before landing; Austin has "by effort of balanced wing." **Cyllenius:** Mercury was born on Mt. Cyllenius in Arcadia.

253-5. **hinc…:** closely modeled on *Od.* 5.50-4, where Hermes on his way towards Calypso's island is compared to a bird. **humilis:** nominative singular, referring to the bird (*quae*) as subject of *volat*.

258. **materno…ab avo:** Atlas was father of Maia, the mother of Mercury.

259. **magalia:** "huts," as in 1.421; cf. *Geo.* 3.340 *mapalia*.

261-4. **conspicit: atque illi…:** "he beholds Aeneas founding… And see! his sword was starred…." We see Aeneas from Mercury's point of view: the god is struck by the magnificence of his clothing, which indicates a man enslaved to a woman (cf. *uxorius* 266 n.) rather than a warrior. **iaspide:** "starred with tawny jasper" (Austin); the word for this yellow-brown jewel is a quadrisyllable here, with the initial "i" treated as a vowel, as in the allusion to this line in Juvenal 5.42-5. Austin calls 261-4 "a glimpse, seldom seen, of Virgil's hero as a happy man." Note too that Aeneas' supervision of the construction that had halted when Dido burned silently with love (86-9) suggests that he and Dido are not completely *regnorum immemores*, as Rumor had reported (194), at least in terms of Carthage. Aeneas can also be thought to be acting like a husband, perhaps even as king of Carthage (Monti 1981, 47).

ensis erat Tyrioque ardebat murice laena
demissa ex umeris, dives quae munera Dido
fecerat, et tenui telas discreverat auro.
continuo invadit: "tu nunc Karthaginis altae   265
fundamenta locas pulchramque uxorius urbem
exstruis? heu, regni rerumque oblite tuarum!
ipse deum tibi me claro demittit Olympo
regnator, caelum et terras qui numine torquet;
ipse haec ferre iubet celeris mandata per auras: 270

262. **ardebat murice:** "blazed" or "glowed with bright purple color"; the *murex* was the shellfish or marine snail from which rich purple dye was acquired, with purple from Dido's Tyre the most highly regarded shade; cf. 134 n. The specifically Carthaginian luxury of Aeneas' purple and gold *laena* is striking. The *laena* was a thick woolen cloak, worn by a *flamen* performing a sacrifice (Cic. *Brutus* 56); the word occurs only here in the *Aeneid*. A brilliant cloak (*coccina* or scarlet, Juvenal 3.283, *hyacinthina*, Persius 1.32) was a sign of luxury, though Homeric chieftains could wear a purple cloak (*Il.* 10.133, Nestor) and Roman generals a *paludamentum* of scarlet, or purple (Pliny *NH* 3.22.3, Valerius Maximus 1.8.8 of Caesar's ghost). Jason at *Arg.* 1.721-68 wears an elaborately decorated purple cloak during his visit to Hypsipyle. Florus 2.21.3 describes Antony's shocking appearance in Egypt, with scepter, scimitar, and purple robe studded with gems. Cicero thrice in the *Verrines* refers scornfully to Verres' purple Greek-style cloak (*cum pallio purpureo*; the Greek cloak may be more shocking than a *laena*), each time in the context of neglecting his duty to spend time with a girlfriend (5.12-13[31], 33[86], quoted above, 52[136]); later Cicero criticizes Antony's wearing of a *lacerna* and Caesar's use of a purple toga (*Phil.* 2.76, 85). See Thomas 2001, 166-7 on translators' attempts to protect Aeneas here, Lyne 1989, 189, Bender 1994 and Heskel 1994; Reed 2006 offers more suggestions for connotations of *ardebat laena*.

264. **fecerat, et...discreverat:** the Latin has two finite verbs where English might use a participle. The clause *et discreverat...* explains that it was made by interweaving gold threads with the wool. This line recurs at a moment of high pathos in 11.75 as Aeneas wraps the body of Pallas in one of two cloaks made by Dido that he had saved.

265. **invadit:** "assails," verbally "attacks," like *adgreditur* (92) but stronger.

266. **uxorius:** a prosaic word (*coniunx* is more common than *uxor* in verse; *uxor* occurs in Vergil only in *Ecl.* 8.29, while forms of *coniunx* appear 60 times in the *Aeneid* alone), which contemptuously suggests that Aeneas is "owned" by his "wife." Cf. Lyne 1989, 43-8, and Syed 2004, 188, who notes that Dio Cassius 50.26.5 has Octavian say before the decisive Battle of Actium that Antony is "enslaved to a woman."

268. **ipse...ipse** (270): extreme emphasis that the message comes straight from Jupiter, *ipse deum* (genitive plural) ... *regnator*. Cf. the similar (but deceptive) claim of authority made by Allecto as she appears to Turnus in 7.428 *ipsa palam fari omnipotens Saturnia iussit*.

269. **caelum...:** *torquet* goes more literally with *caelum* (guides its movement in a circle, cf. 482) than with *terras* (guides its destinies) (cf. zeugma*).

quid struis? aut qua spe Libycis teris otia terris?
si te nulla movet tantarum gloria rerum,
[nec super ipse tua moliris laude laborem,]
Ascanium surgentem et spes heredis Iuli
respice, cui regnum Italiae Romanaque tellus   275
debetur." tali Cyllenius ore locutus
mortalis visus medio sermone reliquit
et procul in tenuem ex oculis evanuit auram.
    At vero Aeneas aspectu obmutuit amens,
arrectaeque horrore comae et vox faucibus haesit.   280
ardet abire fuga dulcisque relinquere terras,
attonitus tanto monitu imperioque deorum.

---

271. **Libycis teris otia terris:** Mercury's replacement for Jupiter's words *inimica in gente moratur* (235) keeps from Aeneas any knowledge of Rome's future wars with Carthage (see 235 n.). **teris...terris:** Vergil frequently uses such assonance* (cf. 238 *parere parabat*), though here paronomasia* or even etymological wordplay* may be suggested. Cf. O'Hara 1996, and Muse 2005, who suggests that Vergil's wordplay here is modeled on Homer's wordplay at *Od.* 15.10 on the first element of the name Telemachus (= "far"); in Homer as in Vergil a god is admonishing a mortal not to forget his mission.

273. This line does not appear in our fourth-century manuscripts, and is an interpolation, an addition to the text by a later reader, suggested by 233.

274. **spes heredis Iuli:** either "the hopes of Iulus your heir," with subjective genitive, or "the hopes placed in Iulus your heir," with objective genitive. *Iuli* is trisyllabic; see 140 n. Mercury omits Jupiter's reference to "Ausonian offspring" (236).

279-95. Aeneas is stunned by Mercury's words; he burns to leave, but ponders anxiously how to tell the queen, and at last sends orders to prepare the fleet for sea, hoping to find the right time to break the news to Dido.

280. **horrore:** partly metaphorical, "dread," partly literal, "bristling." Cf. 2.774 (Aeneas seeing the shade of Creusa); 3.48 (Aeneas hearing Polydorus); 12.868 (Turnus), *Il.* 24.359 (Priam's fear when Hermes approaches), and on the style here see Lelievre 1997.

281. **ardet abire:** "he burns (with desire) to depart"; the infinitive is used with *ardet* here as with verbs expressing desire (cf. 2.10 and 64 and AG §457a). In a reversal, the image of fire (see 2 n.) is used to represent not Dido's passion but Aeneas' desire to leave. **dulcis... terras:** expresses Aeneas' attitude toward his time with Dido, perhaps in slight contrast to the viewpoint expressed by the narrator; cf. Conte 1986, 156, Fowler 2000, 47 (using the term "focalization" and citing a partially corrupt note in Servius), Laird 1997, 286. In more general terms 281-94 express Aeneas' thoughts, though they are in the third person, in what is called "free indirect discourse," a technique extremely popular in modern fiction; see Fowler 2000, 45-7, Mackie 1988, 80-3, Lelievre 1997, Thomas 1999, 225.

heu, quid agat? quo nunc reginam ambire furentem
audeat adfatu? quae prima exordia sumat?
atque animum nunc huc celerem nunc dividit illuc   285
in partisque rapit varias perque omnia versat.
haec alternanti potior sententia visa est:
Mnesthea Sergestumque vocat fortemque Serestum,
classem aptent taciti sociosque ad litora cogant,
arma parent et quae rebus sit causa novandis   290

283-4. **heu, quid agat?**: indirect deliberatives: Aeneas would say to himself *quid agam?* as Ariadne does at Catullus 64.177: *nam quo me referam?* See Reed 2007 for the motif of the distressed heroine like Ariadne, which in the *Aeneid* is applied to Dido, Turnus, and to some extent Aeneas. Dido's *quid ago* in 534 is different (see n.). **quo nunc…:** "with what address can he now approach the passion-frenzied queen?" **ambire:** "to canvass" hints at cunning and treachery; Servius glosses it as *supervenire vel subdole circumvenire* "to circumvent by flattery or guile"; *exordia* (284) also suggests rhetoric and the art of persuasion. See Clausen 1987, 45-6 = 2002, 84-5, Thomas 2001, 168-73 (who comments on translators' strenuous attempts to make Aeneas look better here), Starr 2003, and on Aeneas' reaction here in general see the sympathetic Ross 2007, 16-18.

285-6. = 8.20-1, before Aeneas' dream of the Tiber, where they are followed by a simile linking Aeneas to Medea as she ponders whether to help Jason (cf. Johnson 1976, 84-7, Lyne 1987, 125-32, Reed 2007, 187-9). The description of Aeneas' indecision also recalls Homer, e.g. *Il.* 1.189, and see next n.

287. **haec…:** "to him thus balancing (them) this view seemed better." *Alternanti* may be used intransitively, but *sententias* is easily supplied. Cf. *Il.* 14.23 "to him as he pondered (two alternatives) this seemed to be better…."

288. **Mnesthea:** Greek accusative. The line will be repeated at 12.561 as Aeneas decides to attack Latinus' city.

289-91. **aptent…cogant…parent…dissimulent:** he summons them (telling them to) "make ready…"; subjunctives in indirect command.

290. **quae rebus sit causa novandis:** "what reason there is for changing plans"; *sit* is subjunctive in indirect question; the noun + gerundive *rebus…novandis* is used where English has a gerund + direct object (AG §503). The verb *novare*, like the adjective *novus*, suggests radical or revolutionary change. As Servius Auctus notes, the dative instead of a genitive with *causa* is surprising.

dissimulent; sese interea, quando optima Dido
nesciat et tantos rumpi non speret amores,
temptaturum aditus et quae mollissima fandi
tempora, quis rebus dexter modus. ocius omnes
imperio laeti parent ac iussa facessunt.   295

291-3. **dissimulent:** cf. 305 *dissimulare* and n., 338-9 *ne finge* and n. **sese...temptaturum...:**
accusative and infinitive in indirect statement: "(saying that) he will attempt (to find)."
optima Dido: some think the adjective shows Aeneas' love for Dido, others a sense of
distance (Clausen 1987, 45, 2002, 84-5). **tantos...:** "does not expect such love to be
broken." *Spero* with the present inf. means not "hope" but "expect," and refers not to
something which may happen in the future but to what is already happening in the
present: cf. 305 *dissimulare sperasti* "did you expect to hide"; 338; 2.658; 5.18 (where it is
almost "hope"). **mollissima:** cf. 423 *viri mollis aditus et tempora*, and see Clausen 1987,
144 n. 25: "this is the only instance of the superlative of *mollis* in the *Aeneid*...—surely a
fact bearing on the tone here." Is Aeneas' hesitation a result of concern for breaking the
news gently to Dido, or cowardice that worsens the situation by leading her to think he
would leave without saying anything? Dido will learn of his plans immediately (296), speak
before Aeneas can speak to her (cf. 304 *ultro* and n.), and reproach Aeneas for trying to
hide his departure (305-6 and n.). As Thomas 1999, 173 notes, Dryden in his translation
felt uncomfortable enough about Aeneas' position here to add two lines that are not in the
Latin, the second saying that "Jove will inspire him what to say and when."

294-5. **quis:** nominative, with *modus*. **ocius...laeti:** our first glimpse of how Aeneas' men felt
about the time in Carthage. In *Od*. 10.467-74 Odysseus' men say they have stayed too long
on Circe's island, and in Apoll. Rhod. *Arg*. 1.865-74 Heracles tells the Argonauts that they
must leave the Lemnian women (cf. Clausen 2002, 82-3); for joy in leaving, cf. also *Arg*.
4.888.

At regina dolos (quis fallere possit amantem?)
praesensit, motusque excepit prima futuros
omnia tuta timens. eadem impia Fama furenti
detulit armari classem cursumque parari.
saevit inops animi totamque incensa per urbem   300

296-392: The confrontation between Dido and Aeneas.

Dido learns what is happening and confronts Aeneas; her speeches at 296-330 and 365-87
are brilliantly crafted masterpieces expressing her passion, confusion and anger; combined
with Aeneas' intervening speech they form a scene like the "agon" or contest of words in
Greek tragedy, in which characters passionately defend their positions and no one is ever
persuaded. There are specific debts to the speeches of Medea both in Euripides (when
Jason is abandoning her) and in Apollonius (when she thinks in *Arg.* 4 that she may be
abandoned), and to the lament of Ariadne abandoned by Theseus in Catullus 64.132-
201 (itself modeled in part on the speech of Medea in Euripides). Dido first reproaches
Aeneas for trying to leave secretly, and begs him to stay with her, in what she refers to as a
marriage; she wishes she at least had a child to remind him of her, in words that echo the
wedding song Catullus 61. Aeneas's restrained words at 331-61, which recall two speeches
of Jason's in the *Argonautica,* hide his pain and (most but not all readers think) his love:
Aeneas tells Dido nothing that she wants to hear. He claims that they were never married,
warns her against "enflaming" them both, and says that the gods' commands drive him to
leave for Italy. In Dido's furious second speech she reviles Aeneas for betraying her love,
complains of the gods' unfairness, hopes he will die at sea calling her name, and threatens
to haunt him when she is dead (her formal curse will come later, in 615-29). On these
speeches, on the relationship of Dido and Aeneas, or on gender issues in Book 4 see G.W.
Williams 1968, Highet 1972, 72-80, 132-9, Rudd 1976, Perkell 1981, Wiltshire 1989, 90-
3, Feeney 1990 and 1998, Clausen 1987, 48-9 and 2002, 88-91, Horsfall 1995, Oliensis
1997, Gibson 1999, Starks 1999, Nugent 1999, Hinds 2000, Keith 2000, Nelis 2001, 148-
52, Thomas 2001, 185-9, Ross 2007, 18-9, 32-5, Schiesaro 2008.

296. **At regina:** begins a new section, as at 1 and 504. **dolos:** is the narrator-poet calling what
Aeneas does "treachery" (cf. Aeneas' use of the term for Ulysses and Sinon in 2.44, 62, 152,
196) or does the text again represent Dido's point of view, as Austin suggests? Cf. 172 n. on
culpa.

297. **praesensit:** "divined." **excepit…:** "caught (the news of) his coming departure." *Excipere*
is used in prose with *rumores, voces, sermonem*; the verb implies that the person who catches
the rumor is on the look-out for it.

298. **omnia tuta timens:** "fearing all safety" (*omnia tuta* is neuter plural). *Tuta timere* is "to
fear where all is safe" (cf. Ovid, *Met.* 7.47 *quid tuta times?* [Medea!]); *omnia t. t.* is a stronger
form of the phrase, "to fear where all is *absolutely* safe." Dido at once detected Aeneas' plan,
because even before, when all was safe, she was full of fear and on the watch.

300. **inops animi:** "powerless in mind," with no power to control her rage, cf. the common
use of *impotens.* For the case of *animi,* cf. 203 n.

bacchatur, qualis commotis excita sacris
Thyias, ubi audito stimulant trieterica Baccho
orgia nocturnusque vocat clamore Cithaeron.
tandem his Aenean compellat vocibus ultro:
⌈"dissimulare etiam sperasti, perfide, tantum   305
⌊posse nefas, tacitusque mea decedere terra?
nec te noster amor nec te data dextera quondam
nec moritura tenet crudeli funere Dido?

301-2. **qualis…**: after the verb *bacchatur*, a simile* further likens Dido to a raging worshipper
of Bacchus or Dionysus. The festival of Bacchus was celebrated every other year (*trieterica*
means "every third year" but with inclusive counting) on Mt. Cithaeron near Thebes, when
mystic emblems (*sacra*) were brought forth and with cries to the god the Bacchants, also
called Thyiads or Maenads, rushed over Cithaeron. Cf. 7.385-91, where Queen Amata and
her followers roam the woods in a kind of counterfeit worship of Bacchus. Hughes 2002
notes that Andromache is compared to a Maenad at *Il.* 6.388-9, one of several links she
finds between Aeneas-Dido and Hector-Andromache. **Thyias:** scans as disyllable, with *yi* as
a diphthong, and suggestive of Grk. θύω, "rage" or "run madly." **audito … Baccho:** may
mean "when the voice of Bacchus is heard," but more probably refers to the well-known cry
of his name by his worshippers.

303. **vocat:** Mt. Cithaeron is lightly personified* so as to be subject of *vocat*; we could also call
this a syntactical inversion or enallage*; cf. 226 n. and Conte 2007, 111.

304. **compellat…ultro:** "crucial is *ultro*: Dido speaks first, while Aeneas, who has planned to offer an
explanation, is forced instead into an anguished and halting defence" (Horsfall 1995, 131).

305-6. **dissimulare…tacitus…**: metrically, Dido in 305-13 begins with lines in which
rapidity of speech is expressed through frequent coincidence of ictus and accent (see
appendix on meter), especially in the crucial fourth foot; in contrast, there is much clash
in the last three feet of lines 314-19 (cf. 314 n.). The hissing s's resemble those of the start
of Medea's speech to Jason at Euripides, *Med.* 476. Clausen 2002, 86 notes that Dido
"repeat[s] two words, *taciti* (289) and *dissimulent* (291), from Aeneas' secret instructions
to his men, as if she had overheard him…." The technique is like that of Achilles' use of
the word "kinglier" in *Il.* 9.392, used in Agamemnon's instructions to Odysseus (160), but
dropped by the tactful Odysseus. **perfide:** "faithless one," "traitor," also at 366; at Catullus
64.132-3, Ariadne calls Theseus *perfide* in each of the first two lines of her speech. Starks
1999 suggests that Vergil has Dido throw back in Aeneas' face Roman stereotypes about
Carthaginian treachery.

307. **data dextera quondam:** cf. *dextram* 314; was it a pledge of marriage, as in the models
at *Arg.* 4.99 and Eurip. *Medea* 21, or merely political alliance? Vergil has not shown us the
scene in which the answer to this question might have been made clear. At 7.365-6 Amata
cites Latinus' pledges to Turnus (*totiens data dextera Turno*); were these alliances, or did
they involve a promise of his daughter's hand in marriage? Cf. 172 n. and Monti 1981, 3-8,
27-8, Horsfall on 7.366, and Hersch 2010 index s.v. "*dextrarum iunctio* (handclasp)" on the
Roman wedding. At 10.517 after the death of Pallas Aeneas is anguished at the thought of
right hands given (*dextraeque datae*) to Pallas' father.

quin etiam hiberno moliris sidere classem
et mediis properas Aquilonibus ire per altum, 310
crudelis? quid, si non arva aliena domosque
ignotas peteres, et Troia antiqua maneret,
Troia per undosum peteretur classibus aequor? *with*
your
mene fugis? per ego has lacrimas dextramque tuam te *fleet*
(quando aliud mihi iam miserae nihil ipsa reliqui)? 315
per conubia nostra, per inceptos hymenaeos,
si bene quid de te merui, fuit aut tibi quicquam
dulce meum, miserere domus labentis et istam,

309-10. **hiberno…sidere:** the ancients regularly avoided the danger of seafaring in the winter (cf. Anna's words at 52-3 and n., and the storm that arises at the start of *Aen.* 5 just after the Trojans have left Carthage). **Aquilonibus:** the North Wind is associated with rain and storm.

311. **crudelis:** Vergil, like Homer, often gives emphasis to an adjective by placing it in enjambment* at the beginning of a line with a pause after it. Cf. 72 *nescius,* 185 *stridens,* 366 *perfide,* 496 *impius,* 562 *demens;* 2.345 *infelix,* 372 *inscius,* 529 *saucius;* 5.480 *arduus;* 6.172, 590 *demens,* 822 *infelix.*

311-13. **quid, si…:** these contrary-to-fact clauses make the argument that, even if he were going home, he would not start in such weather (cf. 309-10 and n.), and so his haste must reflect eagerness to escape from her.

314. **mene fugis?:** the powerful simplicity of this question is striking. Clausen 2002, 87 says asking why a lover flees is "an old poetic motif, here first in epic" and gives parallels (cf. Clausen 1987, 145 n. 39); with 6.466 *quem fugis?* Aeneas will echo these words in speaking to the shade of Dido in their encounter in the underworld. **per ego has…:** placing a word between *per* and its object in an oath is common. **te:** direct object of *oro* in 319. The final monosyllable produces an unusual clash of ictus and accent in the sixth foot, and then in 316 the four-syllable final word produces clash in the last two feet (on the meter of 314-19 see 305 n. and Highet 1972, 134-5).

316. **conubia…:** adapted from Ariadne's complaint at Cat. 64.140-1 after she has been abandoned by Theseus: *non haec miseram sperare iubebas, / sed conubia laeta sed optatos hymenaeos,* where *conubia* is also a synonym of *hymenaeos;* in both passages the quadrisyllabic ending produces a Greek-sounding rhythm (see also 314 n.).

317. **si bene quid…:** "if I have done you any service, if anything of mine was ever dear to you": cf. Sophocles *Ajax* 520-1 (Ajax's wife Tecmessa speaks) "But remember me too. A man should remember if he has experienced anything pleasant (*terpnon*)" (cf. Panoussi 2002, 106, and 2009). For *dulce,* cf. 281 *dulcis…terras* and n., and Juturna's words to Turnus at 12.882. Note that *si quid…,* "if…anything" (for the indefinite *quis, quid,* found only after *nisi, si, num,* and *ne,* see AG §310), really means "as surely as…", but in 319 *si quis…locus* expresses doubt.

318. **domus labentis:** "falling house," because Aeneas, who had helped hold it up, was leaving (for the language of collapse see 391 n.).

oro, si quis adhuc precibus locus, exue mentem.
te propter Libycae gentes Nomadumque tyranni   320
odere, infensi Tyrii; te propter eundem
exstinctus pudor et, qua sola sidera adibam,
fama prior. cui me moribundam deseris, hospes?
(hoc solum nomen quoniam de coniuge restat)?
quid moror? an mea Pygmalion dum moenia frater   325
destruat aut captam ducat Gaetulus Iarbas?
saltem si qua mihi de te suscepta fuisset
ante fugam suboles, si quis mihi parvulus aula

320-1. **te propter…**: the postposition or anastrophe of *propter* puts emphasis on *te*, as does
the repetition in 321. **infensi Tyrii**: supply *sunt*; as 294-5 tell us how Aeneas' men viewed
the stay at Carthage, here we have a claim that Dido's people resent her relationship with
Aeneas. **eundem:** = "also," "too," as often.

322. **exstinctus pudor…**: "my honor has been destroyed, and that former fame by which
alone I was approaching heaven." *Sidera adire* is "to win immortality," as Aeneas will (*feres
ad sidera caeli*, 1.259). Catullus' Ariadne, one of the models for Dido's speech, will have her
crown literally become a constellation; this is mentioned not in Cat. 64 but in 66.59-61 in
the poem about Queen Berenice's lock of hair becoming a constellation. By her "former
fame" Dido seems to mean her reputation for fidelity to her dead husband, though the
fame of building Carthage, which will now be destroyed (cf. 325), is not excluded. For
pudor, see 27 n.

323-4. **hospes…de coniuge:** "O guest (since only that name is left in place of 'husband')."
The clause with *quoniam…* explains why she says *hospes*; on guest-friendship, cf. also 10 n.
and 424 n. Servius says that Vergil read this passage to Augustus with intense pathos.

325. **quid moror?:** "why do I delay?" i.e. to die, cf. *moribundam* 323. **an mea…dum…:** "or
(shall I delay) until…?" For *dum* with the subjunctive expressing expectation cf. AG §553.
For Dido's brother, cf. 20-1 n.

327. **suscepta fuisset…:** "had been taken into my arms." The contrary-to-fact condition
has two protases, one past and so with a pluperfect verb, one present with an imperfect
verb. *Suscipere* is used "originally of taking up a new-born child (cf. 9.203), symbolizing
an intent to rear it; then, by an easy transfer, of the begetting or bearing of children"
(Pease). The childlessness of *infelix Dido* adds to the pathos of the situation; see 68-9 n.
on her epithet *infelix*, and recall Anna's argument in 32-3 that Dido should not pass up
this chance to have *dulcis natos*. Hypsipyle in *Arg.* 1.897-8, the other model in Apollonius'
poem (along with Medea) for Dido, mentions the possibility of having a child by Jason, and
in fact she will (cf. Nelis 2001, 161-2, 181-3, Krevans 2002-3). At Ovid, *Heroides* 7.133-8
Dido speculates on whether she may be pregnant.

328. **parvulus:** the only diminutive adjective in the poem, which suggests both Catullus
in general because of his frequent use of diminutives, and the marriage-poem Catullus
61 in particular (*Torquatus…parvulus*, 209; cf. Petrini 1997, 91-3, Gutting 2006, 268-9).
Apuleius, *Met.* 5.13 alludes to this passage tenderly, Juvenal, *Satire* 5.138 with sarcasm.

luderet Aeneas, qui te tamen ore referret,
non equidem omnino capta ac deserta viderer." 330
Dixerat. ille Iovis monitis immota tenebat
lumina et obnixus curam sub corde premebat.
tandem pauca refert: "ego te, quae plurima fando
enumerare vales, numquam, regina, negabo
promeritam, nec me meminisse pigebit Elissae, 335
dum memor ipse mei, dum spiritus hos regit artus.]

329. **tamen:** means "notwithstanding" or "nevertheless," but is hard to translate, because the suppressed thought opposed to it must be supplied or suggested in translation. It may be "to remind me of you by his face in spite of all (your cruelty)," or "though you are far away," or "with his face at least, though he can do so with nothing else." Each of these thoughts is suggested by *tamen* (called "beautiful" by Page), but none of them is right by itself.

330. **capta:** suggests both *decepta*, as in Ovid's short version of the story at *Met.* 14.81, and also a woman captured (and perhaps raped) in the taking of a city. For *deserta*, cf. Ariadne in Catullus 64.57.

331-61. Aeneas, hiding his pain, replies, acknowledging his debt to Dido but denying that they were married. He cites visions of his father, thoughts of his son, and Jupiter's commands as delivered by Mercury, and says he must go.

Aeneas' reply recalls two speeches of Jason's, to Hypsipyle at *Arg.* 1.900-9, and to Medea at 4.395-409. It has struck many readers as cold and lacking in sympathy. The poet's introductory verses (331-2) and Aeneas' warning that Dido not "enflame" them both (360) suggest that it might be dangerous for Aeneas to be anything other than cold, but Aeneas is given little chance here to earn the reader's sympathy. Aeneas shows no affection for Dido (though the narrator tells us in 332 of his *cura*; is this "love" or just "worry"?), and he admits no personal responsibility for the situation. Different readers, then, will find Aeneas here "despicable" (Page) and a man of "incomplete humanity" (Perkell 1981), or a model of "self-control" (Cairns 1989, 52-3) and self-sacrifice (more references above on 296-392). We should strive to keep both views in mind.

332. **obnixus…:** "struggling, he smothered his care/love (cf. previous note) within his heart." Aeneas also hid his pain from his men in a key passage at 1.208-9: *talia voce refert curisque ingentibus aeger / spem vultu simulat, premit altum corde dolorem*; cf. O'Hara 1990, 8-9, 134-7.

333-5. **pauca:** cf. *pauca* 337. His speech is longer than Dido's, but says less than Dido wants to hear. **te…promeritam:** understand *esse*; picks up *si bene quid de te merui* (317). **quae plurima…:** the things which she is able to name in great abundance (the phrase is used at 8.427, of Jupiter's lightning bolts). **Elissae:** Dido's Phoenician name. It is unclear whether the use of the name is supposed to sound more intimate or more formal and distanced; cf. Clausen 2002, 85.

336. **dum memor…mei:** "while I have memory of myself"; cf. *Il.* 22.387-8 (Achilles to Patroclus) and *Arg.* 3.1079-80 (Jason to Medea), as well as Aeneas' promise in 1.607-10, marked by a triple *dum*, that he will always honor and praise Dido.

pro re pauca loquar. neque ego hanc abscondere furto
speravi (ne finge) fugam, nec coniugis umquam
praetendi taedas aut haec in foedera veni.
me si fata meis paterentur ducere vitam 340
auspiciis et sponte mea componere curas,
urbem Troianam primum dulcisque meorum
reliquias colerem, Priami tecta alta manerent,
et recidiva manu posuissem Pergama victis.

---

337. **pro re pauca loquar:** Aeneas' speech begins very formally. The opening 333-6 is the
regular and formal *exordium* or *captatio benevolentiae* prescribed in books on rhetoric, after
which Aeneas adds that he will "speak briefly on the charge," *res* being the subject-matter
of the accusation made against him; cf. Sallust, *Iug.* 102.12 *pauca pro delicto suo verba facit*,
and in imitation of Vergil, Seneca, *Herc. Furens* 401-2 *pauca pro causa loquar/ nostra*, and
see Feeney 1990, 169-71. He then addresses the charge, with the first words of the defense
answering to the first words of the accusation, namely that he never hoped "stealthily to
conceal his flight" (see next n.).

338-9. **ne finge:** *ne* with the present imperative is poetic or colloquial (AG §450a). Aeneas
tells Dido not to "make up" charges that he expected to depart without telling her (305-
6), and he may be sincere, but we have seen that he did tell his men to conceal their initial
preparations while he looked for the best time to tell Dido (287-95, esp. 291 *dissimulent*;
see 305 n. and Thomas 1999, 224-6). **nec coniugis…:** "nor did I ever hold out the
bridegroom's torch, nor join such a compact." **praetendi:** "put forward as a pretence," but
also with the idea of actually "holding out" a marriage torch, even though this was not
a part of a Roman wedding. This claim of Aeneas' is crucial to his view of the situation
(on marriage, cf. 160-72 n.). **foedera:** suggests a political or guest-friendship alliance, in
language applied by Catullus (76.3, 109.6) to his relationship with Lesbia, which Vergil
here uses of a liaison between rulers that involves both love and politics; cf. Monti 1981,
56-62 and below 520 n.

340-1. **meis…auspiciis:** "at my own behest" or "authority." A commander takes the auspices
himself and acts for himself (cf. 102 n.), while his officers only obey orders, as Aeneas does
here. When Aeneas says, in effect, "If I could do what I want," surely Dido would expect
him to say "I would stay here with you." In the classroom exercise described in Suerbaum
1998 and the review by Barchiesi 1998, most students finished the sentence in just that
way. But nothing in Aeneas' speech tells Dido what she wants to hear.

342-4. **dulcisque…:** "and the sweet remnants of my people I would honor: Priam's lofty
halls would still exist and (almost = 'for') I should (before now) with my hand have raised
a restored citadel for the vanquished." The "remnants" are clearly the remains of Troy;
colerem suggests both "honor, cherish" and "inhabit, live in" (cf. *incolerem*). Note the
change of tense in *manerent* and *posuissem*. Courtney 1981 argues, unconvincingly I think,
that *manerent* cannot refer to rebuilding, and that the text is corrupt. The text can be
defended if we see that Aeneas, somewhat illogically, echoes Dido's *Troia antiqua maneret*
in 312. Cf. too Aeneas' apostrophe* at 2.56 *Priamique arx alta maneres*.

sed nunc Italiam magnam Gryneus Apollo,   345⎤
Italiam Lyciae iussere capessere sortes;   ⎦
hic amor, haec patria est. si te Karthaginis arces
Phoenissam Libycaeque aspectus detinet urbis,
quae tandem Ausonia Teucros considere terra
invidia est? et nos fas extera quaerere regna.   350⎤
me patris Anchisae, quotiens umentibus umbris   ⎦
nox operit terras, quotiens astra ignea surgunt,

---

345. **Gryneus:** Apollo had a temple at Grynium, on the coast of Aeolia. Aeneas consulted Apollo through Helenus in 3.369-462, but that was at Buthrotum on the coast of Epirus. There may be a literary allusion that we do not fully understand in the adjective *Gryneus*. Two poetic mentors of Vergil's, the Greek poet Parthenius and the Latin elegist Cornelius Gallus (who like Dido committed suicide), wrote about Grynean Apollo. Parthenius *SH* fr. 620 has the phrase *Grynaios Apollo* in Greek, and Gallus discussed the story of Apollo's Grynean grove, as we see from *Ecl.* 6.72 *Grynei nemoris* and Servius' note there; cf. O'Hara 1993a, and Miller 2009, 100-1, who says this reference to Apollo "looks like an allusion to a variant oracular tour of Asia Minor before Aeneas headed west."

346. **sortes:** "oracles," often written on small tablets or lots. For Apollo's connection with Lycia, cf. 143 n.; Apollo Lykios also appears in the well-known programmatic passage at Callimachus *Aetia* 1.22, telling the poet not to write epic or long poetry.

347-50. **hic amor, haec patria est:** emphatic: "this is my love (not you), this is my homeland." Each demonstrative is attracted into the gender of the following noun (AG §296a). Some have seen allusion here to Amor as the "secret name" of Roma (references at O'Hara 1996, 156, including Serv. on *Aen.* 1.277). **si te…Phoenissam:** the argument answers Dido's suggestion that he was only leaving her for "foreign fields" (311): if Carthage in Libya has a hold on Dido, a Phoenician, what objection can there be that the Trojans feel the same about Ausonia? **quae…invidia est:** "what (cause of) resentment is there that the Teucrians settle…?" "Why resent…?" **et nos:** "we too…."

351. **patris Anchisae:** the genitive is governed by *imago* at the end of 353. We have heard nothing of these dream appearances, and may be as skeptical as Dido, but an epic poet may allude to events not narrated earlier. Servius several times uses a term we find in comments by Greek scholiasts, κατὰ τὸ σιοπώμενον, for events "passed over in silence" but assumed by the subsequent narrative to have happened, e.g. on 5.282, 9.83. And in 6.695-6 Aeneas says that Anchises has frequently appeared to him (we see one appearance in 5.722-40). Cf. Nünlist 2009, 157-73 on the term in Homeric scholia.

admonet in somnis et turbida terret imago;
me puer Ascanius capitisque iniuria cari,
quem regno Hesperiae fraudo et fatalibus arvis.   355
nunc etiam interpres divum Iove missus ab ipso
(testor utrumque caput) celeres mandata per auras
detulit: ipse deum manifesto in lumine vidi
intrantem muros vocemque his auribus hausi.
desine meque tuis incendere teque querellis;   360
Italiam non sponte sequor."
     Talia dicentem iamdudum aversa tuetur
huc illuc volvens oculos totumque pererrat
luminibus tacitis et sic accensa profatur:

354. **me puer Ascanius…:** understand a verb such as *admonet* or *terret* from 353 with *puer* and *iniuria*. **capitis…iniuria cari:** "the wrong to his dear head." *Caput* can be used for a person in strongly emotional language, e.g. 613 *infandum caput* and 640 *Dardanii … capitis* (though most examples display affection and not hatred, as in those two passages), Hor. *Carm.* 1.24.2 *tam cari capitis*, and *caput* paired in comedy with *lepidum* (Ter. *Ad.* 966), *festivum* (*Ad.* 261) and *ridiculum* (*And.* 371). Cf. oaths which are directed against the head as the most vital part, as in 357 and 493 below, so that *caput* = "life." Cf. van Hook (1949).

356: **interpres divum:** as Servius notes, here and in 378 Vergil alludes to and glosses the Greek name for Mercury, Hermes; cf. ἑρμηνεύς, "interpreter, go-between."

357. **testor…:** "I swear by (lit. 'call to witness') your head and mine." Cf. Apoll. Rhod. *Arg.* 3.151 (Aphrodite to Eros) "Be witness now your dear head and mine," Ovid, *Her.* 3.107 *perque tuum nostrumque caput, quae iunximus una.* See also 354 n.

360. **incendere:** not just "stop making us both emotional" (Williams), for the metaphor* of fire applies here as elsewhere in the book. Aeneas seems to fear losing control.

361. **Italiam…sequor:** "A fine half line [whose] powerful terseness is in striking contrast with the wordy rhetoric of the rest of the speech" (Page). There is no reason to think that the half-lines in the *Aeneid* that were incomplete at Vergil's death were meant to be left that way (see 42-4 n.), but Page well notes that "Nothing … could improve these four words thus left rugged and abrupt."

362-92. Dido replies in furious anger, insulting Aeneas, complaining about the gods, stressing what she has done for him, and mocking his citation of messages from the gods. She hopes he will die at sea calling her name, and promises to haunt him when she is dead.

Vergil adapts elements of the speeches of Medea in Euripides, *Med.* 465-519 and in Apoll. Rhod. *Arg.* 4.355-90, and that of Ariadne in Catullus 64.132-201, but with all the furious emotion that Latin rhetoric and skillful manipulation of metrical effects allow.

362. **aversa:** Dido is "turned away" so she looks at him "askance," "out of the corner of her eye"; as again when they meet in the underworld at 6.469. Note how in 362-4 Vergil conveys Dido's emotional state by describing her external appearance.

"nec tibi diva parens generis nec Dardanus auctor,   365
perfide, sed duris genuit te cautibus horrens
Caucasus Hyrcanaeque admorunt ubera tigres.
nam quid dissimulo aut quae me ad maiora reservo?
num fletu ingemuit nostro? num lumina flexit?
num lacrimas victus dedit aut miseratus amantem est?   370
quae quibus anteferam? iam iam nec maxima Iuno
nec Saturnius haec oculis pater aspicit aequis.
nusquam tuta fides. eiectum litore, egentem
excepi et regni demens in parte locavi.
amissam classem, socios a morte reduxi   375

365-6. **nec tibi diva parens…:** Venus; for *Dardanus*, see 163 n. This insult has a long history (and is in sharp contrast to Dido's praise of Aeneas' stock in 12): cf. *Il.* 16.33-5 (Patroclus to Achilles), Catullus 60 and 64.154-7 (Ariadne), and *Ecl.* 8.43-5 (a lover denounces Amor), and then later Ovid, *Her.* 7.37-9 (Dido). See also the discussion in Macrobius, *Sat.* 5.11.14 (in a fifth-century fictionalized dialogue about Vergil) and in Pease's n. here. **perfide:** cf. 305 n.

367. **Caucasus Hyrcanaeque:** *Caucasus* refers to the area between the Black Sea and the Caspian Sea, of which Hyrcania is a part. **admorunt:** = *admoverunt.*

368. **nam…:** "for why conceal (my real thoughts)? Or for what greater wrongs (*maiora* = something like *maiora mala*) do I reserve myself?" The indicative *dissimulo* is like a deliberative subjunctive but is more vivid; cf. 3.88, but 534 below is different (see n.).

369-70. **ingemuit:** the use of the third person may express scorn, or suggest that these lines are a soliloquy in which she forgets Aeneas' presence and argues with herself, before addressing him in the second person again in 380; cf. Highet 1972, 150. **num…num… num:** the tricolon crescendo* with anaphora* beautifully expresses Dido's growing rage. **victus:** "defeated," "yielding."

371. **quae quibus anteferam?:** lit. "what shall I put before what?" Since everything is completely hopeless, she does not know, or care, what thought, word, or deed should come first.

372. **nec Saturnius haec oculis pater aspicit aequis:** even the gods seem to Dido no longer just; she has no idea, of course, of the role Juno and Jupiter have played in her disaster. The unusual rhythm produces coincidence of ictus and accent in the first three words of the line. The epithet *Saturnius* is not used elsewhere in Vergil for Jupiter, though it is applied often to Juno (cf. above 92); it refers to their father Saturnus, and has connotations of the Golden Age and of the Saturnian Italy evoked in *Aeneid* 7-12 (e.g. 8.329) and at times in the *Georgics* (e.g. 2.173 with the n. of Thomas 1988; on the Golden Age in Vergil, see Perkell 2002).

373. **eiectum:** "shipwrecked" (understand *eum*). Dido's complaints are like those of Iarbas against her at 211-18. The double asyndeton* (there is no connector between *eiectum litore* and *egentem*, or *classem* and *socios,* or *locavi* and *reduxi*) marks excited feeling.

(heu furiis incensa feror!): nunc augur Apollo,
nunc Lyciae sortes, nunc et Iove missus ab ipso
interpres divum fert horrida iussa per auras.
scilicet is superis labor est, ea cura quietos
sollicitat. neque te teneo neque dicta refello: 380
i, sequere Italiam ventis, pete regna per undas.
spero equidem mediis, si quid pia numina possunt,
supplicia hausurum scopulis et nomine Dido
saepe vocaturum. sequar atris ignibus absens;

376-7. **nunc...nunc...nunc:** repeating in scorn the *nunc...nunc* of Aeneas (345, 356), here in
another tricolon crescendo* (cf. 369-70 n.). Note too the sarcastic recapitulation of his list
of deities.

378. **horrida:** "awe-inspiring." She mocks the description given by Aeneas at 356-9. In
Odyssey 5, Zeus sent Hermes to the goddess restraining Odysseus, Calypso, while in Vergil
Mercury comes to Aeneas and Dido hears nothing herself.

379. **scilicet:** "certainly," "to be sure," a more formal version of "yeah, right" (cf. irony*).
Dido's scornful words in 379-87 are expressed in hexameters with much clash of ictus and
accent (see appendix on meter), reflecting her troubled emotional state. **ea cura...:** "that
trouble bothers their repose," i.e. trouble about Aeneas. Dido's language recalls the gods of
Epicurus as described by Lucretius (e.g. *DRN* 1.44-9), whose "sacred everlasting calm" is
never marred by *cura* or thought of human sorrow (see 34 n.).

381. **i, sequere...:** mocks *Italiam...sequor* 361.

382. **pia:** "righteous." The noun *pietas* and adjective *pius* are key terms in the *Aeneid*, and
properly describe loyalty, esp. to gods, family, and country. Aeneas is called "a man
outstanding in *pietas*" (*insignem pietate virum* 1.10), and his standard epithet is *pius* (it is
applied to his name 17x); when he meets his mother in disguise, among his first words are *sum
pius Aeneas* (1.378). Here Dido's claim that *pia numina* will punish him is meant (by her) to
be ironic. Note too the bitter recall of "if the gods care for those who are *pius*" in Aeneas' first
speech to Dido in 1.603. On *pietas*, cf. Austin on 1.10, Horsfall on 7.5, Mackie 1988 index
s.vv. *pietas* and *pius*, Wiltshire 1989, 135-8, Garrison 1992, Putnam 1995, Spence 2002.

383. **supplicia hausurum:** supply *te esse*: "that you will drain the cup of vengeance" (lit.
"punishment"). *Haurire* is used even in prose of suffering calamity (cf. *exhausta*, 14),
but here the original meaning of the word may (momentarily) suggest drowning. **Dido:**
probably Grk. accusative, though elsewhere Vergil does not inflect the word: it might be
vocative, as Austin suggests.

384-5. **sequar...:** "though far away I will pursue you with dark torches and, when chill death
has severed (my) limbs from soul, my ghost will haunt you everywhere." Blazing torches are
borne by the Furies (cf. 472 and n., 7.456-7 where Allecto hurls *atro / lumine fumantis...
taedas*), and with them they pursue the guilty, cf. Cicero, *pro Rosc.* 67 *perterreri Furiarum
taedis ardentibus*, Suet., *Nero* 34 *confessus exagitari se materna specie, verberibusque Furiarum ac*

et cum frigida mors anima seduxerit artus,   385
omnibus umbra locis adero. dabis, inprobe, poenas.
audiam et haec manis veniet mihi fama sub imos."
his medium dictis sermonem abrumpit et auras
aegra fugit seque ex oculis avertit et aufert,
linquens multa metu cunctantem et multa parantem   390
dicere. suscipiunt famulae conlapsaque membra
marmoreo referunt thalamo stratisque reponunt.

---

taedis ardentibus. Vergil adapts the words of Medea at Apoll. Rhod. *Arg.* 4.386 ("my Erinyes" = Furies) and her sister Chalciope at 3.704 (Erinys). Servius says that *anima seduxerit artus* is hypallage (also called enallage*) because normally the soul would be severed from the body; cf. 226 n., Conte 2007, 90.

386. **dabis, improbe, poenas:** cf. Ennius *Ann.* fr. 95 Sk. = 1-3 W *nam mi calido dabis sanguine poenas,* Catullus 116.8 *tu dabis supplicium* (alluding to Ennius), Latinus at *Aen.* 7.595 *ipsi has sacrilego pendetis sanguine poenas,* and Aeneas at 8.538: *quas poenas mihi, Turne, dabis!*

388. **auras:** "the day," "the (open) air."

390. **linquens...:** notice the stammering iteration of this line with its marked repetition of *multa,* three words beginning with "m" (cf. alliteration*), and its double *–antem* (consonance*). Similar language marks a similar desire to say more (both times to a dead lover/spouse) at 2.790-1 (Aeneas and Creusa) and *Geo.* 4.501-2 (Orpheus and Eurydice). Feeney 1990, 176: "After the gulf that has opened between them, the enjambment* and isolation of *dicere* harshly expose the inadequacy of mere speech."

391. **conlapsaque:** here and at 664 Vergil uses "a verb normally reserved for the description of collapsing buildings" (Lyne 1989, 41-2); at 664 this is "five lines before the simile that compares the lamentation at Dido's death to that which might attend the sack of her city." The same verb is used when Evander, the Arcadian king living on the future site of Rome whose son's death in battle will enrage Aeneas in Book 10, collapses and is carried away by his *famuli* at 8.584-5 (Clausen 1987, 50, 2002, 92).

392. **marmoreo...:** "carry *back* to her marble chamber and *duly* place upon the couch." Note the different use of *re-* in *referunt* and *reponunt,* for which cf. 403. **thalamo:** dative = *in thalamum,* cf. AG §428h.

At pius Aeneas, quamquam lenire dolentem
solando cupit et dictis avertere curas,
multa gemens magnoque animum labefactus amore   395
iussa tamen divum exsequitur classemque revisit.
tum vero Teucri incumbunt et litore celsas
deducunt toto navis. natat uncta carina,
frondentisque ferunt remos et robora silvis
infabricata fugae studio.   400

393-503: Aeneas prepares to leave, and Dido resolves to die.

Pius Aeneas obeys the gods and returns to his ships, groaning much and close to failing because of love (393-6). As the Trojans prepare to leave, a simile, suggestive both of Apollonius of Rhodes and of the archaic Roman poet Ennius, compares their busy actions on the shore to those of ants hard at work (402-7), and the poet addresses Dido and asks what she was feeling as she watched (408-12). Dido asks Anna, curiously described as in some ways closer to Aeneas than she (421-3), to intercede, and to ask that he at least delay his departure (413-36). Aeneas is unmoved, like an oak whose roots reaching down to Tartarus make it able to withstand heavy winds (the simile has many poetic models), and useless tears fall (437-49). Dido longs for death, and ill omens that include the voice of her dead husband strengthen her resolve, as do dreams in which she is isolated, or pursued by Aeneas as characters in tragedy are pursued by Furies or by their victims (450-73). But she addresses Anna with a feigned look of hope and says she has found a priestess whose magic will either return Aeneas to her or release her from love for him; the rite will involve building a large pyre (474-503).

393. **at pius Aeneas:** Vergil boldly follows Dido's speech by calling Aeneas *pius* (cf. 382 n.), which has struck different readers in different ways, either as an outrageous claim in the face of his disloyalty to Dido (at 693 Juno is called *omnipotens* at her moment of failure), or as a firm explanation of why he is right to leave her. The epithet—like the whole book— highlights the difficulties and potential conflicting loyalties involved in attempts to adhere to *pietas.*

395. **multa…:** "groaning much, his heart weakened by strong love." *Multa* cogn. accusative used adverbially, cf. 390 *multa…cunctantem;* 3.610 *haud multa moratus.* **animum labefactus amore:** *animum* is accusative of specification (AG §397d). Aeneas comes close to failing in his resolve; cf. 22 *animumque labantem* of Dido, and 8.390 *labefacta per ossa,* of Vulcan as he yields to Venus' seduction. *Amore* tells us that Aeneas loves Dido, or (less likely) that he is shaken by her great love for him; still he follows the commands of the gods (*iussa deum*) and returns to the ships (*classem*).

398. **uncta:** "well pitched," with pitch smeared in the cracks to make the vessels waterproof. Cf. *labitur uncta vadis abies* 8.91; both recall Ennius, *Ann.* fr. 376 Sk. = 374 W *labitur uncta carina.*

399-400. **frondentis…remos:** "leafy oars," i.e. boughs made into oars, not smoothly finished because of their eagerness to leave. For the unfinished line 400, cf. 42-4 n.

migrantis cernas totaque ex urbe ruentis.
ac velut ingentem formicae farris acervum
cum populant hiemis memores tectoque reponunt,
it nigrum campis agmen praedamque per herbas
convectant calle angusto: pars grandia trudunt   405
obnixae frumenta umeris, pars agmina cogunt
castigantque moras, opere omnis semita fervet.
quis tibi tum, Dido, cernenti talia sensus,
quosve dabas gemitus, cum litora fervere late
prospiceres arce ex summa, totumque videres   410
misceri ante oculos tantis clamoribus aequor!
improbe Amor, quid non mortalia pectora cogis!
ire iterum in lacrimas, iterum temptare precando
cogitur et supplex animos summittere amori,
ne quid inexpertum frustra moritura relinquat.   415

402-6. **ac velut…cum:** when Aeneas saw the Carthaginians at work on their city Vergil compared them to bees (1.430-36); now the Trojans as they prepare to leave are compared to ants, in a simile* inspired by *Arg.* 4.1452-7. **cum populant:** the ants "despoil" like a conquering army; do the Trojans? Cf. Lyne 1987, 19, Nisbet 1990, 382. The collective nouns *agmen* and *pars* (405, 406) are used with plural verbs (AG §317d). **it nigrum campis agmen:** note the slow and stately movement of this line's five spondees. Servius says it is from an Ennian passage on elephants (frag. 502 Sk. = 513 W); cf. Reed 2007, 99.

408. **quis tibi tum, Dido:** in the apostrophe* at 408-11 we realize that we have been looking down on the Trojans through Dido's eyes; cf. Reed 2007, 99; less satisfying Syed 2004, 238 n. 14, and on both this passage and on apostrophe in Vergil more broadly see Behr 2005, with references. Cf. also Soph. *Phil.* 276-84, where Philoctetes describes how he felt when he saw that the Greeks had abandoned him on Lemnos.

412. **improbe Amor:** another apostrophe,* this time one in which the narrator blames not Dido but Amor; cf. Behr 2005. "O wicked Love": the modern editor must choose whether to capitalize *Amor* and similar terms, but Vergil's readers saw only letters of one type, and so the line between *Amor* and *amor* was not so clearly drawn. Amor is *improbus* because he compels (cf. *cogis*) Dido and everyone else to yield to him; from Dido's point of view it is Aeneas who is *improbus* (386). Cf. the apostrophe to "wicked Eros" at *Arg.* 4.445-7 (Medea is about to kill Absyrtus; cf. Schiesaro 2008, 99-102), and Vergil's own *Ecl.* 8.50 *improbus ille puer* (also Amor, in a context suggesting Medea) and *Aen.* 3.56-7 *quid non mortalia pectora cogis, / auri sacra fames!*; in Book 4, cf. 65 *heu vatum ignarae mentes*, and above 408.

414. **animos:** "pride." **summittere:** cf. *Ecl.* 10.69 (words Vergil puts in the mouth of his friend the poet Gallus) *omnia vincit Amor: et nos cedamus Amori.*

415. **ne quid:** "so that she does not leave anything (*quid* = *aliquid*) unattempted and so die in vain"; if she left anything unattempted which might have saved her, she would die unnecessarily. At 8.205-6 Cacus steals Hercules' cattle, *ne quid inausum / aut intractatum scelerisve dolive fuisset.*

"Anna, vides toto properari litore circum:
undique convenere; vocat iam carbasus auras,
puppibus et laeti nautae inposuere coronas.
hunc ego si potui tantum sperare dolorem,
et perferre, soror, potero. miserae hoc tamen unum   420
exsequere, Anna, mihi; solam nam perfidus ille
te colere, arcanos etiam tibi credere sensus;
sola viri mollis aditus et tempora noras.
i, soror, atque hostem supplex adfare superbum:
non ego cum Danais Troianam exscindere gentem   425
Aulide iuravi classemve ad Pergama misi,

416. **properari:** "the commotion," "stirring," lit. "that haste is being made," cf. 151 n. for the impersonal verb.

418. **puppibus…:** the word *puppes* literally refers to the stern of a ship, but is a frequent synecdoche* for "ship." This line is repeated from *Geo.* 1.304, where the sailors put crowns on their ships as a sign of joy at *entering* port; again we see Aeneas' men delighted to be leaving Carthage (cf. *laeti* 295, and Clausen 2002, 83 n. 22). Curiously, the first-century CE critic Probus, Servius reports, thought that Vergil should have cut this line.

419. **si potui…sperare:** "if I could expect (as I did)"; *potui* is probably to be read literally as a simple past tense (and not, as Servius suggests, as equal to *potuissem*; see Pease for discussion), even though the only hint of her having expected such sorrow is given in 298 *omnia tuta timens*. Dido's claims are probably feigned and merely intended to make her sister and Aeneas believe that she is becoming resigned to her situation; on her whole speech cf. Schiesaro 2008.

422. **colere:** "made his friend." For this infinitive of custom or historic infinitive (AG §463), cf. 11.822 *quicum partiri curas; Geo.* 1.199-200 *sic omnia fatis / in peius ruere*. Vergil alludes here to the alternate version of the Dido story, found e.g. in Varro (see Servius on 4.682 and 5.4), in which Anna, and not the chaste Dido, has a relationship with Aeneas. Ovid, *Fasti* 3.545-654 has Aeneas meet Anna again later, in Italy, and his wife Lavinia grows angry with jealousy. Cf. Pease on 421, Barchiesi 1997, 165-6, Starks 1999, 262, Reed 2007, 97 n. 64, Schiesaro 2008, 96-8.

423. **mollis aditus et tempora:** cf. *aditus et quae mollissima fandi / tempora* 293-4. **noras:** = *noveras*; the past tense may indicate, as Williams says, that "Dido subconsciously puts Aeneas in the past." Courtney 1981 argues that *noris*, a syncopated potential perfect subjunctive now found in a fragment of the *Aeneid* preserved on a sixth-century papyrus (*Pap. Colt* 1), is the better reading.

424. **hostem:** note the progress—in 323 Aeneas is called *hospes* instead of *coniunx* (324) and now is *hostis* (424). The word *hostis* is emphatic: he acts like an enemy, but she, as the next lines show, has given him no cause.

426. **Aulide:** Aulis, where the Greek fleet gathered on its way to Troy and swore allegiance to the mission to get Helen back or sack Troy; contrast the confession of Achaemenides at 3.602, who admits that he fought against Troy and so expects no mercy from the Trojans.

nec patris Anchisae cinerem manisve revelli:
cur mea dicta negat duras demittere in auris?
quo ruit? extremum hoc miserae det munus amanti:
exspectet facilemque fugam ventosque ferentis.   430
non iam coniugium antiquum, quod prodidit, oro,
nec pulchro ut Latio careat regnumque relinquat:
tempus inane peto, requiem spatiumque furori,
dum mea me victam doceat fortuna dolere.
extremam hanc oro veniam (miserere sororis),   435
quam mihi cum dederit, cumulatam morte remittam."

427. **cinerem manisve:** cf. 34 n. Dido alludes not to any actual charge brought against her
(Anchises was buried in Sicily; cf. 3.708-15), but to an imaginary crime great enough to
justify the cruel treatment she has received. Servius attributes to Varro a story in which
Diomedes unearthed Anchises' bones (Horsfall 1981, 144); Horace, *Epod.* 16.13-14 refers
to the idea of a foreign invader scattering the bones of Romulus. Cf. Schiesaro 2008, 91-2.
The manuscripts are divided between *cinerem* and *cineres* here; Conte prints *cineres* because
the other five times V. uses *cinerem* the final syllable is elided.

429. **extremum hoc:** cf. *Ecl.* 10.1 *extremum hunc, Arethusa, mihi concede laborem*, and esp. the
suicidal lover at *Ecl.* 8.60 *extremum hoc munus morientis habeto*.

430. **ventos...ferentis:** "favorable breezes." For *–que ... –que*, see 83 n.

432. **nec pulchro...:** "nor that he give up (lit. 'lack') fair Latium"; *pulchro* is sarcastic.

433. **tempus inane:** "empty time," which will not be full of love as before (*non iam...oro*),
and so may offer (433-4) "repose and room to passion (i.e. rest and time in which to work
itself out) until fortune may teach my conquered soul to grieve." Euripides' Medea asks for
and receives "one day's" delay in her banishment (*Med.* 340, 355), a deadly mistake on the
part of Creon, since it allows her to kill her children and her husband's new bride, Creon's
daughter. Cf. Schiesaro 2008, 66-71 who also cites Sen. *Medea* 285-96.

436. **quam mihi cum dederit:** a difficult line, in part because Dido speaks obscurely and
deceptively. If Aeneas will grant this last favor (*veniam*), Dido "will pay it back with interest
(*cumulatam*) by (or 'at') my death"; the ablative may be either instrumental or temporal
(cf. Schiesaro 2008, 63). For "pay back with interest," or "give back good measure heaped
up," cf. Cicero *ad Fam.* 13.4.1 *cumulatissime mihi gratiam rettulerunt;* Livy 24.48 *bene
cumulatam gratiam referant;* Livy 2.23 *aes alienum ... cumulatum usuris.* Casali 1999-2000
thinks that Vergil suggests that if Aeneas had granted Dido's last request and delayed his
departure, she would have "repaid" him by retracting the brief curse in 381-7, and would
have foregone the more elaborate and largely effective curse below in 607-29. Schiesaro
2008 sees in what Dido asks Anna to say to Aeneas an implied threat. Servius and some
moderns prefer the reading *dederis*, which would call on Anna to grant a favor, which seems
weak, because *extremam veniam* is clearly parallel to *extremum munus* in 429, where the
favor is asked from Aeneas. Highet 1972, 137 calls attention to the twelve "m" sounds in
435-6, half of them in combinations of final "m" followed by initial "m," and says the effect
is "meant to suggest the sound of speech half-stifled by sobs."

Talibus orabat, talisque miserrima fletus
fertque refertque soror. sed nullis ille movetur
fletibus, aut voces ullas tractabilis audit;
fata obstant placidasque viri deus obstruit auris.   440
ac velut annoso validam cum robore quercum
Alpini Boreae nunc hinc nunc flatibus illinc
eruere inter se certant; it stridor, et altae
consternunt terram concusso stipite frondes;
ipsa haeret scopulis et, quantum vertice ad auras   445
aetherias, tantum radice in Tartara tendit:

437-49. Aeneas remains firm and is no more moved by laments and tears than an oak buffeted by winds, but too deep-rooted to be overthrown.

437. **fletus...:** "such tears her sister bears and bears again," i.e. from Dido to Aeneas, and not "bears backwards and forwards," since Aeneas is unmoved.

440. **deus:** both Greek and Latin authors use the singular to refer to the actions or effects of an unspecified deity.

441. **ac velut...cum...haud secus** (447) **... :** "and as when ... even so ... " Note the difference between the use of *ac velut cum* here and in 402. Here the simile* precedes and prepares the way for the thing described, there the simile follows and illustrates the description. **validam...quercum:** names of trees are feminine, even though most nouns of the fourth declension are masculine.

442. **Alpini Boreae:** "Alpine North winds." Names of winds are masculine; Boreas is declined like other first-declension nouns taken from Greek such as *Aeneas* (74 n.). The plural is rare and since *Boreas* is often merely "a gale," perhaps *Boreae* means "gales," without any reference to their direction. But Vergil, who grew up in Northern Italy, may be personifying this wind not in the form of a single power but of a group: the "North winds" rush from the Alps and "with their blasts on this side and on that compete with one another to uproot...." The link between the *flatus* resisted by the tree and the *fletus* resisted by Aeneas resembles wordplay between *flumen* and *flamen* and related words in Lucretius, *DRN* 1.277-97.

443. **it:** i.e. "rises." **altae:** the leaves are called "lofty" (cf. *Geo.* 2.55) here in contrast with *consternunt terram,* so as to suggest the picture of their falling. Some translate "deeply strew."

445-6. **quantum...:** repeated from *Geo.* 2.291. The tree simile* also recalls others in which a tree *does* fall: *Aen.* 2.626-31 (Troy), Catullus 64.105-9 (Minotaur), Apoll. Rhod. *Arg.* 4.1682-6 (a giant), and the ultimate models in *Il.* 13.389-91 = 16.482-4, as well as *Il.* 12.132-4 (gigantic warriors do not fall; cf. *Aen.* 9.679-82). When Jason and Medea first meet they are compared to tall trees whispering together in the wind (*Arg.* 3.968-71). On the simile cf. Briggs 1980, 35-9, Hardie 1986, 280-1, West 1990, 436-7, Nelis 2001, 16, Clausen 1987, 51-2 = 2002, 94-6.

haud secus adsiduis hinc atque hinc vocibus heros
tunditur, et magno persentit pectore curas;
mens inmota manet, lacrimae volvuntur inanes.
   Tum vero infelix fatis exterrita Dido   450
mortem orat; taedet caeli convexa tueri.
quo magis inceptum peragat lucemque relinquat,
vidit, turicremis cum dona imponeret aris
(horrendum dictu), latices nigrescere sacros
fusaque in obscenum se vertere vina cruorem.   455
hoc visum nulli, non ipsi effata sorori.

447. **adsiduis…:** "with ceaseless appeals from this side and from that." Anna presses the case from every angle.

449. **lacrimae…:** whose tears these are is unclear, probably deliberately. The parallel between the tree buffeted with winds and Aeneas with entreaties would suggest that these tears are his, just as the tree may lose leaves but still remain firm. Throughout the passage, however, the contrast is clearly between the tears (*fletus…fletibus*) of Dido and the resolution of Aeneas, so we would have expected that the tears would be hers. The lines have been much discussed; cf. Martindale 1993, 120, Desmond 1994, 79, Horsfall 1995, 125 n. 20, Edwards 2004,106.

450-73. Dido longs for death and her purpose is strengthened by portents and nightmares: in dreams she seems to flee from Aeneas, like Pentheus or Orestes from the pursuing Furies.

450. **fatis:** "doom," "destiny," which she now feels is irresistibly her enemy; construe with *exterrita*, but before encountering *exterrita*, a reader may also think momentarily that Dido is *infelix fatis*. Muecke 1983 suggests that *fata* means messages from the gods in the omens which confirm what Aeneas has said to her — a possible reading, but Vergil is not specific.

452. **quo magis…:** "and that she may more certainly fulfill her purpose and quit the light (i.e. die), she saw…"; *quo* introduces a purpose clause with a comparative adverb (AG §531a). That she sees such a portent helps to strengthen her half-formed resolve (*inceptum*) to die, and the portent is (apparently) sent by destiny or the gods with that object. **lucemque relinquat:** the expression sounds archaic, both here and in 10.855 *lucemque relinquo*. It occurs in Ennius, *Ann.* fr. 137 Sk. = 154 W, *Postquam lumina sis oculis bonus Ancus reliquit,* which is closely imitated at Lucretius, *DRN* 3.1025 (cf. too *DRN* 3.542 and 5.989).

453. **cum dona imponeret:** the *cum* clause with the imperfect subjunctive describes the circumstances in which the main verb *vidit* occurred (AG §546).

454-5. **latices…sacros / fusaque…vina:** possibly hendiadys* for "the holy libation of outpoured wine," but may refer to water and wine mixed together. The libation of wine was a part of the "offerings" (*dona*) at the altar. **obscenum…:** Valerius Maximus 1.6, ext. 1 says that this portent happened to Xerxes, the Persian king who attacked Greece in the early fifth century.

456. **effata:** supply *est*, with *hoc visum* as direct object; both *nulli* and *ipsi…sorori* are dative.

praeterea fuit in tectis de marmore templum
coniugis antiqui, miro quod honore colebat,
velleribus niveis et festa fronde revinctum:
hinc exaudiri voces et verba vocantis　　　　　　460
visa viri, nox cum terras obscura teneret,
solaque culminibus ferali carmine bubo
saepe queri et longas in fletum ducere voces;
multaque praeterea vatum praedicta priorum
terribili monitu horrificant. agit ipse furentem　　　465

457. **templum:** "a chapel" or "shrine" dedicated to the *Di Manes* of her "long-dead husband"; cf. Ovid, *Her.* 7.99-102.

459. **velleribus…:** the line illustrates the "wondrous honor" with which she still "revered" Sychaeus — his shrine was still "garlanded with snowy fillets and festal boughs." In 3.64 the altars of the Manes are *caeruleis maestae vittis atraque cupresso*. The contrast of adjectives is remarkable: "dark" and "snow-white," "funereal" and "festal" (for *festa* certainly suggests "joy," cf. 2.249). She still honored him, not with the signs of gloom and death, but with signs of joy and life.

460-7. **hinc exaudiri…:** notice the solemn effect of the alliteration* in *voces, verba, vocantis, visa, viri*; 465-6 *furentem…ferus*; 466-7 *semper…sola sibi, semper*. The infinitives *exaudiri, queri* and *ducere* all depend on *visa* (*sunt*), with *visa* taking the gender and number of *verba*. For the subjunctive *teneret*, cf. 453 n. We are probably not being encouraged with *visa* to think that the apparitions were imagined by Dido; we are told what she perceives, and nothing more.

463. **longas …voces:** "draw out its long notes into a wail." Williams well comments on the assonance* of long vowels here; for the owl, an omen of death, see Pease's long note, and cf. 12.862-4 when the *Dira* comes to Turnus to tell him that he, too, is fated to lose out to Aeneas.

464. **priorum:** some (including Page) have preferred the reading *piorum* (in part to avoid the triple "*pr-*"), but *priorum* makes Dido's experience fit the pattern of those who understand an old prophecy only when it is too late, like Meliboeus in *Ecl.* 1.16-17, the Odyssean Cyclops (*Od.* 9.507 "prophecies of old") or the Heracles of Sophocles, *Trach.* 1159-73.

465-6. **agit…furentem:** not "drives to frenzy" (*furentem* is not proleptic*), but "pursues her (with her being) frenzied/maddened." Dido's terrifying dream reflects her troubled state of mind and desperate situation. Aeneas pursues her while she flees in frenzied terror; the pursuit echoes the image of Aeneas as hunter in the deer simile of 68-73, and reverses her threat to pursue him as an avenging Fury (384-6) and the idea rejected later of literally following the Trojan ships (537-9). The dream of being alone on a long road reflects her sense of being isolated, hated by both Aeneas and her people. Reed 2007, 191 and Krevans 1993 compare Ilia's dream of wandering alone in Ennius, *Ann.* 34-50 Sk. = 32-48 W; in *Aen.* 12.908-12 Turnus' situation will be compared to a terrifying dream. On Dido's dream see also Schiesaro 2008, 194-206, with references.

in somnis ferus Aeneas, semperque relinqui
sola sibi, semper longam incomitata videtur
ire viam et Tyrios deserta quaerere terra,
Eumenidum veluti demens videt agmina Pentheus
et solem geminum et duplices se ostendere Thebas,   470
aut Agamemnonius scaenis agitatus Orestes,
armatam facibus matrem et serpentibus atris
cum fugit ultricesque sedent in limine Dirae.
　　Ergo ubi concepit furias evicta dolore
decrevitque mori, tempus secum ipsa modumque   475

---

468. **viam:** cognate accusative with a verb (*ire*) that is usually intransitive (AG §390).

469. **Pentheus:** king of Thebes driven mad for opposing the worship of Bacchus; his madness involved "seeing double," cf. Euripides, *Bacch.* 918-19 ("two suns and two Thebes"), and see Austin's n. on wall-paintings of both Pentheus and Orestes.

471. **scaenis agitatus:** "hunted on (or 'across') the stage" (after killing his mother). An unusual passage, because we expect a comparison between Dido and the real Orestes, not Orestes as represented on the stage. The line is unique in the *Aeneid* as an explicit reference to a post-heroic literary genre (we may even hear *scaenis agitatus* as "performed repeatedly on stage"), but follows a long series of allusions to tragic drama that begins with the metaphorical *silvis scaena coruscis* in 1.164 and Venus' wearing of the *cothurnus*, the high boot of the tragic actor, in 1.337 (on tragedy, see Muecke 1983, Hardie 1997, Clausen 2002, Panoussi 2009, and above p. 9, n. 35).

472. **armatam...:** his mother here pursues him in the guise of a Fury (cf. 384), apparently within some house or temple, while the Furies themselves keep ward "on the threshold" to prevent his escape.

474-503. *Dido resolves to die, but to deceive her sister pretends that she has consulted a sorceress who advises her to erect a pyre and burn upon it every memorial of Aeneas.*
Vergil's depiction of Dido's feigned magic combines various models: the pyre is from the pre-Vergilian Dido legend (494 n.), and there are suggestions of Apollonius' Medea, Phaedra's Nurse in Eurip., *Hippolytus* 476-515, Simaetha in Theocritus' *Second Idyll* and Vergil's imitation of that poem in *Ecl.* 8, and the use of love magic in Horace's *Epodes* and in love elegy. On magic here, see Austin 1955, Khan 1995, Kraggerud 1999, Schiesaro 2008, 210-13; on magic in Latin poetry see the list of passages in Maltby on Tibullus 1.2.43-66.

475. **secum ipsa:** i.e. "in her own heart" and not aloud; opposed to *dictis*, cf. *secum* in 1.221, of Aeneas mourning after his speech of encouragement.

exigit, et maestam dictis adgressa sororem
consilium vultu tegit ac spem fronte serenat:
"inveni, germana, viam (gratare sorori)
quae mihi reddat eum vel eo me solvat amantem.
Oceani finem iuxta solemque cadentem   480
ultimus Aethiopum locus est, ubi maximus Atlas
axem umero torquet stellis ardentibus aptum:
hinc mihi Massylae gentis monstrata sacerdos,
Hesperidum templi custos, epulasque draconi
quae dabat et sacros servabat in arbore ramos,   485

477. **consilium vultu…:** "masks her purpose with her face and makes hope bright (or 'sunny')
on her brow." The forehead is often referred to as an index of feeling, e.g. *frons laeta, gravis,
urbana, proterva, tranquilla, sollicita. Frons serena* is the opposite of a "cloudy" or "overcast
brow," cf. Cic. *in Pis.* 9.20 *frontis…nubeculam;* Eurip., *Hipp.* 172. Aeneas at 1.209 hides
his pessimism from his men, *spem vultu simulat, premit altum corde dolorem,* and Jupiter at
1.255 speaks to Venus with a serene appearance: *vultu, quo caelum tempestatesque serenat;*
cf. O'Hara 1990, 133-7. For *spem fronte serenat* as enallage* or an inversion of the expected
spe frontem serenat see 226 n. and Conte 2007, 91.

479. **eo me solvat amantem:** cf. Tibullus 1.2.61-2 *amores / cantibus aut herbis solvere posse
meos.* Here *eo* is ablative of separation after *solvat.*

480. **Oceani finem:** Oceanus was supposed to bound the world on all sides, and seems to do
so especially towards the West "beside the sunset."

482. **axem…:** "turns upon his shoulder the heavens studded with glowing stars." Repeated
at 6.797, and adapted from Ennius, *Ann.* 27 Sk. = 59 W (cf. too fr. 145 Sk. = 162 W), as
Macrobius, *Sat.* 6.1 notes; cf. Lucretius, *DRN* 6.357. *Aptus* is here not "fitted *to*" but "*with*";
so at *Trag.* 350 Jocelyn, Ennius has *apta pinnis* "equipped with wings." Atlas of course has
been described above (247-51).

483. **hinc…:** "a priestess from there…has been shown to me, (once) guardian…and who used
to give…" The impression is that the priestess is no longer in the far West, but at Carthage.
The "gardens," not the temple, of the Hesperides are usually spoken of; *templum* here
means "sacred enclosure." For the Hesperides and the dragon which guarded their golden
apples (cf. *sacros … ramos,* 485), see *OCD* 3rd ed. s.v. and Pease, who notes the parallels
between the story of the apples and that of the Golden Fleece, also guarded by a dragon (cf.
Arg. 4.156-61, and for a mention of the serpent guarding the apples *Arg.* 4.1396-7).

485. **et…servabat…spargens (486):** "and (so) kept safe" the apples "(by) scattering…." The
food must be supposed to induce the dragon to keep guard for her, but see next n.

spargens umida mella soporiferumque papaver.
haec se carminibus promittit solvere mentes
quas velit, ast aliis duras immittere curas,
sistere aquam fluviis, et vertere sidera retro,
nocturnosque movet manis: mugire videbis   490
sub pedibus terram et descendere montibus ornos.
testor, cara, deos et te, germana, tuumque
dulce caput, magicas invitam accingier artis.

---

486. **soporiferum:** a problem. Poppies are perpetually called "sleepy" or "drowsy" (cf. *Geo.* 1.78 *Lethaeo perfusa papavera somno* and of course *The Wizard of Oz*: "poppies will make them sleep"), but to give a dragon "sleepy poppies" in order to keep it awake is odd. Vergil (or Dido, who of course is improvising a ruse) perhaps combines two passages in Apollonius (Heracles carrying off the apples of the Hesperides at *Arg.* 4.1395-449, and Medea drugging the serpent at 4.156-9) to produce a slightly incoherent new story, as Nelis 2001, 142 notes.

487. **se...promittit solvere:** not "promises to" or "promises that she will," but "claims that she does set free hearts." **carminibus:** "incantations" or "magical songs" as in Tibullus 1.2.62 (479 n.), Hor. *Epode* 17.4, Verg. *Ecl.* 8.69-70.

488. **aliis:** supply *mentibus:* she sets free hearts "such as she will, but on others sends...."

489. **sistere aquam fluviis...:** the indirect statement continues, with the claim she has power over rivers (*fluviis* probably is dative; Austin suggests a local ablative) and stars; for such powers, see Apoll. Rhod. *Arg.* 3.532-3, Tibullus 1.2.43-4, and *Ecl.* 8.4 with Clausen's n.

490-1. **mugire videbis / sub pedibus terram:** *mugire* = "low," "rumble," perhaps as in an earthquake; cf. Pease on 491, and 6.256 *sub pedibus mugire solum* (after Aeneas' offerings to the gods of the underworld). **et descendere montibus ornos:** the power of the witch to move trees is somewhat like that used in such malignant acts as drawing the moon from heaven (Prop. 1.1.19) or charming the crops out of a field (*Ecl.* 8.99). But it more closely resembles that of Orpheus to make trees follow his music; cf. Hor. *Carm.* 1.11-12, and especially the description of Hesiod acting like Orpheus in the initiation of Gallus at *Ecl.* 6.71 *rigidas deducere montibus ornos*. Cf. O'Hara 1993a.

492-3. **testor...accingier:** "I call to witness the gods...that unwillingly do I arm myself with magic arts"; cf. *testatus* of Aeneas in 12.496, also of an action said to be taken as a last resort. **accingier:** archaic form of the passive infinitive, cf. 7.70 *dominarier*, 8.493 *defendier*, *Geo.* 1.454 *inmiscerier*. For accusative *artis* after *accingier* used as a middle, cf. 137 n. The verb suggests arming oneself with a weapon, and of course Dido will soon use a sword on herself. **testor, cara, deos et te, germana, tuumque / dulce caput:** adapted from Catullus 66.40, *adiuro teque tuumque caput*, which is itself a translation of Callimachus frag. 110.40 "I swear by your head (in Greek: *karen*) and your life." Konstan 2000 shows that *cara* in 492 echoes the sound of Callimachus' *karen*, "head," which is then translated by *caput* in 493. For more on *caput*, see 354 n.

tu secreta pyram tecto interiore sub auras
erige, et arma viri thalamo quae fixa reliquit   495
impius exuviasque omnis lectumque iugalem,
quo perii, superimponas: abolere nefandi
cuncta viri monimenta iuvat monstratque sacerdos."
haec effata silet, pallor simul occupat ora.
non tamen Anna novis praetexere funera sacris   500
germanam credit, nec tantos mente furores
concipit aut graviora timet quam morte Sychaei.
ergo iussa parat.

494. **tu secreta:** "in isolation, without witnesses." Servius says that this is a figure of speech
in which a quality of a place is transferred to the subject of a verb; we should also note that
adjectives are often used to modify a subject or object of a verb where English would use an
adverb (AG §290). **sub auras:** in the open air, perhaps in an unroofed central courtyard,
or in an interior garden such as is found at the back of many Roman houses; cf. also 504
penetrali in sede sub auras. In the tradition (cf. 198 n.) Dido's suicide on the pyre was how
she escaped Iarbas; her pretense was that the ritual would release her from her vow to
Sychaeus.

495. **arma viri:** one of numerous echoes in the poem of *Aen. 1.1 arma virumque cano*; cf.
Clausen 2002, 97 n. 61.

496. **impius:** the word, in Dido's view, refutes all his claims to *pietas* (cf. 382 n.). For its
emphatic position, cf. 311 n. **exuvias...:** as in the similar magic ritual by the abandoned
lover in *Ecl.* 8.91 (*has olim exuvias mihi perfidus ille reliquit*), having something once worn
or used by the intended victim is crucial (cf. 497 n.). For Vergil's play on substitutions
for bodies, see Bowie 1998. **lectumque iugalem:** Dido never stops thinking that she was
married to Aeneas.

497. **abolere...:** two reasons are given for "consuming" the objects mentioned, (1) that it is
good to get rid of all reminders of a villain, (2) that the priestess so commands, since by
bewitching or ill-treating the *exuviae* you may similarly affect the person himself. It was
common to bewitch, torture, or burn an image of the person, cf. 508 *effigiem; Ecl.* 8.75, 92;
Theocritus 2.53, and Bowie 1998.

500. **novis...:** "veils (her) death with this strange rite"; as often, *novus* means "novel, strange."

501-2. **tantos...furores concipit:** different from *concepit furias* 474: there Dido "conceived
madness" (i.e. grew mad herself), while here Anna cannot "conceive (i.e. imagine) in her
mind such madness" in Dido. **quam morte:** "than (what had occurred) at the death of
Sychaeus."

503. For the unfinished line, cf. 42-4 n.

At regina, pyra penetrali in sede sub auras
erecta ingenti taedis atque ilice secta,   505
intenditque locum sertis et fronde coronat
funerea; super exuvias ensemque relictum
effigiemque toro locat haud ignara futuri.
stant arae circum et crines effusa sacerdos

504-705. Dido's curse of Aeneas and her death.

The pyre is built, the rite is prepared, and Dido prays to whatever divinities care about unequal pacts of love (504-21). Sleep comes to all, but again not to Dido, who runs through alternatives to death and angrily rejects them all (522-53). Mercury then appears for a second time to the sleeping Aeneas and tells him to leave immediately, for a woman "is a changing and variable thing"; the Trojans depart (554-83). Dido sees the ships set sail, and solemnly curses Aeneas in a passage recalling the curses of Polyphemus on Odysseus (*Odyssey* 9) and Ariadne on Jason (Catullus 64), and presaging (and causing) both the troubles Aeneas will have in the second half of the poem, and the centuries of conflict between Carthage and Rome (581-631). Dido mounts the pyre with a sword given to her by Aeneas (a motif borrowed from tragic treatments of Hector and Ajax), reviews her life in a way that recalls the epitaphs of noble Romans (see 653-6 n.), and then after additional lines that recall Ariadne and Medea, she stabs herself (632-62). As Dido sinks dying, the lamentation of her maidens alerts Anna, in a scene reminiscent of the death of Hector and its ties to the Fall of Troy (663-93); Anna laments Dido's act, and reproaches her for what she has done. Juno (here oddly called *omnipotens*) in pity sends Iris from heaven to cut a lock of her hair, and end Dido's pain, since Dido is dying "neither by fate nor by a death she deserved." Dido's spirit passes into the air (693-705). On Dido's death, see Perkell 1994, Johnson 1976, 59-75, Tatum 1984, Rauk 1995, Clausen 1987= 2002, and Keith 2000, 114-17; on the curse, see 584-631 n.

504. **At regina:** beginning a new section of the book, as at 1 and 296.

506. **intenditque locum sertis et…:** "both hangs (or 'decorates') the place with garlands, and…." The ordinary construction would be *intendere serta loco,* but here *intendere* is allowed to govern *locum* in the secondary sense of "cover" or "adorn." On such enallage* cf. 226 n. and Conte 2007, 87-8.

507-8. **super:** adverb. **exuvias…effigiem:** cf. above 497 n.; Hor. *Serm.* 1.8.30 *lanea et effigies erat, altera, cerea.* **haud ignara futuri:** litotes*: "well-knowing what was to happen," i.e. what was her real purpose in opposition to her feigned one. Cf. 8.627 *haud vatum ignarus venturique inscius aevi.*

509. **crines effusa:** the participle is middle and governs *crines* (cf. 137 n.).

ter centum tonat ore deos, Erebumque Chaosque   510
tergeminamque Hecaten, tria virginis ora Dianae.
sparserat et latices simulatos fontis Averni,
falcibus et messae ad lunam quaeruntur aënis
pubentes herbae nigri cum lacte veneni;
quaeritur et nascentis equi de fronte revulsus   515
et matri praereptus amor.

510-11. **ter centum tonat:** *tonat* is transitive here in the secondary sense of "call" or "name
with a voice of thunder." Many take *ter* with *tonat*, but it is better to take *ter centum*
together, as the parallel position of *tergeminam* and *tria* shows: the number "three" is of
regular recurrence in magic rites and "three hundred" is put for any vague number (cf.
Geo. 1.15), although *centum* may also allude (as Servius suggests) to the name Hecate (cf.
Greek ἑκατόν, "hundred"). **Erebum:** sometimes a god of darkness, sometimes a name
for the underworld (as at *Aen.* 6.247); could be taken in either sense here. **Chaos:** neuter,
the underworld personified; invoked also at 6.265. **tergeminam:** "three-fold"; cf. 6.800
septemgemini … Nili "sevenfold Nile," 6.287 *centumgeminus* "hundredfold." The goddess
who was Luna in heaven, Diana on earth, and Hecate in hell was symbolized by a three-
faced image set up at places where three roads met, cf. 609; Ovid, *Fasti* 1.141. As Hecate or
the Moon (cf. *ad lunam* 513) she was often called on by witches.

512. **simulatos…:** "feigned (as being the waters) of Avernian fount." The pretense is an
accepted part of magical ritual, not a part of Dido's deception of Anna. For Lake Avernus
with its entrance to the underworld, cf. 6.107, 118.

513-15. **ad lunam:** "by moonlight." **quaeruntur…quaeritur** (515): "are sought" i.e. brought
forth, presumably from the witch's supplies. The perfect participles *messae* (< *metior*),
revulsus and *praeruptus* tell how she had earlier acquired them. **aënis:** "of bronze." Bronze
was known before iron and so was retained in many ceremonial usages when for ordinary
purposes iron had taken its place. Macrobius *Sat.* 5.19 thinks that Vergil borrows from a
lost tragedy of Sophocles, *The Rootcutters*, where Medea cuts plants with a bronze sickle;
Nelis 2001, 143 thinks of Medea gathering the drug that will help Jason at *Arg.* 3.844-57.

514. **pubentes…:** usually "ripening" or "growing to maturity." Conington says it "seems to
include the two notions of downiness and luxuriance," while Williams translates "juicy."
The herbs are full of sap or juice (*lac*) which, though white, is "black poison."

516. **amor:** "a love-charm"; a bold use of *amor* for something which produces love. The
reference is to *hippomanes*, a piece of flesh supposed to be found on the forehead of a "foal
at birth" (*nascentis equi*) from which it was bitten by the mother, unless "snatched away
beforehand" (*praereptus*) to be used as a love charm. Vergil describes a different kind of
hippomanes at *Geo.* 3.280 (cf. Thomas ad loc. and O'Hara 1996, 277-8). For the unfinished
line, cf. 42-4 n.

ipsa mola manibusque piis altaria iuxta
unum exuta pedem vinclis, in veste recincta,
testatur moritura deos et conscia fati
sidera; tum, si quod non aequo foedere amantis   520
curae numen habet iustumque memorque, precatur.
    Nox erat et placidum carpebant fessa soporem
corpora per terras, silvaeque et saeva quierant
aequora, cum medio volvuntur sidera lapsu,
cum tacet omnis ager, pecudes pictaeque volucres,   525
quaeque lacus late liquidos quaeque aspera dumis
rura tenent, somno positae sub nocte silenti.

---

517. **mola manibusque piis:** the adjective *piis* in sense goes with both nouns, "with holy hands and offering." The *mola salsa* or mixture of meal and salt was sprinkled on the altar (*Ecl.* 8.82 *sparge molam*), and for *pius* cf. 5.745 *farre pio*, Horace, *Carm.* 3.23.20 *farre pio et saliente mica*, [Tibull.] 3.4.10. The reference to Dido's hands as *piae* is interesting, given the prominence of *pietas* in Book 4 (cf. nn. on 382, 393, 496, 596-9).

518. **unum...:** "with one foot unsandaled"; the participle is middle and governs *pedem* (cf. 137 n.). Having one foot wearing a sandal and one foot bare may be meant, as Servius suggests, to bind Aeneas and free Dido (cf. 479, 487-8, and *Ecl.* 8.80-1), but a simpler explanation would be that the bare foot keeps her "in touch with the earth and underworld powers" (Pease, who also mentions other theories).

520. **tum...:** "then she prays to whatever righteous and mindful power has concern (*curae* is pred. dative; cf. AG §382) for those who love in an unequal pact." Dido will find reciprocal love in the underworld: 6.474 *aequatque Sychaeum amorem.* For the lovers' *foedus* esp. in Catullus see 338-9 n.

522-53. *Night brings rest to all the world, but not to Dido, who reviews her options and resolves to die.*

Note the placid and restful rhythm of 522-7. The contrast between the peace of night and Dido's restless misery is adapted from the description of Medea at *Arg.* 3.744-51, soon before a passage in which Medea plans but does not carry out suicide (785-90); cf. too *Aen.* 8.26-7 (Aeneas; see 4.285-6 and n.) and 9.224-5 (before the Nisus and Euryalus episode), and the list of passages in Pease.

523. **quierant:** = *quieverant* < *quiesco*, "had sunk to rest."

524. **cum medio...:** "when the stars wheel midway in their motion": *lapsu* suggests motion which is smooth and steady.

526. **quaeque...quaeque:** both relative pronouns have *volucres* as antecedent. Note the smooth liquids in *lacus late liquidos.* The line is adapted from Lucretius, *DRN* 2.344-6: *Et variae volucres, laetantia quae loca aquarum / concelebrant circum ripas fontisque lacusque, / et quae pervolgant nemora avia pervolitantes.*

[lenibant curas et corda oblita laborum.]
at non infelix animi Phoenissa neque umquam
solvitur in somnos oculisve aut pectore noctem   530
accipit: ingeminant curae rursusque resurgens
saevit amor magnoque irarum fluctuat aestu.
sic adeo insistit secumque ita corde volutat:
"en, quid ago? rursusne procos inrisa priores
experiar, Nomadumque petam conubia supplex,   535
quos ego sim totiens iam dedignata maritos?

---

528. This line does not appear in our fourth-century manuscripts, or in Servius, but only in later manuscripts, and is an interpolation suggested by 9.225, where it occurs with *laxabant* for *lenibant*.

529. **at non…**: supply *quierat* from *quierant* above (ellipsis*). For the case of *animi*, cf. 203 n.

530. **solvitur:** both of the actual "unloosing" or relaxing of the limbs in sleep and also because sleep would set Dido free from cares. **oculisve aut:** for *–ve aut*, cf. 87-8 n. and Austin's note here on 529ff.

531. **rursusque resurgens:** the sound of *rursus* repeated in *resurgens* illustrates the words *ingeminant curae.*

532. **magnoque irarum fluctuat aestu:** the phrase recalls Lucretius, *DRN* 6.73-4 *magnos irarum volvere fluctus* (see Dyson 1997 on the wrath of the gods in Lucretius and Vergil, and cf. 34 n.), and Catullus 64.62 on Ariadne, *et magnis curarum fluctuat undis.* At *Aen.* 8.19 Aeneas will be described in similar language, *magno curarum fluctuat aestu*, just before a simile modeled on one that Apollonius used of Medea; cf. 522-53 n., Petrini 1997, 55, Reed 2007, 64-5.

533. **sic adeo:** the emphasis thrown on *sic* by *adeo* marks excitement: after all the turmoil of her passion this is at last the outcome. **insistit:** cf. 12.47 *sic institit ore;* the word marks vigor and movement, as in *viamque insiste Geo.* 3.164.

534. **en, quid ago?:** the present indicative is sometimes substituted for the deliberative subjunctive (AG §444a), but since actual deliberative subjunctives follow in *experiar* and *petam*, Dido's *quid ago* is not *quid agam* "what am I to do?" (cf. 283, of Aeneas) but "what am I doing?" Dido criticizes herself for idly debating any longer, where there is no alternative but death, then she runs through all possible alternatives and shows that they are useless. **rursusne…:** having rejected her African suitors before, Dido worries that she would be ridiculed (*inrisa*) if she were to make trial of them again. Cf. 27 n. for Kaster's idea that *pudor* can involve people who "know that their present behavior falls short of their past or ideal selves." Allecto mocks Turnus as an object of laughter at 7.425, *i nunc, ingratis offer te, inrise, periclis.*

536. **sim…dedignata:** concessive subjunctive.

Iliacas igitur classis atque ultima Teucrum
iussa sequar? quiane auxilio iuvat ante levatos
et bene apud memores veteris stat gratia facti?
quis me autem, fac velle, sinet ratibusve superbis   540
invisam accipiet? nescis heu, perdita, necdum
Laomedonteae sentis periuria gentis?
quid tum? sola fuga nautas comitabor ovantis?
an Tyriis omnique manu stipata meorum
inferar et, quos Sidonia vix urbe revelli,   545
rursus agam pelago et ventis dare vela iubebo?
quin morere ut merita es, ferroque averte dolorem.
tu lacrimis evicta meis, tu prima furentem
his, germana, malis oneras atque obicis hosti.

---

537. **igitur:** "then," implies that the former suppositions have been rejected and *therefore* a fresh one must be put. **ultima:** "utmost," "extreme." Dido's sense of her dignity is different from the subservience of Ariadne (Catullus 64.158-63) or Ovid's Dido (*Her.* 7.168), who are both ready to accept a lesser role to be with a man.

538-9. **quiane...:** "(should I do so) because ...." After *iuvat* supply *eos* and *esse* after *levatos*. *Bene* may go with *memores* or *stat* or *facti;* it probably affects them all, but goes strictly with the last. The language is that of reciprocal relationships between Roman aristocrats.

540. **quis me...:** "but who—assume that I wish—will allow me to?" **fac velle:** supply *me* (ellipsis*), as subject of *velle* in indirect statement.

541-2. **necdum:** note the force—"and do you not *yet* understand?" **Laomedonteae...periuria gentis:** Laomedon, Priam's father, refused to reward Apollo and Poseidon for building the walls of Troy as he said he would, and mention of him always has the potential to associate the Trojans with treachery. Cf. *Geo.* 1.502 *Laomedonteae luimus periuria Troiae* with Thomas' n., *Aen.* 3.3, 248. The six-syllable word *Laomedonteae* helps produce a rare four-word hexameter.

543-6. **sola fuga:** both words are emphatic. Should she join the Trojans "alone in flight," or accompanied by all her people, whom she would uproot again (544-6)?

547. **quin morere...:** "no, die, as you have deserved, and with the sword end sorrow." With *merita* (Dido's view) contrast the words of the narrator, perhaps representing Juno's view, at 696 *merita nec morte*, and see also 663-92 n.

548. **tu...tu:** sudden change of addressee (and subject) as Dido turns from talking to herself to addressing her absent sister, in an apostrophe* with anaphora*.

non licuit thalami expertem sine crimine vitam   550
degere more ferae, tales nec tangere curas;
non servata fides cineri promissa Sychaeo."
Tantos illa suo rumpebat pectore questus:
Aeneas celsa in puppi iam certus eundi
carpebat somnos rebus iam rite paratis.   555
huic se forma dei vultu redeuntis eodem
obtulit in somnis rursusque ita visa monere est,

550-1. non licuit…: after Dido in 548-9 mentions Anna's pushing her towards Aeneas, she laments that she was not allowed "to lead my life blamelessly, far from bridal chambers, like a wild animal (*more ferae*), or not to know (lit. 'touch, encounter') such cares." She regrets that she was not allowed (perhaps because of Anna's pressure, or even the initial marriage to Sychaeus) to live a life without the emotional attachments (*curas*) of marriage (*thalami*), as wild animals do. The phrase *more ferae* has been much discussed by scholars. The similar *more ferarum* occurs three times in Lucretius, at *DRN* 4.1264 of sexual positions likely to lead to conception (see Brown ad loc.), at 5.932 of the simple life of early man (*volgivago vitam tractabant more ferarum*) and at 6.198 of stormwinds. Dido's wish to be free of *curae* thus resonates with Epicurean thinking, as elsewhere in *Aen.* 4; see 34 n. The phrase *more ferarum* at Hor. *Serm.* 1.3.109 describes men who take women by force as animals do. It is perhaps also noteworthy that the phrase *barbaros et ferarum more viventes* is used of "Hiarbas" (see 198 n.) and his people in the version of the Dido story told in Justin's epitome of Pompeius Trogus 18.6.

552. non servata fides: Williams says "this summarising line contains indeed the whole truth, as Dido well knows," but Dido will never know the whole truth of how gods and circumstances have conspired against her. Her self-criticism and her conviction that she must die represent one way of looking at her situation, but not the only way; cf. 663-92 n. **cineri … Sychaeo:** "the ashes of Sychaeus." *Sychaeus* is an adjective formed from a proper name, used instead of a genitive; cf. Harrison on 10.156-7 *Aeneia puppes*.

554-83. In a dream Mercury reappears and warns Aeneas to leave Carthage immediately. Aeneas and his men depart.

This second visit of Mercury (on which see Feeney 1998, Schiesaro 2008) is modeled in part on Hermes' return in *Iliad* 24.677-91 to warn Priam to leave Achilles' tent, with borrowings too from the nocturnal visit of the shade of Patroclus to Achilles (*Il.* 23.65-107). The cutting of the cable (579-80) recalls models in Homer and Apollonius.

554. certus eundi: "resolved to depart"; the poetic construction is an extension of the genitive after adjectives of knowledge or ignorance. Note the different construction *certa mori* in 564. Aeneas' resolve allows him to sleep peacefully, unlike Dido (cf. 522 *carpebant*).

556. forma dei: "the shape of the god"; Page suggests that this was only a phantom "in all things like to Mercury," and not the actual god who had been sent before, but it may be that we are simply getting Aeneas' point of view here, while for the first visit we had Mercury's (so Harrison 1985). It may also be relevant that Aeneas is asleep here (*in somnis* 557), while he was awake before.

omnia Mercurio similis, vocemque coloremque
et crinis flavos et membra decora iuventa:
"nate dea, potes hoc sub casu ducere somnos,   560
nec quae te circum stent deinde pericula cernis,
demens, nec Zephyros audis spirare secundos?
illa dolos dirumque nefas in pectore versat
certa mori, variosque irarum concitat aestus.
non fugis hinc praeceps, dum praecipitare potestas?   565
iam mare turbari trabibus saevasque videbis
conlucere faces, iam fervere litora flammis,
si te his attigerit terris Aurora morantem.
heia age, rumpe moras. varium et mutabile semper
femina." sic fatus nocti se immiscuit atrae.   570
    Tum vero Aeneas subitis exterritus umbris
corripit e somno corpus sociosque fatigat

---

558. **coloremque:** polysyndeton* (in 558-9), and also a hypermetric line (see appendix on meter), with the final *-que* elided before the vowel at the beginning of the next line; cf. 629 and n.; 1.332, 448; 2.745; 5.753. In 5.422 such a line suggests size, in 6.602 an overhanging rock. Cf. Austin here and on 1.332, Harrison on 10.895; Seneca is quoted as saying Vergil used such verses because they sounded like Ennius (Gellius, *Attic Nights* 12.2.10).

560. **nate dea:** used often of Aeneas, but cf. esp. 2.289 *heu fuge, nate dea*, the first words of the apparition of Hector to the sleeping Aeneas, telling him to leave Troy.

565. **praecipitare potestas:** supply *tibi est*.

566. **iam:** "soon." **turbari trabibus:** perhaps "crowded with craft" with *trabs*, lit. "tree-trunk" or "lumber," used for "ship." **saevas:** "fierce," as indicating danger.

568. **si te his attigerit terris Aurora morantem:** in Euripides, *Med.* 352 a similar phrase is part of Creon's threat to Medea (cf. 433 n.).

569. **rumpe moras:** "break off delay"; also at *Geo.* 3.43 and *Aen.* 9.13 (Iris appearing to Turnus). **varium...:** "woman is always a varying and changeful thing." The neuter seems to indicate contempt and *mutabilis* is usually used of inanimate objects; cf. Lyne 1989, 48-51, and Schiesaro 2008, 86-90, who sees "a traditional analogy between woman and the sea," both capable of suddenly becoming dangerous. Is Mercury right, because Dido's mood indicates that she is dangerous (to someone other than herself?), or is the god lying here, because it is Aeneas who has been "changeable" and Dido whose love has been unwavering? And is the slander on women here to be attributed to Vergil or merely to his character Mercury? Keith 2000, 24 reads the comment in the light of epic's traditional attitude towards women; cf. also Schiesaro 2008. Does Mercury save Aeneas here, or does his visit make things worse, and in fact lead to Dido's curse and, ultimately, the Punic Wars (see 615-29 n.)? Dido at Ovid, *Her.* 7.51 wishes Aeneas were more *mutabilis*.

571. **subitis...:** "startled by the sudden vision" or "phantom." For the plural, cf. 5.81.

praecipitis: "vigilate, viri, et considite transtris;
solvite vela citi. deus aethere missus ab alto
festinare fugam tortosque incidere funis   575
ecce iterum instimulat. sequimur te, sancte deorum,
quisquis es, imperioque iterum paremus ovantes.
adsis o placidusque iuves et sidera caelo
dextra feras." dixit vaginaque eripit ensem
fulmineum strictoque ferit retinacula ferro.   580
idem omnis simul ardor habet, rapiuntque ruuntque;
litora deseruere, latet sub classibus aequor,
adnixi torquent spumas et caerula verrunt.

---

575. **tortos:** "twisted," i.e. with twisted strands. **incidere funis:** "to cut the cables"; cf. the same phrase 3.667 of hurried flight, and below 580 where *retinacula* is equivalent to *funes*, the cables or ropes by which the ship is made fast to some object on shore.

577. **quisquis es:** "whoever you are," "whatever your name." Aeneas had no doubt that it was Mercury, but, as mortals' names for the gods may be wrong or displeasing to them, ancient prayers often added a phrase like this which apologizes for any mistake in the name, and asks the proper power, whatever his or her name, to accept the prayer; cf. Turnus at 9.22 (after addressing Iris by name), and Nisus at 9.209.

578. **adsis…:** "be present and graciously assist us"; for *adsis* or similar forms used in prayers, cf. Harrison on 10.254-5 and cf. *Arg.* 2.693, "be gracious, lord (Apollo), be gracious, you who have appeared to us."

579-80. **ensem / fulmineum:** "his lightning sword." The adjective emphasizes how fast he drew it, and may suggest a connection with the lightning of Jupiter both here and at 9.441 (see Hardie there), reinforcing that in leaving Dido, Aeneas is returning to Jupiter's plan. Vergil imitates both *Arg.* 4.207-8, where Jason cuts a rope when leaving Colchis after securing the fleece, and Apollonius' model at *Od.* 10.126-7, where Odysseus draws his sword to cut a cable and get his ship away from the monstrous Laestrygonians who have been killing his men.

581. **idem omnis simul ardor habet:** cf. *idem omnis simul ardor agit* 7.393, *sic omnis amor unus habet* 12.282, and the model for the line here, *Od.* 10.130, which describes Odysseus' shipmates fleeing the Laestrygonians (Clausen 1987, 111-12 = 2002, 214).

583. **adnixi…:** repeated from 3.208.

Et iam prima novo spargebat lumine terras
Tithoni croceum linquens Aurora cubile.   585
regina e speculis ut primum albescere lucem
vidit et aequatis classem procedere velis,
litoraque et vacuos sensit sine remige portus,
terque quaterque manu pectus percussa decorum
flaventisque abscissa comas "pro Iuppiter! ibit   590
hic," ait "et nostris inluserit advena regnis?
non arma expedient totaque ex urbe sequentur,
diripientque rates alii navalibus? ite,
ferte citi flammas, date tela, impellite remos!
quid loquor? aut ubi sum? quae mentem insania mutat?   595

584-631. Dido sees the Trojan ships at sea and laments that she had not earlier used violence against Aeneas. She curses Aeneas, calling for him to suffer in Italy and for eternal enmity between Rome and Carthage.

Dido's curse, which the reader must realize is largely to be fulfilled (see 615-29 n.), recalls those of Odysseus by Polyphemus in *Od.* 9.529-35, of Agamemnon and Menelaus by Ajax in Sophocles, *Ajax* 835-44, of Jason by Medea in *Arg.* 4.382-90, and of Theseus by Ariadne in Catullus 64.192-201, as well as the prelude to the duel in *Il.* 3.277. It must also be read against the popular tradition of cursing one's enemies or those who had committed an injustice, including lovers. Thousands of such curses survive on lead tablets (see OCD 3rd ed. s.v. curses). On Dido's curse, see O'Hara 1990, 94-102, Kraggerud 1999, Khan 1995 with Harrison 1995, Horsfall 1995, 124, Panoussi 2009, 193-6.

584-5. Tithoni: Tithonus is the Trojan lover of Dawn. This two-line description of dawn recurs at 9.459-60, as the Trojans learn of the deaths of Nisus and Euryalus, and is inspired by *Il.* 11.1 (= *Od.* 5.1), *Il.* 24.695, *Arg.* 4.183, and Lucretius, *DRN* 2.144, *primum Aurora novo cum spargit lumine terras.*

589-90. pectus percussa…abscissa: the middle sense of *percussa* and *abscissa* allows them to take direct objects (cf. 137 n.).

590-1. ibit / hic…: "shall this wanderer depart and have mocked…?" i.e. depart and so succeed in mocking. **advena:** in scorn, as at *Ecl.* 9.2-3 *advena nostri…possessor agelli*, and of Aeneas at *Aen.* 12.261. At *Aen.* 7.38-9 the narrator somewhat surprisingly refers to the Trojans who have arrived in Italy as an *advena…exercitus* (cf. O'Hara 2007, 96, with references).

592. expedient…sequentur: understand Dido's people as subjects.

594. citi: the adjective modifies the implied subject of the imperative, where English would probably use an adverb (cf. 494 n. and AG §290).

595. mutat: "changes," i.e. from a *mens sana* to a *mens insana*. Dido experiences a brief return to calmness and sad regret, like that of the rejected lover Corydon in *Ecl.* 2.69 *a, Corydon, Corydon, quae te dementia cepit!*

infelix Dido, nunc te facta impia tangunt?
tum decuit, cum sceptra dabas. en dextra fidesque,
quem secum patrios aiunt portare penatis,
quem subiisse umeris confectum aetate parentem!
non potui abreptum divellere corpus et undis   600
spargere? non socios, non ipsum absumere ferro
Ascanium patriisque epulandum ponere mensis?

596-9. **infelix Dido:** Laird 1997, 289: "Dido is the only personage in the *Aeneid* to address
herself by name. Homer's characters never address themselves in the second person, let
alone by name. But the device is found in a poem by Catullus," Poem 8, *Miser Catulle*....
facta impia: Vergil does not say whose "disloyal deeds" these are, and many have thought
Dido refers to her own betrayal of Sychaeus. But because Dido goes on to talk about her
decision to share power with Aeneas, and about his *dextra fidesque*, Casali 1999 (cf. too
Monti 1981, 62-9, rejected by Horsfall 1995, 127) argues that the whole passage makes
better sense as an allusion to the story that Aeneas was able to escape from Troy (events
to which 598-9 refer) because he abandoned or even betrayed Troy to the Greeks. See
12.15, where Turnus calls Aeneas the "deserter of Asia," and cf. Servius on 1.242 and
488, and Vergil's contemporary Dionysius of Halicarnassus, *Roman Antiquities* 1.48, who
cites earlier authors on various sides of the issue. Thus Dido would be saying "you should
have thought about those (stories of Aeneas') disloyal deeds then, when you were handing
over the sceptre." Cf. too [Tibull.](the brackets mean this is an anonymous poem in the
Tibullan corpus) 3.6.42, *ingrati referens impia facta viri*, of Theseus' desertion of Ariadne
in Catullus. **tangunt:** cf. 1.462, *sunt lacrimae rerum et mentem mortalia tangunt*; the echo
(just one word, but *tangunt* appears in Vergil in only these two passages) may be significant.

598. **quem:** sc. *eius quem* "(the hand and faith) of that man who, they say, ..." **secum patrios
aiunt portare penatis:** in 2.293-4 Hector tells Aeneas to take the *penates*, the household
gods of Troy, out of the city as it is being sacked.

599. **subiisse umeris:** cf. 2.708 *ipse subibo umeris* (Aeneas about to lift Anchises, as here, in
a scene familiar in Greek and Roman art), and for the accusative after *subire*, cf. 12.899
vix illum...subirent, of men trying to lift a heavy stone. **confectum aetate parentem:** cf.
confecto aetate parenti Catullus 68.118.

600-1. Dido's imagined scenarios for killing Aeneas and his men remind us of scenes from
Greek myth, especially as treated in Greek and Roman tragedy. Lines 600-1 resemble one
version (though not Apollonius') of how Medea killed her brother Apsyrtus, and scattered
pieces of his corpse on the sea to slow her father's pursuit (cf. Schiesaro 2008, 103-4). Then
601-2 suggest a crime like that of Atreus, who served his brother's children to him as a
meal, or that of Procne and Philomela, who served Tereus his child (cf. *Ecl.* 6.78-81, Ovid,
Met. 6.412-674).

verum anceps pugnae fuerat fortuna - fuisset:
quem metui moritura? faces in castra tulissem
implessemque foros flammis natumque patremque   605
cum genere exstinxem, memet super ipsa dedissem.
Sol, qui terrarum flammis opera omnia lustras,
tuque harum interpres curarum et conscia Iuno,
nocturnisque Hecate triviis ululata per urbes
et Dirae ultrices, et di morientis Elissae,   610
accipite haec, meritumque malis advertite numen
et nostras audite preces. si tangere portus
infandum caput ac terris adnare necesse est,

603-6. **verum…**: "but (if I had fought them) the outcome of the combat would have been doubtful." The sequence of thought is complex. Lines 600-2 suggested that it would have been better to fight Aeneas. *Verum…fortuna* (603) introduces an objection to this. Then *fuisset…* (603) says that even if this were true, she had no one to fear, since she was ready to die (*moritura*). Then *faces…dedissem* (604-5) confirms this argument, for if she had fought with him, she would have destroyed him before dying herself. In 603 the indicative *fuerat* is put for the subjunctive for the sake of vividness and because the indicative is necessary to bring out the contrast with the subsequent *fuisset*.

605-6. **implessem…exstinxem:** = *implevissem…exstinxissem*, which are more difficult forms to use in the hexameter. **foros:** "gangways" or "decks" of a ship. **memet…dedissem:** "have flung myself upon the pile," a phrase modeled on what is said of Medea at *Arg.* 4.391-3.

607. **Sol…:** the start of Dido's curse resembles both *Il.* 3.277, and (as part of a series of allusions to Ajax that will culminate in 6.450-76) Soph. *Aj.* 845-9, where Ajax cries out to the Sun when he is about to commit suicide (cf. Panoussi 2002, 112 and 2009, 193-6).

608. **tuque…:** "and you, O Juno, mediator and witness of these woes." *Interpres* means (1) one who acts as agent between two others, (2) one who explains what is dark or mysterious. So *Iuno pronuba* (59, 166) is *interpres* because (1) she brings man and woman together in wedlock and (2) explains its mysteries and "troubles" (*curae*). Again Dido's ignorance of Juno's real role is striking.

609. **nocturnisque Hecate triviis:** cf. 511 n. for the worship of Diana/Hecate at crossroads (*trivia*); she was often called Trivia, as at Cat. 34.15, *Aen.* 6.13, etc. **ululata:** "worshipped with wails", cf. this verb at 168 for the shrieking of the Nymphs in the "marriage" in the cave.

610. **di morientis:** probably the *di Manes* (cf. 34 n.).

611. **accipite…:** "listen to these things, turn your (divine) regard to ills that have earned it." After *accipite* supply *animis* (for which cf. 5.304) or more probably *auribus. Malis* should be understood both with *meritum* and *advertite:* they were to have regard *for* her ills because that regard had been earned *by* those ills.

613. **infandum caput:** "that accursed one"; cf. 354 n., but the notion that his name is literally "unspeakable" is also felt.

> et sic fata Iovis poscunt, hic terminus haeret:
> at bello audacis populi vexatus et armis,   615
> finibus extorris, complexu avulsus Iuli
> auxilium imploret videatque indigna suorum
> funera; nec, cum se sub leges pacis iniquae
> tradiderit, regno aut optata luce fruatur,
> sed cadat ante diem mediaque inhumatus harena.   620
> haec precor, hanc vocem extremam cum sanguine fundo.
> tum vos, o Tyrii, stirpem et genus omne futurum

614. **hic terminus haeret:** "that boundary stands fixed." A Roman image of immovability, derived from the "boundary-stones" which everywhere marked their fields under the protection of the god *Terminus*; cf. Lucretius, *DRN* 1.77 *alte terminus haerens;* Horace, *Carm. Saec.* 25-6 *stabilisque rerum / terminus.*

615-29. Those who are about to die are thought to be gifted with prophetic power (*Il.* 16.843-54, 22.355, *Aen.* 10.739-46), and Dido's curse will largely be fulfilled (references above 584-631 n.), though not always in the worst way possible. The later books of the *Aeneid* tell how Aeneas was "harassed in war" by the bold Rutulians, and driven to leave his son (temporarily); how he "implores aid" from the Greek Evander (Book 8), and accepts a peace that sacrifices the name of Troy (12.828). Other sources relate that after a brief reign of three years he fell in battle and his corpse was undiscovered (cf. *Aen.* 1.259-66, which focuses on apotheosis, and contrast the words of Anchises in 6.763-6 about "long life" for Aeneas; cf. O'Hara 2007, 81-2). The latter part of the curse looks to Roman history, with a clear reference to Hannibal and the Punic wars in 622-9. The curse means both that the poem is providing the "aetion" or origin-story for Carthage's long opposition to Rome, and that Aeneas' troubles in the second half of the poem can to some extent be attributed to his actions in Carthage, just as Odysseus' suffering and loss of his men follow from the Cyclops' curse.

615. **audacis:** used of Aeneas' opponents in Italy at 7.409, 9.3, 126, 519, 10.276, but cf. too 7.114 of the Trojans, 9.625 (Ascanius of his own actions).

616. **finibus extorris:** Aeneas is an "exile from his homeland," but the phrase could also suggest his trip to see Evander and then the Etruscans in *Aen.* 8.

617. **indigna:** "cruel," "undeserved."

618. **cum se…:** "when he will have surrendered himself beneath the conditions of an unequal peace." Cf. the unequal compromise between Jupiter and Juno at 12.791-840, in which the Trojan name will die out and the Italian contribution predominate.

620. **sed cadat…:** "but let him die before his day and (lie) unburied amid the sand" (in the second clause, some verb like *iaceat* must be supplied from *cadat*). **ante diem:** used of Dido's death in 697. "To die in one's prime and to die unburied—these were the most dreadful things that a man could suffer in ancient times" (Austin ad loc.).

exercete odiis, cinerique haec mittite nostro
munera. nullus amor populis nec foedera sunto.
exoriare aliquis nostris ex ossibus ultor   625
qui face Dardanios ferroque sequare colonos,
nunc, olim, quocumque dabunt se tempore vires.
litora litoribus contraria, fluctibus undas
imprecor, arma armis: pugnent ipsique nepotesque."
    Haec ait, et partis animum versabat in omnis,   630
invisam quaerens quam primum abrumpere lucem.
tum breviter Barcen nutricem adfata Sychaei,

---

623. **exercete…:** "hound with hate, and offer that tribute (or 'gift') to my dust." *Exercere* is "keep busy," "allow no rest to," "torment," but Conte 2007, 115 says *genus … exercete odiis* may be enallage* for the usual construction *exercete odium.*

624. **sunto:** future imperative, 3rd plural, archaic in tone (AG §448a).

625-6. **exoriare…:** = *exoriaris,* 2nd singular present, hortatory subjunctive (AG §439a) of a deponent: "Arise, you unknown Avenger, from my bones, to pursue…." With abrupt change of addressee, Dido vividly speaks both to and of the avenger, whom every Roman would know to be Hannibal, who attacked Italy and threatened Rome in the Second Punic War. **nostris ex ossibus:** because in his hatred of Rome Hannibal was Dido's true descendant. **qui…colonos:** relative clause of purpose; *sequare* is 2nd singular present subjunctive.

629. **imprecor:** "I invoke." **ipsique nepotesque:** imitates *seque suosque* at the end of Ariadne's curse at Catullus 64.201 (Wills 1997, 265-6, Clausen 2002, 101). Vergil's hypermetric line (cf. 558 and appendix on meter) at the *end* of a speech is remarkable, and marks the rush and vehemence of her words, with no break between her words and what follows. Williams rightly speaks of how the meter suggests "the never-ending hatred of Dido."

631. **invisam…:** "seeking how with all speed (lit. 'as soon as possible') to be rid of hateful day." *Abrumpere lucem* is a variation of *abrumpere vitam* (8.579), with *lucem* meaning "the light of day" or "life" (cf. *luce* in 31) and *abrumpere* "to break off" what would otherwise continue.

632-62. *Sending an old nurse to distract her sister, Dido mounts the pyre and draws a sword given her by Aeneas; gazing on the memorials around her, she recalls the greatness of her life and with a curse on her betrayer stabs herself.*

Borrowings from tragedy, especially Sophocles' *Ajax* (647 n.) and Euripides' *Alcestis* (648-51 n., 659 n.), deepen the pathos, and there are again echoes of Medea and Ariadne (657-8 n., 659 n.), as well as one important suggestion of Cleopatra (644 n.).

632. **Barcen nutricem:** the "nurse" or "foster-mother" was held in high esteem, cf. 5.645, 7.1-7 (Aeneas' nurse Caieta), Euripides' *Hippolytus,* and Lyne on [Verg.] *Ciris* 206-385. As Servius Auctus notes, Barca was the family name of Hannibal (cf. also Barcaei in 43 and n.).

namque suam patria antiqua cinis ater habebat:
"Annam, cara mihi nutrix, huc siste sororem:
dic corpus properet fluviali spargere lympha,   635
et pecudes secum et monstrata piacula ducat.
sic veniat, tuque ipsa pia tege tempora vitta.
sacra Iovi Stygio, quae rite incepta paravi,
perficere est animus finemque imponere curis
Dardaniique rogum capitis permittere flammae."   640
sic ait. illa gradum studio celerabat anili.
at trepida et coeptis immanibus effera Dido
sanguineam volvens aciem, maculisque trementis
interfusa genas et pallida morte futura,
interiora domus inrumpit limina et altos   645
conscendit furibunda rogos ensemque recludit

633. **suam:** the reflexive here refers to the subject not of its own clause but of the previous clause, as often happens when the clause in which the reflexive appears reproduces the thought of the subject of the other clause (AG §300.2).

635. **dic...properet:** "tell her to hurry to..." (*ut* is often omitted after *dic*, AG §565); cf. 5.550-1.

637. **sic:** "so," i.e. when she has done what lines 635-6 require. Dido wishes to gain time.

638. **Iovi Stygio:** the "underworld Jupiter" is Pluto; at 6.138 *Iunoni infernae* = Proserpina.

639-40. **finemque...:** "and put an end to my troubles by giving (lit. 'and to give') to the flame the funeral pyre of that Trojan person." The periphrasis *Dardanium caput* is probably meant to mark abhorrence, cf. 354 n. and 614 n. The clause introduced by -*que* in 640 is explanatory. The *rogus* is that on which his *effigies* (508) is placed.

642. **coeptis immanibus effera:** "maddened by her awful purpose," "wild with the enormity of what she has begun."

643-4. **sanguineam volvens aciem:** "rolling her bloodshot eyes" (cf. *sanguineam torquens aciem* of Amata at 7.399, *volvens oculos* of Aeneas at 12.939). **maculisque trementis / interfusa genas:** cf. 137 n. for the passive participle with "middle" sense, as well as 509 *crines effusa*, and 12.64-5 *Lavinia ... flagrantis perfusa genas*. Here both *maculis* and *interfusa* suggest that her face is marked with dark or red spots. **pallida morte futura:** cf. *pallentem morte futura* at 8.709, of Cleopatra after the battle of Actium on the shield of Aeneas; the echo links the two North African queens (cf. Introduction above, and nn. on 86, 193, 215). On Cleopatra in Augustan poetry cf. Keith 2000, 118-22 and index, with further references; on the *Aeneid* see Hardie 2006.

Dardanium, non hos quaesitum munus in usus.
hic, postquam Iliacas vestis notumque cubile
conspexit, paulum lacrimis et mente morata
incubuitque toro dixitque novissima verba: 650
"dulces exuviae, dum fata deusque sinebat,
accipite hanc animam meque his exsolvite curis.
vixi et quem dederat cursum fortuna peregi,
et nunc magna mei sub terras ibit imago.
urbem praeclaram statui, mea moenia vidi,   655
ulta virum poenas inimico a fratre recepi,
felix, heu nimium felix, si litora tantum
numquam Dardaniae tetigissent nostra carinae."

---

647. **non hos…:** "a gift not begged (or perhaps 'sought') for such a purpose." In 507 *ensem relictum* seems to describe a sword left behind by chance, but here the sword is clearly a gift which Dido had asked Aeneas for, and which was to be a fatal gift. As Servius notes, Vergil adapts the model of the gifts exchanged by Hector and Ajax after their duel in *Iliad* 7: Ajax will kill himself with the sword given by Hector (cf. Sophocles, *Ajax* 661-5, 1026-35), and Hector will be dragged around Troy by Achilles, tied with the baldric given to him by Ajax (cf. Tatum 1984, 446, Panoussi 2002, 103, Panoussi 2009, 183).

648-51. Dido throws herself on the bed like Euripides' Alcestis, who is about to die to save her husband, at Eur. *Alc.* 175-80. For *Iliacas vestis* in 648 and *dulces exuviae* in 651 as suggestive of Hypsipyle, from whom Jason departs on better terms in Apollonius, see Krevans 2002-2003. **novissima verba:** "last words."

653-6. The monumental simplicity and grandeur of these lines make them recall the simple epitaphs of the Scipios and other Republican nobles; see the first several examples in Warmington, *ROL* vol. 1, and cf. Clausen 1987, 58-60 = 2002, 107-8, Perkell 1994, 67, and Thomas 1998, 283-5 on Turnus and the Scipios.

653. **vixi:** "I have lived my life." The word conveys the idea that the life thus lived has not been an empty and useless one, cf. Horace, *Carm.* 3.29.41-3 *ille potens sui / laetusque deget, cui licet in diem / dixisse "vixi,"* i.e. "I have lived" and not merely existed, and *Carm.* 3.26.1-2 *vixi puellis nuper idoneus / et militavi non sine gloria.*

654. **et nunc…:** cf. the words used by Turnus at 12.648-9: *sancta ad vos anima atque istius inscia culpae / descendam, magnorum haud umquam indignus avorum.* A number of echoes link Turnus and Dido.

657-8. **felix, heu nimium felix … tetigissent:** an echo of several earlier poems. Cf. the abandoned Ariadne's words at Catullus 64.171-2 *utinam ne tempore primo / Gnosia Cecropiae <u>tetigissent</u> litora puppes*, Silenus' words on Pasiphae in *Ecl.* 6.45 *et <u>fortunatam</u>, si numquam armenta <u>fuissent</u>*, and their models in Eurip. *Med.* 1-6, Apoll. Rhod. *Arg.* 4.26-33, Ennius *Medea Exul* 208-9 J = 253-4 W. Cf. Clausen 1987, 58-60 = 2002, 107-10, Reed 2007, 117.

dixit, et os impressa toro "moriemur inultae,
sed moriamur," ait. "sic, sic iuvat ire sub umbras.   660
hauriat hunc oculis ignem crudelis ab alto
Dardanus, et nostrae secum ferat omina mortis."
dixerat, atque illam media inter talia ferro
conlapsam aspiciunt comites, ensemque cruore
spumantem sparsasque manus. it clamor ad alta   665
atria: concussam bacchatur Fama per urbem.
lamentis gemituque et femineo ululatu
tecta fremunt, resonat magnis plangoribus aether,

659. **os impressa toro:** probably "pressing her lips upon the couch," i.e. in a kiss. So Medea in Apoll. Rhod. *Arg.* 4.26 and Alcestis in Eurip. *Alc.* 183; cf. Reed 2007, 79-80. **moriemur …:** "I shall die unavenged but (still) let me die"; (it is, however, possible to put a question mark after *inultae*, as in Propertius 2.8.17-18, *sic igitur prima moriere aetate, Properti? / sed morere).* **inultae:** emphatic: to die unavenged or to leave the dead unavenged (cf. 656) was repugnant to ancient sentiment; cf. Aeneas' words at 2.670 *numquam omnes hodie moriemur inulti.*

660. **sic, sic iuvat…:** *iuvat* is a strong word, cf. 2.27; 3.606; *Geo.* 3.292. The meaning of *sic, sic* is uncertain. Some take it as summing up all that precedes ("with this sword, on this couch, etc."); others refer it specifically to *inultae* ("even so" = unavenged). Some even suggest that she stabs herself at each utterance of the word. Cf. the words of Anchises at 2.644-5 in what he (wrongly) thinks to be a similarly hopeless situation: *sic o sic positum adfati discedite corpus. / ipse manu mortem inveniam* and Wills 1996, 118-9.

662. **omina:** anything seen when setting out on a journey was specially ominous, cf. Hor. *Carm.* 3.27.1-20. At 5.1-7 the sight of the flames of Carthage indeed has a grim effect on the Trojans.

663-92. Dido sinks dying: a wail arises among her maidens and alarms Anna, who laments, and reproaches Dido for what she has done.
The responses of Anna, and of the city, to Dido's suicide, suggest a perspective different from Dido's: that she did not deserve to die, and should not have killed herself (Perkell 1994). On Dido's death, see references above 504-705 n. Keith 2000, 114-17 notes that prolonged physical agony in the *Aen.* occurs only with the deaths of Dido and Camilla, i.e. only with women.

663-4. **dixerat, atque…:** "she had spoken and right away, amid such words…." **ferro:** "on the sword." **conlapsam:** see 391 n.

665. **sparsas:** this may suggest either hands spattered with blood or hands loosened and so spread wide in death (Servius).

666. **concussam…:** "rumor rushes wildly through the startled town." **bacchatur:** cf. 300-1 (Dido) *per urbem / bacchatur.*

667. **lamentis…:** note the wild and imitative rhythm of 667, with hiatus before the final four-syllable *ululatu,* as in 9.477, where Euryalus' mother laments his death. Recall too the wailing of the nymphs in 168.

non aliter quam si immissis ruat hostibus omnis
Karthago aut antiqua Tyros, flammaeque furentes   670
culmina perque hominum volvantur perque deorum.
audiit exanimis trepidoque exterrita cursu
unguibus ora soror foedans et pectora pugnis
per medios ruit, ac morientem nomine clamat:
"hoc illud, germana, fuit? me fraude petebas?   675
hoc rogus iste mihi, hoc ignes araeque parabant?
quid primum deserta querar? comitemne sororem
sprevisti moriens? eadem me ad fata vocasses:
idem ambas ferro dolor atque eadem hora tulisset.
his etiam struxi manibus patriosque vocavi   680
voce deos, sic te ut posita, crudelis, abessem?

669-70. non aliter...: in the climax of the imagery likening Dido's fall to the sack of a city (cf. Lyne 1987, 19-20, Hardie 1986, 283 and 2006, 33), Vergil borrows this simile* (as Macrobius *Sat.* 4.6. noted) from *Il.* 22.410-13, where the wailing for Hector is as if Troy were fallen. At the actual destruction of Carthage in 146 BCE, Scipio Aemilianus thought of Troy, quoted Hector's famous words from *Il.* 6.448-9 about the necessity for Troy to fall, and said that even Rome would meet this fate (Appian, *Rom. Hist.* 8.19.132, Polybius 38.21-2). For suggestions of the *Iliad* in *Aen.* 4, cf. 149 n., and for the fire imagery cf. 2 n.

671. perque...perque: effective repetition: the flames "roll on" in wave after wave.

672. audiit: recalls Grk. ἤκουσε of *Iliad* 22.447, where Andromache hears the mourning at Hector's death.

673. Repeated, of Turnus' sister Juturna, in 12.871, just before his death.

674. nomine: Vergil follows Homeric usage in saying "address by name" and then not actually giving the name in 675 (cf. e.g. *Il.* 1.361).

675. hoc illud...: "Was this then your purpose?" **me:** emphatic, "was it me you sought to deceive (lit. 'assailed with a trick')?" (cf. 12.359 *bello ... petisti*).

678. vocasses: = *vocare debebas* or *utinam vocasses*; the form = *vocavisses*. "To the same doom you should have invited me," or "if only you had invited...." Cf. 8.643; 10.854; 11.161-2 (Evander to his dead son) *Troum socia arma secutum / obruerent Rutuli telis; animam ipse dedissem.*

680-1. his... manibus: *his* is deictic and rhetorical, calling attention to her hands as she speaks. **struxi:** i.e. the pyre. **vocavi / voce:** "called aloud upon." **posita:** > *pono*, "lay out" (for burial). **crudelis:** vocative, of Dido.

exstinxti te meque, soror, populumque patresque
Sidonios urbemque tuam. date vulnera lymphis
abluam et, extremus si quis super halitus errat,
ore legam." sic fata gradus evaserat altos,   685
semianimemque sinu germanam amplexa fovebat
cum gemitu atque atros siccabat veste cruores.
illa gravis oculos conata attollere rursus
deficit; infixum stridit sub pectore vulnus.
ter sese attollens cubitoque adnixa levavit,   690
ter revoluta toro est oculisque errantibus alto
quaesivit caelo lucem ingemuitque reperta.

682-3. **populumque patresque / Sidonios**: the "people" and the "Fathers" constitute the whole nation; the phrase is modeled on the well-known *Senatus Populusque Romanus* (so too 8.679 *cum patribus populoque*).

683-4. **date vulnera lymphis / abluam…:** "grant me to wash her wound with water and gather with my mouth whatever latest breath flickers over hers." The words are in strong contrast with her previous passionate speech; her passion is over, she has but one care—to perform the last acts of tenderness and love to her dying sister. For this contrast and for the construction *date abluam*, cf. 6.883-6. Similar constructions are 5.163 *stringat sine*, 717 *habeant … sine*. Servius suggests *date* = *permittite*. Some prefer to call *date vulnera lymphis* "a rhetorical inversion quite in Virg.'s manner, like *dare classibus austros* 3.61" (Conington; cf. 226 n. on enallage*). **extremus…:** the next of kin customarily receive in the mouth the last breath of the dying in order to continue the existence of the spirit; cf. Cic. *Verr.* 2.5.45 *matres… filiorum suorum postremum spiritum ore excipere;* Ovid, *Met.* 12.424, and *Star Trek III: The Search for Spock.*

685. **sic fata…evaserat:** "so saying (i.e. while so speaking)…she had climbed"; *fata* is like a present participle here.

686. **semianimem:** four syllables; the "i" of *semi-* is treated as a consonant.

689. **deficit:** "swoons": the sign of life shown in lifting her eyes disappears. **infixum stridit sub pectore vulnus:** recalls 4 *infixi pectore vultus* and 67 *tacitum vivit sub pectore vulnus.* Earlier wound metaphors* here become literal, just as Dido's pyre makes literal the earlier fire imagery.

692. **quaesivit…:** Dido's eyes "roam" vaguely in search of the light, and then, when they have at last turned heavenward and found it, she "groans deeply," perhaps as though regretful that she is still alive.

Tum Iuno omnipotens longum miserata dolorem
difficilisque obitus Irim demisit Olympo
quae luctantem animam nexosque resolveret artus.   695
nam quia nec fato merita nec morte peribat,
sed misera ante diem subitoque accensa furore,
nondum illi flavum Proserpina vertice crinem
abstulerat Stygioque caput damnaverat Orco.

693-705. *Juno in pity sends Iris from heaven to cut a lock of Dido's hair and end her pain.*

693. **Iuno omnipotens:** an epithet used often of Jupiter (cf. 220 and n.), but of Juno elsewhere only in Allecto's deceptive words to Turnus at 7.428. Juno's *lack* of power, however, is evident here; she has been unable to protect Dido (though was this ever really her goal, e.g., in her plan with Venus earlier in the book?) or to stop Aeneas, and will ultimately fail to protect Carthage.

694. **Irim:** often the messenger of Jupiter (9.803) or esp. Juno (cf. 5.606, 9.2); cf. Feeney 1998, and for the rainbow Johnson 1976, 66-72 and Perkell 1994, 68-70 with further references.

695. **quae…:** "to separate her struggling soul from (lit. 'and') the limbs that cling to it" (relative clause of purpose). The soul was supposed to be intertwined with the body, and so to have difficulty in disentangling itself, cf. Lucretius, *DRN* 2.950 *vitalis animae nodos a corpore solvit.*

696. **nec fato:** suggests that while Aeneas had to leave Dido, the story did not have to end with her death. **merita nec morte:** here the narrator, perhaps reflecting Juno's viewpoint, explicitly contradicts Dido's words *quin morere ut merita es* (547); the narrator's condemnation of Dido's *culpa* in 172 is similarly challenging, but presents an opposing viewpoint.

697. **ante diem:** Dido dies "before her time"; her curse called for Aeneas to fall *ante diem* (620), and he will indeed die and/or be taken up to heaven within three years.

698-9. **nondum illi flavum Proserpina vertice crinem / abstulerat:** the need for Proserpina (wife of Pluto and queen of the underworld = Greek Persephone) to cut a lock from the hair of the dying seems to be a Vergilian invention, despite the efforts of Macrobius *Sat.* 5.19.2 to make it traditional; Horace, *Carm.* 1.28.19-20, often cited by modern commentators, does not mention hair, as noted by Rauk 1995. Vergil adapts the words of Death at Euripides *Alc.* 74-6: both Dido and Alcestis are being likened to sacrificial victims, from whom some hair is plucked before death (cf. 6.245). The cutting of the lock here may interact with the allusion at 6.460 to Catullus 66, the *Lock of Berenice*, in which the queen cuts off and dedicates a lock of her hair (Hardie 2006, 34).

ergo Iris croceis per caelum roscida pennis   700
mille trahens varios adverso sole colores
devolat et supra caput adstitit. "hunc ego Diti
sacrum iussa fero teque isto corpore solvo."
sic ait et dextra crinem secat: omnis et una
dilapsus calor atque in ventos vita recessit.   705

702-3. **hunc:** supply *crinem.* **sacrum:** the basic meaning of this word is the one relevant here, "consecrated to a deity" (*OLD* 1). Similar language at Eurip. *Alc.* 76.

705. **in ventos…:** "her life passed into the air." Cf. the deaths of Lausus (*tum vita per auras…* 10.819) and of both Camilla and Turnus: *vitaque cum gemitu fugit indignata sub umbras* (11.831 = 12.952, the last line of the poem).

Appendix A: Vergil's Meter[1]

Dactylic hexameter was the meter of Greek epic, and beginning with Ennius' *Annales* (early second century BCE),[2] it became the meter of Roman epic as well. Its basic rhythm can be felt in the following line from the opening of Longfellow's *Evangeline*:

Thís is the fórest priméval. The múrmuring pínes and the hémlocks

Here five dactyls (búm-ba-ba) are followed by a final disyllabic foot. These metrical units (as with English verse more generally) are created through the use of natural word stress to create patterns of stressed and unstressed syllables. Thus a dactyl in English poetry is a stressed syllable followed by two unstressed syllables (e.g. "Thís is the" and "múrmuring"). Classical Latin meter, however, differs in an important way. Metrical feet are based not on word stress but on the quantity of individual syllables (i.e. whether they are long or short). Thus, in Latin a dactyl contains one long syllable followed by two short ones (– ◡◡).

As the name indicates, "dactylic hexameter" literally describes a line that contains six (Gr. *hex*) measures or feet (Gr. *metra*) that are dactylic (– ◡◡).[3] In actual practice, however, spondees (– –) could substitute for dactyls within the first four feet,[4] and the line's ending was largely regularized as – ◡◡ / –x. The Latin dactylic hexameter can thus be notated as follows:

---

1   For more on Vergil's meter, see Jackson Knight 1944, 232-42, Duckworth 1969, 46-62, Nussbaum 1986, and Ross 2007, 143-52.

2   The earliest Latin epics by Livius Andronicus and Naevius were composed in Saturnian verse, a meter that is not fully understood.

3   The word "dactyl" comes from the Greek word *dactylos*, "finger." A metrical dactyl with its long and two short syllables resembles the structure of a finger: the bone from the knuckle to the first joint is longer than the two bones leading to the fingertip.

4   More technically the two short syllables of a dactyl are "contracted" into one long, and a spondee is formed.

$$- \smile\smile / - \smile\smile / - \smile\smile / - \smile\smile / - \smile\smile / - x$$

(Here, "/" separates metrical feet; "–" = a long syllable; "$\smile$" = a short syllable; and "x" = an *anceps* ("undecided") syllable, one that could be either long or short, but in an actual line will be one or the other.)

Very rarely (and never in *Aen.* 4) a spondee is used in the fifth foot, in which case the line is called "spondaic."

To *scan* a line (i.e. to identify a line's rhythm and meter), long and short syllables must be identified. A syllable can be *long* in two ways: by *nature*, if it contains a vowel that is inherently long or is a diphthong[5]; or *by position*, if it contains a naturally short vowel followed either by a double consonant (*x* or *z*) or, in most cases, by two consonants—even if one or both consonants are in the next word.[6] In general, all other syllables are *short*, although at times a syllable is lenghtened in the "arsis," the first long of a foot that receives a special metrical emphasis known as the *ictus* (see discussion below, and notes on 4.64, 146, 213, 222). If, however, a word ending in a vowel, diphthong, or vowel-plus-*m* is followed by a word that begins with a vowel, diphthong, or *h*, the first vowel or diphthong is *elided* (cf. *credo* in 4.12 below; elided syllables are enclosed in parentheses in the examples below). As a result the two syllables merge and are scanned as one — a phenomenon called *elision*. *Elision* occurs frequently in Vergil, though at times a final vowel is left unelided in what is called *hiatus* (see 4.235 *spe inimica*). When an extra syllable at the end of one line is elided before the next, it produces a *hypermetric* line (see 4.558, and the wonderful example at 629).

By applying these rules, we may scan hexameter lines as follows:

āt rē/gīnă grā/vī iăm/dūdūm / saūcĭă / cūrā

(*Aen.* 4.1)

---

5   One can determine if a vowel is long by nature by looking the word up in a Latin dictionary to see if it has a macron over it or by checking inflected endings in a grammar (for example, some endings, like the first and second declension ablative singular (-*a*, -*o*), are always long; others, like the second declension nominative neuter plural (-*a*), are always short).

6   An exception to this general rule: if a short vowel is followed by a mute consonant (*b, c, d, g, p, t*) and a liquid (*l* or *r*), the resulting syllable can be either short or long. Cf. 2.663 where the first syllables of *patris* and *patrem* are short and long respectively: *natum ante ora pătris, pātrem qui obtruncat ad aras*. It should also be noted that *h* is a breathing, not a consonant; it therefore does not help make a vowel long by position.

crēd(o) ĕquĭ/dēm, nēc / vānă fĭ/dēs, gĕnŭs / ēssĕ dĕ/ōrŭm.
(*Aen.* 4.12)
pūlvĕrŭ/lēntă fŭ/gā glŏmĕ/rānt mōn/tīsquĕ rĕ/līnquūnt.
(*Aen.* 4.155)
īt nī/grūm cām/pīs āg/mēn prāē/dāmquĕ pĕr / hērbās
(*Aen.* 4.404)

A long syllable generally takes twice as long to pronounce as a short. The flow of a line is affected not only by its rhythm but also by the placement of word breaks. A word break between metrical feet is called a *diaeresis*, while a word break within a metrical foot is called a *caesura*[7]:

īmpŭlĭt. / āgnōs/cō vĕtĕ/rīs vēs/tīgĭă / flāmmāē.
(*Aen.* 4.23)

Here, diaeresis occurs after *impulit* and after *vestigia*, while caesura occurs after *agnosco* and *veteris*.[8] In Latin word breaks are important mainly because they affect the interplay between the ictus and accent (see below), but scholars have also drawn attention to how they seem to divide most lines. The most important caesura in any given line often coincides with a sense break and is called the *main* or *principal caesura*.[9] It most frequently falls in the third foot, but also occurs not uncommonly in the second or fourth (or sometimes both). The slight pause implied in the main caesura helps shape the movement of each verse by breaking it into two (or more) parts. Here are the first seven lines of the *Aeneid*, scanned and with the principal caesurae marked ("||"):

ārmă vĭ/rūmquĕ că/nō, || Trō/iāē quī / prīmŭs ăb / ōrīs

Ītălĭ/ām fā/tō prŏfŭ/gūs || Lā/vīniăquĕ / vēnĭt

lītŏră, / mūlt(um) īll(e) / ēt tēr/rīs || iāc/tātŭs ĕt / āltō

---

7   When a *diaeresis* occurs just before the fifth foot, it is often called a *bucolic diaeresis* because this type of diaeresis was used frequently in pastoral poetry: e.g. *nos patriam fugimus; tu, Tityre,* || *lentus in umbra* (Vergil, *Eclogues* 1.4).
8   In the combinations *qu, gu, su* (e.g. *–que, sanguis, suesco*), note that the *u* is consonantal but that the combinations themselves count as a single consonant for the purposes of scansion.
9   Readers may differ on where (or even if) there is a main caesura in a given line.

vī sŭpĕ/rūm, || sāē/vāē mĕmŏ/rēm Iū/nōnĭs ŏb / īrăm,

mūltă quŏ/qu(e) ēt bēl/lō pās/sūs, || dūm / cōndĕrĕt / ūrbĕm

īnfēr/rētquĕ dĕ/ōs Lătĭ/ō, || gĕnŭs / ūndĕ Lă/tīnŭm

Ālbā/nīquĕ pă/trēs || āt/qu(e) āltāē / mōēnĭă / Rōmāē. (*Aen.* 1.1-7)

(Note that in line 2, *Laviniaque* is pronounced as four (not five) syllables, with the second "i" treated as a consonant; cf. 4.686 n.)

In addition to metrical length, words also have a natural accent.[10] This accent will either coincide with or clash with the metrical stress (*ictus*), which falls on the first long syllable of each foot. Coincidence of word accent and metrical stress produces fluidity in the verse; clashing of word accent and metrical stress creates tension. For example:

$$x \quad x \quad / \quad x \quad / \quad /$$

īnfān/dūm, rē/gīnă, iŭ/bēs rĕnŏ/vārĕ dŏ/lōrĕm (*Aen.* 2.3)

$$/ \quad x \quad x \quad x \quad / \quad /$$

īmpŭlĭt. / āgnōs/cō vĕtĕ/rīs vēs/tīgĭă / flāmmāē. (*Aen.* 4.23)

(Naturally accented syllables are in boldface; "/" = ictus that coincides with word accent; "x" = ictus that clashes with word accent.)

In these two lines, there are clashes in three of the first four feet (wherein the word accent generally does not coincide with the verse accent), followed by coincidence in the final two feet.[11] In creating clashes, the placement of "strong" caesurae is particularly important. When a caesura falls after the first syllable of a foot, it is called "strong" (as after *cano* in 1.1 above); if it falls after the second syllable in a dactylic foot, it is called "weak" (as

10 Disyllabic words have their accent on their initial syllable: *cáris, dábant, mólis.* For words of three syllables or longer, the word accent falls: on the penultima (second to last syllable), if it is long (*ruébant, iactátos*) but on the antepenultima (the syllable preceding the penultima), if the penultima is short (*géntibus, mária, pópulum*).

11 Classical Latin speakers would presumably have pronounced the word accents in reading lines, while still maintaining the basic rhythm of hexameter. Otherwise, the ictus would have transformed the basic sound of the word.

after *arma* in 1.1). In practice, "if a word of two or more syllables ends after the first long of a foot (that is, producing a strong caesura), there will be a clash between accent and ictus in that foot," because the final syllable of such words is not accented.[12] The strong caesurae in 4.23 (above) and in 4.33, 35 (below) display this principle well.

One of Vergil's artistic feats was to manage the sequence of clash and coincidence of ictus and word accent in such a way as to achieve a rhythmically varied and pleasing line. In general we find that Vergilian hexameters are characterized by the clash of ictus and word accent in the first four feet and by the coincidence of ictus and word accent in the last two feet, which results in a pleasing resolution of stress at line end.[13]

/   x   x   x   /   /

nec dulcis **na**tos **Ve**neris nec **prae**mia **no**ris?   (4.33)

/   x   x   x   /   /

est(o): **ae**gram **nul**li **quon**dam **fle**xere **ma**riti,   (4.35)

---

12   Ross 2007, 146. For word accentuation, see n. 10 (above).

13   Vergil can also make lines stand out and sound unusually smooth or harsh by using lines with much coincidence in the first four feet (cf. nn. on 4.81, 305), or by using final monosyllables or four-syllable words to produce clash in the fifth or sixth feet (cf. nn. to 4.132, 314).

Appendix B: Stylistic Terms

Vergil's skillful use of language is a defining element of his artistry. He often employs rhetorical figures and stylistic devices to reinforce the content of his poetry. Although the initial goals of the beginning student involve knowing how to translate Vergil into good English, careful attention should be paid both to what Vergil says *and* to exactly how he says it in Latin. The following list defines many of the stylistic terms and features that are encountered in studying Vergil. For discussion of the examples cited from Book 4, see the commentary notes. For more information on the terms, see Lanham 1991 and Brogan 1994. Fuller information on Vergilian style can be found in Jackson Knight 1944, 225-341, Camps 1969, 60-74, O'Hara 1997, and Conte 2007, 58-122. Stylistic analyses of Vergilian passages are presented in Horsfall 1995, 237-48 and Hardie 1998, 102-14. This appendix is adapted from that of Ganiban 2008.

Alliteration: the repetition of the initial consonant sound in neighboring words. E.g., *magno misceri murmure* (4.160). **Alliteration** is often used to create **onomatopoeia**, and occurs frequently with **assonance** and **consonance**.

Anaphora (Gr. "bringing back"): the repetition of a word at the beginning of consecutive sentences or clauses. E.g., *num fletu ingemuit nostro? num lumina flexit? / num lacrimas victus dedit aut miseratus amantem est?* (4.369-70).

Apostrophe (Gr. "turning away"): a sudden shift of address to a figure (or idea), absent or present. E.g., Dido addresses *pudor* as *te* in 27, and the narrator addresses *improbe Amor* at 412.

Assonance (Lat. "answer with the same sound"): the repetition of vowel sounds in neighboring words or phrases. E.g., the long vowels describing the song of the owl at 4.463.

Asyndeton (Gr. "unconnected"): the omission of connectives between words, phrases, or sentences. E.g. Dido's words *eiectum litore, egentem / excepi* (4.373-4).

Consonance (Lat. "sound together with"): the repetition of consonant sounds in neighboring words or phrases. Cf. 4.390, and see **alliteration, assonance**.

Dicolon Abundans: see **Theme and Variation**.

Ellipsis (Gr. "leaving out"): the omission of a syntactically necessary word or words, the meaning of which must be inferred. E.g., *dextra* (supply *manu*) (4.60), *tu coniunx* (supply *Iovis es*), *tibi fas* (supply *est*) *animum temptare precando* (113), *fac velle* (supply *me*) (540).

Enallage (Gr. "interchange"): a distortion in normal word order, whereby a word, instead of modifying the word to which it belongs in sense, modifies another grammatically. E.g., Jupiter's command to Mercury, *celeris defer mea dicta per auras* (4.226), where it is Mercury and not the air that will be swift.

Enjambment (Fr. "crossing over," "straddling"): the continuation of the sense or syntactic unit from one line to the next. E.g., *pastor agens telis liquitque volatile ferrum / nescius* (4.71-2), *linquens multa metu cunctantem et multa parantem / dicere* (290-1).

Epanalepsis (Gr. "taking up again"): the repetition of a syntactically unnecessary word or phrase from a preceding line. E.g., *umbras, / pallentis umbras* (4.25-6), *magnas it Fama per urbes, / Fama* (173-4).

Etymological wordplay: allusion to the etymological meaning of a word. E.g., *cura* as if from *cor urit*, "burns the heart" (4.1-2), and *viri virtus* (3). Cf. **paronomasia**.

Golden Line: in dactylic hexameter, an artful arrangement of two substantive/ adjective pairs with a verb in between. It usually takes the form of ABCab, where Aa and Bb are both adjective-noun phrases, while C is a verb. E.g.,

     A   B   C   a   b

aurea purpuream subnectit fibula uestem. (4.139)

Hendiadys (Gr. "one through two"): the expression of one idea through two terms joined by a conjunction. E.g., *thalami taedaeque* (4.18) where "marriage-bed" and "torch" = "marriage."

Hyperbaton (Gr. "transposed"): a distortion of normal word order. E.g., *ille meos, primus qui* (4.28-9) = *ille, qui primus me sibi iunxit, meos amores abstulit*.

Hypotaxis: see **Parataxis**.

Interpretatio: see **Theme and Variation**.

Irony (Gr. "dissembling"): saying one thing but with its opposite implied or understood. E.g., *egregiam vero laudem et spolia ampla refertis / tuque puerque tuus* ... (4.93-4), where Juno says it is a great accomplishment for Venus and Cupid, two gods, to overcome Dido; cf. also Dido's words at 379-80.

Litotes (Gr. "simplicity"): the description of something by negating its opposite. E.g., *nec me adeo fallit* (4.96), *haud ignara futuri* (4.508).

Metaphor (Gr. "transference"): the application of a word or phrase from one field of meaning to another, thereby suggesting new meanings. E.g., in 4.1-2 Dido's love for Aeneas is described both as a "wound" and as "fire"; at 369 Aeneas tells Dido not to "enflame" them both.

Metonymy (Gr. "change of name"): the substitution of one word for another somehow closely related. E.g., in 4.242 *Orcus = Dis*, lord of the Underworld, and by **metonymy** his name is used for the Underworld itself.

Onomatopoeia (Gr. "making of a word" or "name"): the use or formation of words that imitate natural sounds. E.g., *magno misceri murmure* (4.160) "to be troubled with mighty murmurings"; and *ululent* (4.168, cf. too 609).

Parataxis (Gr. "placing side by side"): the sequential ordering of independent clauses (as opposed to **hypotaxis**, the subordination of one clause to another). A famous example is Caesar's *veni, vidi, vici*. An example from *Aeneid* 1: *et iam iussa facit, ponuntque ferocia Poeni / corda* (1.302-3). Though the two halves of the sentence are independent, in sense one is subordinated to the other: "after he has performed the commands, the Phoenicians set aside their fierce hearts." Vergil leaves it to the reader to sense such logical relationships. Cf. too 4.154-5. **Parataxis** is particularly characteristic of Vergil and epic more generally.

Paronomasia (Gr. "slight alteration of name"): wordplay or pun. E.g., *Libycis teris otia terris* (4.271), which may involve **etymological wordplay.**

Personification: (Lat. *persona*, "mask"): treating an inanimate object or abstract quality as though it were a living thing. E.g., the description of Rumor at 173-97 and Dido's address to Pudor at 27.

Polyptoton (Gr. "in many cases"): the repetition of a word in its inflected cases. E.g., *absens absentem* (4.83), *auro...aurum, aurea* (4.138-9).

Polysyndeton (Gr. "much-connected"): the repetition or excessive use of conjunctions. E.g., *Cretesque Dryopesque fremunt pictique Agathyrsi* (4.146).

Praeteritio (Lat. "passing by"): the figure in which a speaker pretends or claims to "pass over" a topic, but nevertheless discusses it in whole or in part. E.g., Anna asks why she should even mention the threat from Dido's brother (but she does): *quid bella Tyro surgentia dicam / germanique minas?* (4.43-4)

Prolepsis (Gr. "anticipation"): the use of a word or phrase that anticipates a later event. E.g., *furentem / incendat reginam* (1.659-60), where the force of *furentem* is not "set the raging queen on fire" but "set her on fire so that she rages." For Book 4 cf. notes on 22, 465.

Simile (Lat. "similar"): a figurative comparison between two different things. It is an important component of epic style. E.g., in Book 4 Dido in love is compared to a wounded deer (68-73), Aeneas to Apollo (143-50).

Synecdoche (Gr. "understanding one thing with another"): a type of **metonymy** that uses the part for the whole (or the reverse). E.g., in Book 4 two words for part of a ship, *carinae* (46) and *puppes* (418), are used to mean "ship."

Theme and Variation: the restatement of an initial phrase in different language, so that the same action or thing is seen from two slightly different perspectives. E.g., a description of dawn: *postera Phoebea lustrabat lampade terras / umentemque Aurora polo dimoverat umbram* (4.6-7).

Transferred Epithet: see **Enallage**.

Tricolon (Gr. "having three limbs"): the grouping of three parallel clauses or phrases. When the third element is the longest, the resulting *tricolon* is called *abundans, crescens,* or *crescendo.* E.g., *num fletu ingemuit nostro? num lumina flexit? / num lacrimas victus dedit aut miseratus amantem est?* (4.369-70), and again *nunc augur Apollo, / nunc Lyciae sortes, nunc et Iove missus ab ipso / interpres divum fert horrida iussa per auras* (4.376-7). These are both examples of **tricolon crescendo**.

Zeugma (Gr. "yoking"): the governing of two words by one verb or adjective, which is strictly appropriate for just one of them. E.g., *crudelis aras traiectaque pectora ferro/ nudavit* (1.355-6), where Sychaeus figuratively "reveals" his murder at the altar (*aras*) but literally "bares" his pierced chest (*traiectaque pectora*). Cf. 4.131, and perhaps 4.200-2.

Bibliography

Adler, E. 2003. *Vergil's Empire: Political Thought in the Aeneid.* Lanham, MD.

Allen, G. 2000. *Intertextuality.* London.

Allen & Greenough: see Mahoney 2001.

Anderson, W.S. 2005. *The Art of the Aeneid.* Second edition. Wauconda, IL.

_____ 2006. "Ancient Illustrations of the *Aeneid*: The Hunts of Books 4 and 7," *Classical World* 99.2: 157-165

Armstrong, D., Fish, J., Johnston, P. A., and Skinner, M. (eds.) 2004. *Vergil, Philodemus, and the Augustans.* Austin.

Austin, R.G. 1955. *P. Vergili Maronis Aeneidos Liber Quartus.* Oxford.

Barchiesi, A. 1984. *La traccia del modello: effetti omerici nella narrazione virgiliana.* Pisa.

_____ 1997. *The Poet and the Prince: Ovid and Augustan Discourse.* Berkeley.

_____ 1998. Rev. of A. Radke (ed.) 1998. *Candide Iudex. Beiträge zur augusteischen Dichtung. Festschrift für Walter Wimmel zum 75. Geburtstag* (Stuttgart 1998). http://ccat.sas.upenn.edu/bmcr/1998/1998-11-28.html.

Behr, F. 2005. "The narrator's voice: a narratological reappraisal of apostrophe in Virgil's Aeneid," *Arethusa* 38.2: 189-221.

Bender, H. 1994. "*De Habitu Vestis*: Clothing in the *Aeneid*," pp. 146-52 in J.L. Sebesta and L. Bonfante (eds.), *The World of Roman Costume.* Madison.

Bowie, A.M. 1998. "*Exuvias effigiemque*: Dido, Aeneas and the Body as Sign," pp. 57-79 in D. Montserrat (ed.), *Changing Bodies, Changing Meanings: Studies on the Human Body in Antiquity.* London/New York.

Briggs, W.W. 1980. *Narrative and simile from the Georgics in the Aeneid.* Leiden.

_____ 1981. "Virgil and the Hellenistic epic," *Aufstieg und Niedergang der römischen Welt* 2.31.2: 948-84.

Brogan, T.V.F. (ed.) 1994. *The New Princeton Handbook of Poetic Terms.* Princeton.

Brown, R.D. 1987. *Lucretius on Love and Sex: A Commentary on De Rerum Natura IV, 1030-1287.* Leiden/New York.

Burden, M. (ed.) 1998. *A Woman Scorn'd. Responses to the Dido Myth*. London.

Cairns, F. 1989. *Virgil's Augustan Epic*. Cambridge.

Caldwell, L. 2008. "Dido's *Deductio*: *Aeneid* 4.127-65," *Classical Philology* 103.4: 423-34.

Camps, W.A. 1960. *An Introduction to Virgil's Aeneid*. Oxford.

Casali, S. 1999. "Facta Impia (Virgil, *Aeneid* 4.596-9)," *Classical Quarterly* 49: 203-11.

_____ 1999-2000. "Staring at the Pun: *Aeneid* 4.435-36 Reconsidered," *Classical Journal* 95: 103-118.

Clausen, W.V. 1987. *Virgil's Aeneid and the Tradition of Hellenistic Poetry*. Berkeley, CA.

_____ 1994. *A commentary on Virgil, Eclogues*. Oxford.

_____ 2002. *Vergil's Aeneid. Decorum, Allusion and Ideology*. Munich and Leipzig. Revised and expanded version of *Virgil's Aeneid and the Tradition of Hellenistic Poetry* (Berkeley, 1987).

Coleman, R. 1977. *Virgil: Eclogues*. Cambridge.

Commager, S. 1981. "Fateful Words. Some Conversations in *Aeneid* 4," *Arethusa* 14: 101-14.

Conington, J. 1963. *The Works of Virgil with a Commentary*. Rev. by Henry Nettleship. Hildesheim. Reprint of 1883-84 London edition.

Conrad, C. 1965. "Traditional Patterns of Word-Order in Latin Epic from Ennius to Vergil," *Harvard Studies in Classical Philology* 69: 195-258.

Conte, G.B. 1986. *The Rhetoric of Imitation: Genre and Poetic Memory in Virgil and Other Latin Poets*. Ithaca and London.

_____ 1999. "The Virgilian paradox: an epic of drama and sentiment," *Proceedings of the Cambridge Philological Society* 45: 17-42.

_____ 2007. *The Poetry of Pathos: Studies in Virgilian Epic*. Oxford.

Courtney, E. 1981. "The Formation of the Text of Vergil," *Bulletin of the Institute of Classical Studies* 28: 13-29.

Crook, J. 1996. "Political history: 30 B.C. to A.D. 14," in *The Augustan Empire: 43 B.C. – A.D. 69. The Cambridge Ancient History*, vol. X. Second edition, eds. A. Bowman, E. Champlin, and A. Lintott. Cambridge: 70-112.

Desmond, M. 1994. *Reading Dido. Gender, Textuality, and the Medieval Aeneid*. Minneapolis and London.

Duckworth, G. 1969. *Vergil and Classical Hexameter Poetry: A Study in Metrical Variety*. Ann Arbor

Dyer, R.R. 1989. "*Vergil's Fama: A New Interpretation of Aeneid 4.173 ff.*," *Greece & Rome* 36: 28-32.

Dyson, J. 1996. "Dido the Epicurean," *Classical Antiquity* 15.2: 203-21.

_____ 1997. "*Fluctus Irarum, Fluctus Curarum*: Lucretian *Religio* in the *Aeneid*," *American Journal of Philology* 118.3: 449-57.

Edmunds, L. 2001. *Intertextuality and the Reading of Roman Poetry*. Baltimore.

Edwards, M.W. 2004. *Sound, Sense, and Rhythm: Listening to Greek and Latin Poetry*. Princeton.

Estevez, V.A. 1982. "*Oculos ad moenia torsit*: On *Aeneid* 4.220," *Classical Philology* 77: 22-34.

Farrell, J. 1991. *Vergil's Georgics and the Traditions of Ancient Epic: The Art of Allusion in Literary History*. Oxford.

_____ 1997. "The Virgilian intertext," pp. 222-38 in Martindale 1997.

_____ 2005. "The Augustan Period: 40 BC-AD 14," in *A Companion to Latin Literature*, ed. S. J. Harrison. Oxford: 44-57.

Feeney, D.C. 1990. "The Taciturnity of Aeneas," pp. 167-90 in Harrison 1990. Reprinted from *Classical Quarterly* 33 1983, 204-219.

_____ 1991. *The Gods in Epic: Poets and Critics of the Classical Tradition*. Oxford.

_____ 1998. "The Appearance(s) of Mercury and the Motivation of Aeneas," pp. 105-130 in Burden 1998.

Fletcher, K.F.B. 2006. "Vergil's Italian Diomedes," *American Journal of Philology* 127: 219-59.

Fowler, D.P. 1990. "Deviant Focalisation in Virgil's *Aeneid*," pp. 40-63 in *Roman Constructions: Readings in Postmodern Latin*. Oxford. Reprinted from *Proceedings of the Cambridge Philological Society* 36 1990, 42-63.

_____ 1997. "On the shoulders of giants: intertextuality and classical studies," *Materiali e Discussioni* 39: 13-34. Reprinted in *Roman Constructions: Readings in Postmodern Latin*. Oxford, 2000, 115-137.

_____ 2000. "Philosophy and Literature in Lucretian Intertextuality," pp. 138-155 in *Roman Constructions: Readings in Postmodern Latin*. Oxford.

Fratantuono, L. 2007. *Madness Unchained: A Reading of Virgil's Aeneid*. Lanham, MD.

Gale, M. 2000. *Virgil on the Nature of Things: The Georgics, Lucretius and the Didactic Tradition*. Cambridge.

Galinsky, K. 1988. "The anger of Aeneas," *American Journal of Philology* 109: 321-48.

_____ 1996. *Augustan Culture: An Interpretive Introduction*. Princeton.

_____ 2003. "Greek and Roman drama and the *Aeneid*," in *Myth, History, and Culture in Republican Rome: Studies in Honour of T. P. Wiseman*, eds. D. Braund and C. Gill. Exeter: 275-94.

_____ (ed.) 2005. *The Cambridge Companion to the Age of Augustus*. Cambridge.

Ganiban, R. 2008. *Vergil, Aeneid, Book 2*. Newburyport, Mass.

Garrison, J. 1992. *Pietas from Vergil to Dryden*. University Park, PA.

George, E.V. 1974. *Aeneid VIII and the Aitia of Callimachus*. *Mnemosyne* Suppl. 27. Leiden.

Gibson, R.K. 1999. "Aeneas as *Hospes* in Vergil, *Aeneid* 1 and 4," *Classical Quarterly* 49.1: 184-202.

Goold, G.P. 1990. "Servius and the Helen Episode," pp. 60-126 in Harrison 1990. Reprinted from *Harvard Studies in Classical Philology* 74 1970, 101-68.

Gordon, P. 1998. "Dido the Phaeacian: Lost Pleasures of an Epicurean Intertext," *Classical Antiquity* 17.2: 188-211.

Gransden, K.W. 1984. *Virgil's Iliad: An Essay on Epic Narrative*. Cambridge.

Gurval, R.A. 1995. *Actium and Augustus*. Ann Arbor.

Gutting, E. 2006. "Marriage in the *Aeneid*: Venus, Vulcan, and Dido," *Classical Philology* 101.3: 263-79.

Hardie, P.R. 1986. *Virgil's Aeneid. Cosmos and Imperium*. Oxford.

_____ 1991. "The *Aeneid* and the *Oresteia*," *Proceedings of the Virgil Society* 20: 29-45.

_____ 1993. *The Epic Successors of Virgil*. Cambridge.

_____ 1994. *Virgil: Aeneid Book IX*. Cambridge.

_____ 1997. "Virgil and Tragedy," pp. 312-26 in Martindale 1997.

_____ 1998. *Virgil. New Surveys in the Classics* 28. Oxford.

_____ 2006. "Virgil's Ptolemaic relations," *Journal of Roman Studies* 96: 25-41.

Harrison, E.L. 1985. "Vergil's Mercury," pp. 1-47 in *Vergilian bimillenary lectures* 1982, edd. A.G. McKay, A. Gordon, College Park, Md. Vergilius Supplementary volume.

Harrison, S.J. (ed.) 1990. *Oxford Readings in Vergil's Aeneid*. Oxford.

_____ 1991. *Vergil, Aeneid* 10. With Introduction, Translation, and Commentary. Oxford.

_____ 1995. Response to Khan 1995, pp. 29-37 in *Religion and Superstition in Latin Literature: Nottingham Classical Literature Studies* 3, ed. A. Sommerstein. Bari.

Hejduk, J. 2009. "Jupiter's *Aeneid: Fama* and *Imperium*," *Classical Antiquity* 28.2: 279-327.

Heinze, R. 1993. *Virgil's Epic Technique*. Translation by H. and D. Harvey and F. Robertson of *Vergils epische Technik* (Leipzig, 3rd ed. 1928). Berkeley.

Hersch, K. 2010. *The Roman Wedding: Ritual and Meaning in Antiquity*. Cambridge.

Heskel, J. 1994. "Cicero as Evidence for Attitudes to Dress in the Late Republic," pp. 133-45 in *The World of Roman Costume*, edd. J. L. Sebesta and L. Bonfante. Madison.

Hexter, R. 1992. "Sidonian Dido," pp. 332-84 in Hexter and D. Selden (eds.), *Innovations of Antiquity*. New York and London.

Heyworth, S. 2005. "Pastoral," in *A Companion to Latin Literature*, ed. S.J. Harrison. Oxford: 148-58.

Highet, G. 1972. *The Speeches in Vergil's Aeneid*. Princeton.

Hinds, S. 1998. *Allusion and Intertext: Dynamics of Appropriation in Roman Poetry*. Cambridge.

_____ 2000. "Essential epic: genre and gender from Macer to Statius," pp. 221-44 in M. Depew and D. Obbink (eds.), *Matrices of Genre: Authors, Canons, and Society*. Cambridge, Mass.

Horsfall, N.M. 1981. "Virgil and the Conquest of Chaos," *Antichthon* 15: 141-50.

_____ 1990. "Dido in the Light of History," pp. 127-44 in Harrison 1990.

_____ (ed.) 1995. *A Companion to the Study of Virgil*. Leiden.

Hughes, L. 2002. "Aeneas and Dido, an Homeric Homilia?" *Latomus* 61: 339-51.

Hunter, R.L. 2006. *The Shadow of Callimachus: Studies in the Reception of Hellenistic Poetry at Rome*. Cambridge.

Jackson Knight, W.F. 1944. *Roman Vergil*. London.

Johnson, W.R. 1976. *Darkness Visible: A Study of Vergil's "Aeneid."* Berkeley and Los Angeles.

_____ 2005. "Introduction," in *Virgil: Aeneid*, S. Lombardo, Indianapolis, IN: xv-lxxi.

Johnston, P.A. 1980. *Vergil's Agricultural Golden Age: A Study of the Georgics.* Leiden.

Jones, A.H.M. 1970. *Augustus.* London.

Kaster, R. 1997. "The Shame of the Romans," *Transactions of the American Philological Association* 127: 1-19.

Keith, A.M. 2000. *Engendering Rome: Women in Latin Epic.* Cambridge.

Kennedy, D. 1992. "'Augustan' and 'Anti-Augustan': reflections on terms of reference," in *Roman Poetry and Propaganda in the Age of Augustus*, ed. A. Powell. Bristol: 26-58.

Khan, H.A. 1995. "Demonizing Dido: A Rebounding Sequence of Curses and Dreams in *Aeneid* 4," pp. 1-28 in A. H. Sommerstein (ed.), *Religion and Superstition in Latin Literature*: Nottingham Classical Literature Studies 3. Bari.

Knauer, G.N. 1964a. *Die Aeneis und Homer: Studien zur poetischen Technik Vergils mit Listen der Homerzitate in der Aeneis.* Göttingen.

_____ 1964b. "Vergil's Aeneid and Homer," *Greek, Roman and Byzantine Studies* 5: 61-84. Reprinted in *Oxford Readings in Vergil's Aeneid*, ed. S. J. Harrison 1990. Oxford: 390-412.

Konstan, D. 1986. "Venus' Enigmatic Smile," *Vergilius* 32: 18-25.

_____ 2000. "A Pun in Virgil's *Aeneid*: 4.492-3?" *Classical Philology* 95: 74-6.

Kraggerud, E. 1999. "Samson Eitrem and the death of Dido: A literary reappraisal of a magical scene," pp. 103-113 in D. Jordan, H. Montgomery, E. Thomassen (eds.), *The World of Ancient Magic. Papers from the first International Samson Eitrem Seminar at the Norwegian Institute at Athens 4-8 May 1997.* Bergen.

Krevans, N. 2002-3. "Dido, Hypsipyle, and the bedclothes," *Hermathena* 173/174: 175-83.

Laird, A. 1997. "Approaching Characterisation in Virgil," pp. 282-93 in Martindale 1997.

Lanham, R.A. 1991. *A Handlist of Rhetorical Terms.* Berkeley.

Lelievre, F.J. 1997. "*Aeneas Amens*: Sound, Meter, Thought in *Aeneid* 4," *Vergilius* 43: 19-21.

Lord, M.L. 1969. "Dido as an example of chastity: the influence of example literature," *Harvard Library bulletin* 17.1 (January 1969) 22-44.

Lyne, R.O.A.M. 1987. *Further Voices in Vergil's Aeneid.* Oxford.

_____ 1989. *Words and the Poet: Characteristic Techniques of Style in Vergil's 'Aeneid.'* Oxford.

Mack, S. 1978. *Patterns of Time in Vergil.* Hamden, Connecticut.

Mackie, C.J. 1988. *The Characterization of Aeneas.* Edinburgh.

Mahoney, A. (ed.) 2001. *Allen and Greenough's New Latin Grammar.* Newburyport, MA. Revised version of 1903 edition.

Maltby, R. 2002. *Tibullus: Elegies: Text, Introduction and Commentary.* Leeds.

Martindale, C. 1993. "Descent into Hell: Reading Ambiguity, or Virgil and the critics," *Proceedings of the Virgil Society* 21: 111-50.

_____ (ed.) 1997. *The Cambridge Companion to Virgil.* Cambridge.

McDonough, C.M., R.E. Prior, M. Stansbury 2004. *Servius' Commentary on Book Four of Virgil's Aeneid.* Wauconda, IL.

Monti, R.C. 1981. *The Dido Episode and the Aeneid: Roman Social and Political Values in the Epic.* Leiden.

Morgan, G. 1994. "Dido the Wounded Deer," *Vergilius* 40: 67-8.

Muecke, F. 1983. "Foreshadowing and Dramatic Irony in the Story of Dido," *American Journal of Philology* 104: 134-55.

Muse, K. 2005. "'Don't Dally in this Valley': Wordplay in *Odyssey* 15.10 and *Aeneid* 4.271," *Classical Quarterly* 55.2: 646-9.

Mynors, R.A.B. (ed.) 1990. *Virgil: Georgics.* Oxford.

Nappa, C. 2005. *Reading After Actium: Vergil's Georgics, Octavian, and Rome.* Ann Arbor.

Nelis, D. 2001. *Vergil's Aeneid and the Argonautica of Apollonius Rhodius.* Leeds.

Newton, F. 1957. "Recurrent Imagery in *Aeneid* IV," *Transactions of the American Philological Association* 88: 31-43.

Nisbet, R.G.M. 1990. "*Aeneas Imperator*: Roman Generalship in an Epic Context," pp. 378-89 in Harrison 1990.

Nugent, S.G. 1999. "The Women of the *Aeneid*: Vanishing Bodies, Lingering Voices," pp. 251-70 in Perkell 1999.

Nünlist, R. 2009. *The Ancient Critic at Work: Terms and Concepts of Literary Criticism in Greek Scholia.* Cambridge.

Nussbaum, G.B. 1986. *Vergil's Meter: A Practical Guide for Reading Latin Hexameter Poetry.* Bristol.

Nuttall, A.D. 1998. "Inconstant Dido," pp. 89-104 in Burden 1998.

O'Hara, J. J. 1990. *Death and the Optimistic Prophecy in Vergil's "Aeneid."* Princeton.

_____ 1993. "Dido as 'Interpreting Character' at *Aeneid* 4.56-66," *Arethusa* 26: 99-114.

_____ 1993a. "Medicine for the Madness of Dido and Gallus: Tentative Suggestions on *Aeneid* 4," *Vergilius* 39: 12-24.

_____ 1996. *True Names. Vergil and the Alexandrian Tradition of Etymological Wordplay.* Ann Arbor.

_____ 2007. *Inconsistency in Roman Epic: Studies in Catullus, Lucretius, Vergil, Ovid and Lucan.* Cambridge.

Oliensis, E. 1997. "Sons and Lovers. Sexuality and Gender in Virgil's Poetry," pp. 294-311 in Martindale 1997.

Osgood, J. 2006. *Caesar's Legacy: Civil War and the Emergence of the Roman Empire.* Cambridge.

Otis, B. 1964. *Virgil: A Study in Civilized Poetry.* Oxford.

Panoussi, V. 2002. "Vergil's Ajax: Allusion, Tragedy, and Heroic Identity in the *Aeneid*," *Classical Antiquity* 21.1: 95-134.

_____ 2009. *Greek Tragedy in Vergil's Aeneid: Ritual, Empire, and Intertext.* Cambridge.

Pavlock, B. 1985. "Epic and tragedy in Vergil's Nisus and Euryalus episode," *Transactions of the American Philological Association* 115: 207-24.

Pease, A.S. 1935. *Publi Vergili Maronis Aeneidos Liber Quartus.* Cambridge, Mass.

Pelling, C. 1996. "The Triumviral period," in *The Augustan Empire: 43 B.C. – A.D. 69.* The Cambridge Ancient History, vol. X. Second edition, eds. A. Bowman, E. Champlin, and A. Lintott. Cambridge: 1-69.

Perkell, C. 1981. "On Creusa, Dido, and the Quality of Victory in Virgil's *Aeneid*," *Women's Studies* 8: 201-23. Repr. in *Reflections of Women in Antiquity*, ed. H. Foley 1981, 335-77.

_____ 1989. *The Poet's Truth: A Study of the Poet in Virgil's Georgics.* Berkeley.

_____ 1994. "Ambiguity and Irony, the Last Resort?," *Helios* 21.1: 63-74.

_____ 2002. "The Golden Age and Its Contradictions in the Poetry of Vergil," *Vergilius* 48: 3-39.

_____ (ed.) 1999. *Reading Vergil's Aeneid. An Interpretive Guide.* Norman, Oklahoma.

Petrini, M. 1997. *The Child and the Hero: Coming of Age in Catullus and Vergil.* Ann Arbor.

Pöschl, V. 1950. *Die Dichtkunst Vergils: Bild und Symbol in der* Aeneis. Innsbruck. = (1962) *The Art of Vergil. Image and Symbol in the* Aeneid. Translated by G. Seligson. Ann Arbor.

Powell, A. (ed.) 1992. *Roman Poetry and Propaganda in the Age of Augustus*. Bristol.

Putnam, M.C.J. 1965. *The Poetry of the Aeneid*. Cambridge, MA.

_____ 1979. *Virgil's Poem of the Earth: Studies in the Georgics*. Princeton.

_____ 1993. "The languages of Horace, *Odes* 1.24," *Classical Journal* 88.2: 123-35.

_____ 1995. "'Pius' Aeneas and the Metamorphosis of Lausus," pp. 134-51 in Putnam, *Virgil's Aeneid: interpretation and influence*. Chapel Hill.

Quint, D. 1993. *Epic and Empire. Politics and Generic Form from Virgil to Milton*. Princeton.

Rauk, J. 1995. "Macrobius, Cornutus, and the Cutting of Dido's Lock," *Classical Philology* 90.4: 345-54.

Reed, J. 2006. "*Ardebat Laena: Aeneid* 4.262," *Vergilius* 52: 55-75.

_____ 2007. *Virgil's Gaze: Nation and Poetry in the Aeneid*. Ann Arbor.

Rosenmeyer, P. 1999. "Tracing *Medulla* as a *Locus Eroticus* in Greek and Latin Poetry," *Arethusa* 32: 19-47.

Ross, D. O., Jr. 1969. *Style and Tradition in Catullus*. Cambridge, Mass.

_____ 1987. *Virgil's Elements: Physics and Poetry in the Georgics*. Princeton.

_____ 2007. *Virgil's Aeneid: A Reader's Guide*. Oxford: Blackwell.

Rudd, N. 1990. "Dido's Culpa," pp. 145-90 in Harrison 1990.

Schiesaro, A. 2008. "Furthest Voices in Virgil's Dido," *Studi italiani di filologia classica n.s.* 6: 60-109, 194-245.

Schmidt, E.A. 2001. "The Meaning of Vergil's *Aeneid*: American and German Approaches," *Classical World* 94.2: 145-71

Scullard, H.H. 1982. *From the Gracchi to Nero: A History of Rome from 133 B.C. to A.D. 68*. Fifth edition. London.

Segal, C. 1990. "Dido's Hesitation in *Aeneid* 4," *Classical World* 84: 1-12.

Shotter, D. 2005. *Augustus Caesar*. Second edition. London.

Skulsky, S. 1985. "*Invitus, regina. . .* : Aeneas and the Love of Rome," *American Journal of Philology* 106: 447-55.

Smith, R.A. 2003. "Dido as Vatic Diva: A New Voice for the Persona of the Lost Lover." *Classical Journal* 98.4: 433-36.

Southern, P. 1998. *Augustus*. New York.

Sparrow, J. 1931. *Half-lines and Repetitions in Virgil*. Oxford.

Spence, S. 1999. "'Varium et mutabile'. Voices of authority in *Aeneid* 4," pp. 80-95 in Perkell 1999.

_____ 2002. "*Pietas* and *Furor*: Motivational Forces in the *Aeneid*," pp. 46-52 in W.S. Anderson and L.N. Quartarone (eds.), *Approaches to Teaching Vergil's Aeneid*. New York.

Stahl, H.-P. (ed.) 1998. *Vergil's Aeneid: Augustan Epic and Political Context*. London.

Starks, J.H. 1999. "*Fides Aeneia*: The Transference of Punic Stereotypes in the *Aeneid*," *Classical Journal* 94.3: 255-83.

Starr, R.J. 1991. "Explaining Dido to Your Son: Tiberius Claudius Donatus on Vergil's Dido," *Classical Journal* 87: 25-34.

_____ 2003. "Aeneas the Rhetorician: *Aeneid* IV, 279-295," *Latomus* 62.1: 36-46.

Suerbaum, W. 1998. "*Si fata paterentur*. Gedanken an alternatives Handeln in Vergils Aeneis," pp. 353-74 in A.E. Radke (ed.): *Candide Iudex. Beiträge zur augusteischen Dichtung. Festschrift für Walter Wimmel zum 75. Geburtstag*. Stuttgart.

Syed, Y. 2004. *Vergil's Aeneid and the Roman Self: Subject and Nation in Literary Discourse*. Ann Arbor.

Syme, R. 1939. *The Roman Revolution*. Oxford.

Tatum, J. 1984. "Allusion and Interpretation in *Aeneid* 6.440–76," *American Journal of Philology* 105: 434–52.

Thomas, R.F. 1986. "Virgil's *Georgics* and the art of reference," *Harvard Studies in Classical Philology* 90: 171-98. Reprinted in Thomas 1999, 114-41.

_____ 1988. *Virgil: Georgics*. Cambridge

_____ 1992. Rev. of Harrison 1991, *Vergilius* 38: 134-44.

_____ 1998. "The Isolation of Turnus. *Aeneid* Book 12," pp. 271-302 in H.-P. Stahl (ed.), *Vergil's 'Aeneid': Augustan Epic and Political Context*. London.

_____ 1999. *Reading Virgil and His Texts: Studies in Intertextuality*. Ann Arbor.

_____ 2001. *Virgil and the Augustan Reception*. Cambridge.

Treggiari, S. 1991. *Roman Marriage. Iusti Coniuges from the Time of Cicero to the time of Ulpian*. Oxford.

van Hook, La Rue 1949. "On the Idiomatic Use of KARA, KEFALH and Caput," pp. 413-14 in *Commemorative Studies in Honor of Theodore Leslie Shear, Hesperia* Supplements Vol. 8.

Van Sickle, J. 1992. *A Reading of Virgil's Messianic Eclogue.* New York.

Vernant, J.-P. and Vidal-Naquet, P. 1988. *Myth and Tragedy in Ancient Greece,* tr. J. Lloyd. New York.

Volk, K. (ed.) 2008a. *Virgil's Eclogues.* Oxford.

————— (ed.) 2008b. *Virgil's Georgics.* Oxford.

Wallace-Hadrill, A. 1993. *Augustan Rome.* London.

————— 2008. *Rome's Cultural Revolution.* Cambridge/New York.

Weber, C. 2002. "The Dionysus in Aeneas," *Classical Philology* 97.4: 322-43.

West, D. 1990. "Multiple-Correspondence Similes in the *Aeneid,*" pp. 429-44 in Harrison 1990.

White, P. 1993. *Promised Verse: Poets in the Society of Augustan Rome.* Cambridge, MA.

————— 2005. "Poets in the new milieu: realigning," in *The Cambridge Companion to the Age of Augustus,* ed. K. Galinsky. Cambridge: 321-39.

Wigodsky, M. 1972. *Vergil and Early Latin Poetry.* Wiesbaden.

Wilkinson, L.P. 1969. *The Georgics of Virgil: A Critical Survey.* Cambridge.

Williams, C.A. 1999. *Roman Homosexuality: Ideologies of Masculinity in Classical Antiquity.* New York, Oxford.

Williams, G.W. 1968. *Tradition and Originality in Roman Poetry.* Oxford.

————— 1983. *Technique and Ideas in the Aeneid.* New Haven & London.

Wills, J. 1997. *Repetition in Latin Poetry. Figures of Allusion.* Oxford.

Wiltshire, S.F. 1989. *Public and Private in Vergil's* Aeneid. Amherst.

Wlosok, A. 1999. "The Dido tragedy in Virgil: a contribution to the question of the tragic in the *Aeneid,*" transl. of Wlosok 1976, in *Virgil: Critical Assessments of Classical Authors,* vol. 4, ed. P. Hardie. London: 158-81. Originally published as "Vergils Didotragödie: ein Beitrag zum Problem des Tragischen in der Aeneis," in *Studien zum antiken Epos,* eds. H. Görgemanns and E. A. Schmidt. Meisenheim: 228-50.

Zanker, P. 1988. *The Power of Images in the Age of Augustus,* tr. A. Shapiro. Ann Arbor.

List of Abbreviations

abl.	= ablative
acc.	= accusative
adj.	= adjective
adv.	= adverb
cf.	= *confer*, i.e. compare
comp.	= comparative
conj.	= conjunction
dat.	= dative
dep.	= deponent
f.	= feminine
gen.	= genitive
i.e.	= *id est*, that is
indecl.	= indeclinable
indef.	= indefinite
interj.	= interjection
intr.	= intransitive
interrog.	= interrogative
m.	= masculine
n.	= neuter
nom.	= nominative
num.	= numeral
opp.	= opposed
part.	= participle
pass.	= passive
perf.	= perfect
pers.	= personal
pl.	= plural
poss.	= possessive
prep.	= preposition
pron.	= pronoun
rel.	= relative
sing.	= singular
subst.	= substantive
superl.	= superlative
tr.	= transitive
v.	= verb

Vocabulary for *Aeneid* 4

Revised from the MacMillan/St. Martin's Press school edition
by Rev. H. M. Stephenson, originally published in 1888.

A

ā, ab, prep. with abl. *from, by*

abeō, -īre, -īvi and **-iī, -itum,** *depart*

abluō, -luere, -luī, -lūtum, *wash off, wash*

abnuō, -nuere, -nuī, *nod assent to, refuse*

aboleō, -ēre, -ēvī, -itum, *efface, destroy*

abripiō, -ripere, -ripuī, -reptum, *tear away, seize by force*

abrumpō, -ere, -rūpī, -ruptum, *break, break off,* 631

abscindō, -ere, -scidī, -scissum, *cleve away, tear*

abscondō, -ere, -di or **-didī, -ditum,** *conceal*

absens, -entis, part. of **absum** as adj., *absent*

absum, -esse, afuī, *be away*

absūmō, -ere, -mpsī, -mptum, *destroy*

ac, conj. short form of **atque,** only used before consonants, *and;* see **atque**

accendō, -dere, -dī, -sum, *kindle, enflame*

accingō, -cingere, -cinxī, -cinctum, *gird on, arm;* in pass. by sense constrn., *employ as weapon, arm self with,* with acc., 493

accipiō, -cipere, -cēpī, -ceptum, *receive, listen to, welcome*

ācer, acris, acre, adj., *keen, spirited*

acervus, -ī, m., *heap*

aciēs, -eī, f., *line, line of sight, eye*

ad, prep. with acc., *to, near, at;* **ad lunam,** 513, *by moonlight*

adeō, -īre, -īvi or **-iī, -itum,** *go up to; approach; soar to,* 322

adeō, adv., *to such an extent, indeed*

adfātus, -ūs, m., *address*

[adfor], -ārī, -ātus sum, defective, *address*

adgnoscō, -gnoscere, -gnōvī, -gnitum, *recognize*

adgredior, -ī, -gressus sum, *attack, assail, accost*

adhuc, adv., *still*

adigō, -igere, -ēgī, -actum, *drive, hurl*

adimō, -ere, -ēmī, -emptum, *take away*

aditus, -ūs, m., *approach; approach to his heart,* 423, etc.

adloquor, -loquī, -locūtus, *address, speak to*

admoneō, -ēre, -uī, -itum, *warn*

admōrunt for **admoverunt,** see **admoveō,** 367

admoveō, -movēre, -mōvī, -mōtum, *move to;* **admorunt ubera,** 367, *put their breasts to your lips*

adnītor, -ī, -nīsus or **-nixus sum,** *lean upon; use effort, strive*

adnō, -are, *swim to, float to*

adnuō, -nuere, -nuī, -nūtum, *nod assent*

adquīrō, -quirere, -quīsīvī, -quīsītum,
  gain
adsiduus, -a, -um, unceasing
adstō, -stāre, -stitī, stand by
adsum, -esse, -fuī, be at hand, here,
  present
adsurgō, -surgere, -surrexī,
  -surrectum, rise towards, up
advēna, -ae, m. and f., stranger
adversor, -arī, -avī, -atum, be opposed
adversus, -a, -um, adj., opposite
advertō, -tere, -tī, -sum, turn to, turn
  the mind to, attend
Aenēās, -ae, m., Aeneas, 74, 117, etc.
aēnus, -a, -um, adj. of bronze [aes]
aequō, -āre, -āvī,- ātum, make equal;
  aequatis velis, 586, with leveled
  line of sail
aequor, -oris, n., level surface, open sea,
  sea, ocean, water
aequus, -a, -um, adj., equal, favorable
aestus, -ūs, m., heat; boiling movement
  of the sea, surge, swell, tide
aetās, -tātis, f., age
aeternus, -a, -um, adj., eternal
aethēr, -eris, acc. aethera, m., upper
  air, sky
aetherius, -a, -um, adj., belonging to
  the aether or to the sky, heavenly
Aethiops, -opis, m., Ethiopian
Āfricus, -a, -um, adj., African; Africa
  terra, 37, land of Africa
Agamemnonius, -a, -um, adj., of
  Agamemnon
ager, -grī, m., field, land
aggerō, -āre, -āvī, -ātum, pile, heap
  one on another; ag. iras, wrath on
  wrath, 197
agitō, -āre, -āvī, -ātum, stir, hunt (freq.
  of ago)
agmen, -inis, n., troop, marching line;
  band, herd, 154

agō, -ere, ēgī, actum, work, form, do;
  drag, drive, drive before one; absol.
  71, hunt; se agere, agī, move; age,
  come! 223
aiō, ais, ait, aiunt. defective, say
āla, -ae, f., feather, wing; troop of
  hunters, 121 n.
ālātus, -a, -um, adj., winged
albescō, -bescere, grow white
aliēnus, -a, -um, adj., belonging to
  another, strange
aliquis or aliquī, aliqua, aliquod,
  pron. adj., some
aliquis, aliquid, pron. indef., some one
aliter, adv., otherwise
alius, -a, -ud, adj., other, some
alō, alere, aluī, altum or alitum, rear,
  cherish, nurse
Alpīnus, -a, -um, adj., of the Alps
altāria, -ium, n. pl., altar
altē, adv., on high
alter, -tera, -terum, adj., one or other
  of two
alternō, -are, do by turns; in V., only
  in pres. part. and intr., alternate,
  waver
altum, -ī, n., the deep sea, the deep
altus, -a, -um, adj., high; deep; lofty
amans, -ntis, pres. part. of amō, as
  subst. m. and f., a lover
amārus, -a, -um, adj. bitter
ambiō, -īre, -īvī and -iī, -ītum, go
  round, canvass, visit seeking
  sympathy
ambō, -ae, -ō, adj., both
āmens, -ntis, adj., distracted, mad,
  aghast
āmittō, -ere, mīsī, missum, lose
amnis, -is, m., river
amō, -āre, -āvī, -ātum, love
amor, -ōris, m., love; love charm, 516 n.
amplus, -a, -um, adj., large, spacious,

grand

an, conj., *or?* introduces second of two questions. The first is sometimes not expressed but implied.

anceps, -cipitis, adj., *with two heads, double; doubtful*

Anchīsēs, -ae, *Anchises,* father of Aeneas, 351

angustus, -a, -um, adj., *narrow*

anīlis, -e, adj., *of an old woman*

anima, -ae, f., *breath, life, soul*

animus, -ī, m., *mind, heart,* pl., *spirit, courage*

Anna, -ae, f., sister of Dido, 9, 20, etc.

annōsus, -a, -um, adj., *full of years*

ante, adv. and prep. with acc., *before; in front of;* **ante...quam,** *before,* conj.

antīquus, -a, -um, adj., *ancient, old*

aper, -prī, m. *boar*

apex, -icis, m., *crest, head*

Apollō, -inis, m., *Apollo,* 144 etc.

aptō, -āre, -āvī, -ātum, *get ready, equip*

aptus, -a, -um, adj., *fitted; studded,* 482

apud, prep. with acc., *by, among, in the mind of*

aquilō, -ōnis, m., *north-wind, storm-wind, Roman name for Boreas*

aquōsus, -a, -um, adj., *watery, rainy*

āra, -ae, f., *altar*

arbōs or **arbor, -oris,** f., *tree*

arcānus, -a, -um, adj., *secret*

ardeō, -dēre, -sī, -sum, *blaze, burn* with desire; **ardens,** *blazing*

ardor, -ōris, m., *heat, ardor, eagerness*

arduus, -a, -um, adj. *high, lofty, steep, tall, towering*

arēna, -ae, f., *sand*

arēnōsus, -a, -um, adj., *sandy*

arguō, -guere, -guī, -gūtum, *make clear, expose*

arma, -ōrum, n. pl., *arms*

armō, -āre, -āvī, -ātum, *arm, equip*

armus, -ī, m., *shoulder*

arō, -āre, -āvī, -ātum, *plough, till*

arrigō, -rigere, -rexī, -rectum, *erect, set up on end*

ars, artis, f., *art*

artus, -ūs, m., *limb*

arundō, -inis, f., *reed, shaft*

arvum, -ī, n., *ploughed land, field*

arx, arcis, f., *place of defense, citadel, height, tower*

Ascanius, -iī, m. son of Aeneas and Creūsa, also called Iūlus, 156, 234, etc.

aspectus, -ūs, m. *sight, appearance*

asper, -era, -erum, adj., *rough*

aspiciō, -ere, -spexī, -spectum, *see, behold*

ast = **at**

astrum, -ī, n., *star*

at or **ast,** conj., *but, moreoever, yet, meanwhile*

āter, -tra, -trum, adj., *black*

Atlās, -ntis, m., *Atlas,* son of Iapetus and Clymene, who supported the sky on his shoulders, identified with Mt. Atlas in W. Africa, 247, 481

atque or **ac** only before consonants, conj., *and also, and;* stronger form of **-que; simul atque,** *as soon as*

ātrium, -ī, n., *hall, court*

attingō, -tingere, -tigī, -tactum, *reach, find*

attollō, -ere, *rear, lift*

attonō, -āre, -uī, -itum, *astound*

auctor, -ōris, m., *originator, author, founder*

audax, -ācis, adj., *bold*

audeō, -dēre, -sus, *be bold, dare*

audiō, -īre, -īvi and **-iī, -ītum,** *hear*

auferō, -ferre, abstulī, ablātum, *take away, carry off*

augur, -uris, m., *one who interprets omens, augur, prophet*

aula, -ae, *courtyard, hall*

Aulis,- idis, f., harbor in Boeotia where Agamemnon assembled the fleet against Troy, 426

aura, -ae, f., *air, breeze*

aureus, -a, -um, adj., *golden*

auris, -is, f., *ear*

Aurōra, -ae, f., the goddess of the dawn

aurum, -ī, n., *gold*

Ausonius, -a, -um, adj., *Italian.* The Ausones were a tribe in ancient times inhabiting Latium, 236, 349

auspex, -icis, m., *interpreter of bird-omens, guide;* **dis auspicibus,** 45, *under heaven's auspices*

auspicium, -iī, n., *auspice*

aut, conj. *either, or*

autem, conj. *but, however, moreover*

auxilium, -iī, n., *aid*

āvellō, -ere, -vellī or **-vulsī, -vulsum,** *tear away, tear out*

Avernus, -ī, m., *belonging to lake Avernus* in Campania, 512

āvertō, -ere, -tī, -sum, *turn away, divert, avert*

avis, -is, f., *bird*

avus, -ī, m., *grandfather, ancestor*

axis, -is, m., *axis,* round which the heavens revolved; hence, *the heavens,* 482

B

bacchor, -ārī, -ātus sum, *behave like a bacchanal, rush wildly*

Bacchus, -ī, m., *Bacchus,* god of wine; the cry of 'Bacchus', 302

barba, -ae, f., *beard*

Barcaeī, -ōrum, m. pl., *inhabitants of Barce,* town in Cyrenaica, 43

Barcē, -ēs, f., *nurse of Sychaeus,* 632

bellum, -ī, n., *war*

bene, adv., *well*

bidens, -tis, f., lit., *with two teeth;* hence a two-year-old *sheep,* at which age sheep have two prominent cutting teeth.

bis, num. adv., *twice*

Boreas, -ae, m., *north-wind* = Roman Aquilo, *storm-wind,* 442

breviter, adv., *shortly, in few words*

būbō, -ōnis, f., *owl*

C

cadō, -ere, cecidī, cāsum, *fall, perish, die;* of sun, *set*

caecus, -a, -um, adj., *blind; hidden*

caedēs, -is, f., *bloodshed, murder*

caelum, -ī, n., *sky*

caerulus, -a, -um, adj. *deep blue, dark-colored;* n. pl. as subst., *the blue sea,* 583

callis, -is, m., *path*

calor, -ōris, m., *heat*

campus, -ī, m., *plain*

candeō, -ēre, -uī, *be bright, white;* **candens,** *white*

canis, -is, m. and f. *dog, hound*

canō, -ere, cecinī, cantum, *sing, chant; rehearse, tell of*

capessō, -ere, -essīvi or **-essiī, -essītum,** *seize, make for* (freq. of **căpio**)

capiō, -ere, cēpī, captum, *take, hold, contain, capture, captivate, enthrall; cheat, betray,* 330

capra, -ae, f., *she-goat*

caput, pitis, n. *head, life, soul*

carbasus, -ī, f., *canvas, sail;* also plur. **carbasa, -ōrum,** n.

careō, -ēre, -uī, *be without, forgo*

carīna, -ae, f., *keel, ship*

carmen, -inis, n., *song; note,* 462; *spell, incantation,* 487

carpō, -pere, -psī, -ptum, *pull to pieces,*

crop, enjoy, consume
Carthāgō, -inis, f., *Carthage,* 97, etc.
carus, -a, -um, adj., *dear*
castīgō, -āre, -āvī, -ātum, *chastise, keep in order*
castra, -ōrum, n. pl., *camp*
cāsus, -ūs, m., *falling, chance, crisis,* 560
caterva, -ae, f., *troop*
Caucasus, -ī, m., mountain range between the Euxine and Caspian, 367
causa, -ae, f., *cause, pretext*
cautēs, -is, f., *rock, crag*
celer, -eris, -ere, adj., *swift*
celerō, -are, -avī, -atum, *quicken, hasten*
celsus, -a, -um, adj., *lofty*
centum, num. adj., indecl. *hundred*
Cerēs, -eris, f., *Ceres,* 58; see **legifer**
cernō, -ere, crēvī, crētum, *see, descry*
certamen, -inis, n., *strife*
certatim, adv., *with contending, vying with one another, emulously* (**certo**)
certō, -āre, -āvī, -ātum, *strive, struggle with all one's might*
certus, -a, -um, adj., *secure, determined; to be relied on,* 125; with gen., 554 n., *resolved on*
cerva, -ae, f., *doe*
cervus, -ī, m., *stag*
Chaōs, only in nom. acc. and abl. Chaō, n., a Power of the underworld, parent of Night and Erebus, 510
chlamys, -ydis, f., broad woolen *upper garment* worn in Greece, *cloak, mantle*
chorus, -ī, m., *dance, troop of dancers*
cieō, -ēre, cīvī, citum, *rouse, summon*
cingō, -ere, -nxī, -nctum, *gird, close in, surround*
cinis, -eris, m., *ash, embers*

circum, adv. and prep. with acc., *around*
circumdō, -dāre, -dedī, -datum, *put around, surround, gird*
Cithaeron, -ōnis, m., mountain on borders of Attica and Boeotia, 303
citus, -a, -um, *quick*
clāmō, -āre, -āvī, -ātum, *call on*
clāmor, -ōris, m., *shouting, yell, cry*
clārus, -a, -um, adj., *bright*
classis, -is, f., *fleet*
coepī, coeptum, coepisse, active or defect. transitive, *begin*
coeptum, -ī, n., *something started, undertaking*
Cōēus, -ī, m., Titan, son of Uranus and Gaea, 179
cōgō, -ere, coēgī, coactum, *muster, force, marshal; compel,* with double acc. 412
colō, colere, coluī, cultum, *cultivate, tend, pay honor to, worship*
colōnus, -ī, m., *settler*
color, -ōris, m., *color, hue*
coma, -ae, f., *hair*
comēs, -itis, m. and f., *companion*
comitātus, -ūs, *retinue, attendents*
comitor, -ārī, -ātus, *accompany*
commisceō, -ēre, -uī, -mixtum, *mingle together*
commoveō, -movēre, -mōvī, -mōtum, *stir* or *shake violently*
commūnis, -e, adj., *shared, common, joint*
compellō, -āre, -āvī, -ātum, *address*
complexus, -ūs, m., *embrace*
compleō, -ēre, -ēvī, -ētum, *fill up, crowd*
compōnō, -ere, -posuī, -positum, *put together, settle*
concipiō, -cipere, -cēpī, -ceptum, *conceive, shape, realize*

concitō, -āre, -āvī, -ātum, *rouse*

concutiō, -cutere, -cussī, -cussum, *shake violently, convulse*

condō, -ere, -didī, -ditum, *put (into), hide*

conficiō, -ere, -fēcī, -fectum, *perform, complete, finish; wear out*

confiō, -fierī, used as pass. of **conficio**

cōniciō, -icere, -iēcī, -iectum, *hurl, shoot* (con, iăcio)

coniugium, -iī, n., *marriage, wedlock*

coniunx, -ugis, m. and f., *consort, spouse*

conlābor, -labī, -lapsus, *fall together, faint, sink helpless*

conlūceō, -ēre, *shine together, in numbers; shine brilliantly*

cōnor, -ārī, -ātus sum, *attempt, endeavor*

conscendō, -scendere, -scendī, -scensum, *climb, mount*

conscius, -a, -um, adj., *conscious, privy to a secret*, with gen., *conscious of*

consīdō, -ere, -sēdī, -sessum, *settle, take seat*

consilium, -ī, n., *counsel, purpose*

consistō, -ere, -stitī, -stitum, *halt, make stand*

conspiciō, -ere, -spexī, -spectum, *catch sight of, behold*

consternō, -sternere, -strāvī, -strātum, *cover by strewing, bestrew, spread*

consulō, -sulere, -suluī, -sultum, *consult*

contendō, -tendere, -tendī, -tentum, *contend, strike*

continuō, adv., *immediately, forthwith*

contrā, adv. and prep. with acc., *against, in reply*

contrārius, -a, -um, adj., *opposite, opposed to*

cōnūbium or cōnubium, -ī, n., *marriage*; see 126 n. for prosody

convectō, -āre, *bring together, convey in quantities, convey hurriedly*

conveniō, -venīre, -vēnī, -ventum, *come together, assemble*

convexus, -a, -um, adj., *hollow, convex*; neut. pl. *dome, vault*

convīvium, -ī, n., *banquet*

cor, cordis, n., *heart, mind*

cornu, -ūs, *horn*

corōna, -ae, f., *chaplet*

corōnō, -āre, -āvī, -ātum, *crown*

corpus, -oris, n., *body*

corripiō, -ere, -uī, -reptum, *raise hastily, catch*

crastinus, -a, -um, adj., *of tomorrow*

crēdō, -ere, -didī, -ditum, *believe, confide*

Crēs, Crētis, m., *a Cretan*

crescō, -ere, crevī, crētum, *grow*

Crēsius, -a, -um, adj., *of Crete*

crīmen, -inis, n., *accusation, blame*

crīnis, -is, m., *hair*

croceus, -a, -um, adj., *saffron-colored, yellow*

crūdēlis, -e, adj., *cruel*

cruor, -ōris, m., *blood* spilt, *gore*

cubīle, -is, n., *couch*

culpa, -ae, f., *fault*

cum, prep. with abl., *with*

cum, conj., *when, since*

cumulō, -āre, -āvī, -ātum, *heap*, cumulatus, 436, *with interest*

cunctor, -ārī, -ātus, *linger, hesitate*

cunctus, -a, -um, adj., *all together, one and all*

cupīdō, -inis, f., *lust, desire*

cupiō, cupere, cupīvī, cupītum, *desire*

cūr, conj., *why*

cūra, -ae, f., *care, love*; **curae** (dat.) esse, *be an object of care*, 59; **curae**

habere, *have care for, care for*
cūrō, -āre, -āvī, -ātum, *care for*
cursus, -ūs, m., *course, running,*
voyage, speed
custōs, -ōdis, m. and f., *guardian,*
sentinel
Cyllēnius, -a, -um, adj., *of Cyllene,* Mt.
in Arcadia, epithet of Mercury
born there, 252, etc.
Cynthus, -ī, m., Mt. in Delos,
birthplace of Apollo, 147
Cytherēa, -ae, f., *goddess of Cythĕra,*
Venus, from the island of Cythera
on the coast of which she first
landed when she arose out of the
foam of the sea, 128
D
damnō, -āre, -āvī, -ātum, *condemn*
Danaī, -um, m. pl., *the Greeks,* so
called from Danaus, the founder
of Argos
Dardanius, -a, -um, adj., *connected*
with Dardanus, Dardanian, Trojan
Dardānus, -ī, m., *Dardanus,* son of
Jupiter and founder of the royal
line of Troy, 365
dē, prep with abl., *from, about,*
according to, made of
dea, -ae, f., *goddess*
dēbeō, -ēre, -uī, -itum, *owe, am due*
dēcēdō, -cēdere, -cessī, -cessum,
withdraw
deceō, -ēre, -uī, *become, befit;* generally
impers., **decet**
dēcernō, -ēre, -crēvī, -crētum, *resolve,*
decide
dēcipiō, -ere, cēpī, ceptum, *deceive*
dēclīnō, -āre, -āvī, -ātum, *droop*
decōrus, -a, -um, adj., *good-looking,*
handsome
dēcurrō, -currere, -currī, -cursum,
run down

decus, -oris, n., *grace, beauty,*
ornament
dēdignor, -arī, -atus, *disdain*
dēdūcō, -ere, xī, ctum, *lead down, haul*
down
dēfendō, -fendere, -fendī, -fensum,
defend
dēferō, -ferre, -tulī, -lātum, *carry*
down, report
dēficiō, -ficere, -fēcī, -fectum, *fall*
short, fail, weaken
dēgener, -generis, adj., *degenerate,*
unheroic
dēgō, degere, dēgī, *spend, pass*
dēhiscō, -hiscere, *yawn, gape, open*
dēiciō, -icere, -iēcī, -iectum, *throw*
down, dislodge
deinde, adv., *next; after what has*
happened; in the near future, soon
dēligō, -ere, -lēgī, -lectum, *choose*
Dēlos, -ī, acc. Delum, 144, f., *Delos,*
one of the Cyclades islands, where
Apollo was born
dēlūbrum, -ī, n., *shrine*
dēmens, -tis, adj., *infatuated, mad,*
distracted
dēmittō, -ere, -mīsī, -missum, *send*
down, let down, admit; **demissus,**
263, *hanging, falling*
dēripiō, -ere, -uī, -reptum, *tear down,*
pull hastily down
desaeviō, -vire, -vii, -vītum, *spend or*
work out one's wrath
descendō, -scendere, -scendī,
-scensum, *descend, come down*
dēsecō, -secāre, -secuī, -sectum, *cut off*
dēserō, -serere, -seruī, -sertum,
abandon; **desertus,** *abandoned,*
unpeopled
dēsinō, -sinere, -sīvī and -siī, -situm,
cease, stop
despiciō, -spicere, -spexī, -spectum,

look down on, slight, scorn
destruō, -struere, -struxī, -structum,
pull down, destroy
dēsuper, adv., *from above*
detineō, -tinēre, -tinuī, -tentum, *hold back, detain*
dētorqueō, -torquēre, -torsī, -tortum, *turn away, bend*
deus, -ī, m., *god*
dēveniō, -venīre, -vēnī, -ventum, *come down to;* in poetry often without prep., *reach*
dēvolō, -āre, -āvī, *fly down*
dexter, -era and **-ra, -erum** and **-rum,** adj., *right-handed, propitious;* **sidera dextra,** 579, *fair weather*
dextera or **dextra, -ae,** f., *right-hand; pledge*
Diāna, -ae, f., daughter of Jupiter and Latona, sister of Apollo, 511
dīcō, -ere, -xī, -ctum, *say, mention*
dicō, -āre, -āvī, -ātum, *dedicate, assign*
Dictaeus, -a, -um, adj., *belonging to Dicte,* a mountain in Crete; *Cretan,* 171
dictum, -ī, n., *word* (**dico**)
Dīdō, ūs and **ōnis,** f., *Dido,* Carthaginian queen, 60, etc.
diēs, -ēī, m. and f. in sing,; **m** in pl., *day*
difficilis, -e, adj., *difficult, hard*
diffugiō, -fugere, -fūgī, *fly in different directions*
diffundō, -fundere, -fūdī, -fūsum, *scatter, sow, broadcast*
dignor, -ārī, -ātus sum, *deem worthy; deign*
dignus, -a, -um, adj., *worthy*
dīgredior, -ī, -gressus sum, intransitive, *part, disperse*
dīlābor, -lābī, -lapsus, intr., *glide away, depart*
dīligō, -ligere, -lexī, lectum, *love*

dimoveō, -ēre, -mōvī, mōtum, *divide, dislodge*
Dīra, -ae, f., *Fury,* 473, 610
dīrus, -a, -um, adj., *dreadful, fearful, terrible, hideous, fell*
Dis, Dītis, *Pluto,* as Zeus (Dis) of the lower world, 702
discernō, -cernere, -crēvī, -crētum, *distinguish, pick out*
dissimulō, -āre, -āvī, -ātum, *dissimulate, conceal*
dīva, -ae, f., *goddess*
dīvellō, -vellere, -vellī or **-vulsī, -vulsum,** *tear asunder, tear apart*
dīversus, -a, -um, adj., *in different directions*
dīvēs, -itis, adj., *rich*
dīvidō, -ere, -vīsī, -visum, *divide*
dīvus, -a, -um, adj., *divine*
dīvus, -ī, m. gen. pl., **divum** *god*
dō, dare, dedī, datum, *give, allow, give away, grant, shed* tears, *pay* penalty, *heave* groans, *set* sail; **me d.,** 606, *fling* myself
doceō, -ēre, -uī, doctum, *teach, tell*
doleō, -ēre, -uī, -itum, trans. and intr., *grieve, be indignant, grieve at*
dolor, -ōris, m., *pain, indignation, agony*
dolus, -ī, m., *deceit, strategem, trick*
dominus, -ī, m., *owner, lord*
domus, -ūs, f., irregular; *house, home*
dōnum, -ī, n., *gift*
dōtālis, -e, adj., *belonging to a dowry; as her dowry,* 104
dracō, -ōnis, m., *serpent, dragon*
Dryopes, -um, m. pl., Pelasgian tribe originally settled in the neighborhood of Parnassus, 146
dubius, -a, -um, adj., *doubtful, wavering*
dūcō, dūcere, dūxī, ductum, *lead,*

draw, prolong, guide, lead off
ductor, -ōris, m., *leader, chief*
dulcis, -e, adj., *sweet, dear, pleasant*
dum, conj., *while, until*
dūmus, -ī, m., *thorn*
duō, -ae, -ō, num. adj., *two*
duplex, -icis, *double, two*
dūrus, -a, -um, adj., *hard, rugged*
dux, ducis, m. and f., *leader, guide*
E
e or **ex,** prep. with abl., *from, out of, made of*
ecce, interj., *lo! behold!*
edō, edere or **esse, ēdī, ēsum,** *eat*
efferō, efferre, extulī, ēlātum, *bring forth, lift*
efferus, -a, -um, adj., *wild, maddened*
effigiēs, -eī, f., *image, statue*
effor, -ārī, -fātus sum, *speak out, tell*
effundō, -ere, fūdī, fūsum, *pour out, let stream,* **crines effusa,** 509, *with hair let down*
egeō, -ēre, -uī, *be in need*
ego, meī, first pers. pron., *I*
ēgregius, -a, -um, adj., *outstanding, excellent*
ēiciō, ēicere, ēiēcī, ēiectum, *cast out*
Elissa, -ae, f., *another name of Dido,* 335, 610
en, interj., *see! behold!*
Enceladus, -ī, m., *one of the giants who fought against Jupiter; slain with a thunderbolt and buried under Aetna; son of Uranus and Gaea,* 578
enim, conj., *for, indeed*
ēniteō, -ēre, -uī, *shine out*
ensis, -is, m., *sword*
ēnumerō, -āre, -āvī, -ātum, *recount*
eō, īre, īvī or **iī, itum,** *go;* of noise, *arises, is heard*
epulor, -ārī, -ātus, intr., *feast,* tr. 602

eques, -itis, m., *horseman*
equidem, adv., *for my own part,* strengthened form of **quidem,** but always used with first pers. in classical Latin.
equus, -ī, m., *horse*
Erebus, -ī, m., *the Underworld,* or a *god of darkness,* 26, 510
ergō, adv., *therefore*
ērigō, -rigere, -rexī, -rectum, *erect, rear*
ēripiō, -ere, -uī, -reptum, *seize, snatch*
errō, -āre, -āvī, -ātum, *wander*
ēruō, -uēre, -uī, -utum, *root up*
et, conj. and adv., *and, both, also*
etiam, adv., *also, even*
Eumenides, -um, f. pl., *Eumenides,* avenging *Furies* = **Dirae,** 469
ēvādō, -ere, -sī, -sum, *go forth, from,* with acc., 685, *clear, surmount*
ēvānescō, -nescere, -nuī, *vanish, melt away*
ēvincō, -vincēre, -vīcī, -vāsum, *overpower*
ēvocō, -āre, -āvī, -ātum, *call forth, summon*
ex, see **e**
exanimis, -e, adj., *lifeless, fainting, with sinking heart*
exaudiō, -īre, -īvī, -itum, *hear from out of* something
exciō, -īre, -īvi or **-iī, -ītum** and **excieō, -ēre, -itum,** *rouse*
excipiō, -ere, -cēpī, -ceptum, *receive, take up, answer, catch, overhear, discover* (ex, capio)
excubiae, -ārum, f. pl., *watchkeeping, watch-fires, sentries*
exerceō, -ēre, -uī, -itum, *keep in motion, work, practice; press forward,* 100; *harass*
exhauriō, -haurīre, -hausī, -haustum,

draw off; bear to the end, 14
exigō, -igere, -ēgī, -actum, work out,
plan
exiguus, -a, -um, adj., small, scanty
exordium, -ī, n., beginning
exorior, -īrī, -ortus sum, arise
expediō, -īre, -īvī or **-iī, -ītum,**
disentangle; get ready (**ex, pes**)
experior, -perīrī, -pertus, try
expers, -tis, adj., without share,
ignorant of (**ex, pars**)
exposcō, -ere, -poposcī, demand
earnestly, entreat
exquīrō, -ere, -quīsīvī, -quīsītum, seek
for earnestly
exscindō, -scindere, -scidī, -scissum,
destroy, root out
exsequor, -sequī, -secūtus, follow out,
perform
exsolvō, -solvere, -solvī, -solūtum,
release
exspectō, -āre, -āvī, -ātum, await,
tarry for; intr. linger, 225
extinguō, -stinguere, -stinxī,
-stinctum, obliterate, wipe out
exstruō, -ere, struxī, structum, build
up, rear
exta, -ōrum, n. pl., the outer and more
important vital organs, heart,
lungs, liver, of victims
extemplō, adv., immediately
exterreō, -ēre, -uī, -itum, terrify
exterus, -a, -um, adj., outside, foreign
extorris, -e, adj., exiled
extrēmus, -a, -um, sup. adj., outmost,
utmost, last, furthest; superl. of
exterus
exuō, -uēre, -uī, ūtum, uncover, bare,
discard
exuviae, -ārum, f. pl., relics, mementos
F
facessō, -cessere, -cessī, -cessītum,

take in hand eagerly, fulfil (**facio**)
facilis, adj., easy
faciō, -ere, fēcī, factum, do, make; fac,
suppose, 540
factum, -ī, n., deed
fallō, fallere, fefellit, falsum, deceive,
cheat, frustrate
falx, -cis, f., sickle, knife
fāma, -ae, f., report, news, name; care
for her good name, 91; personified,
Rumor, 173, etc.
famula, -ae, f., handmaid
famulus, -ī, m., manservant
far, farris, n., the grain spelt, a kind of
wheat
fās, n. indecl., that which allowed by the
law of the gods, privilege; fas est, it
is allowed by heaven
fātālis, -e, adj., fated, given by fate
(**fatum**)
fateor, -ērī, fassus sum, confess
fatīgō, -āre, -āvī, -ātum, worry, give no
rest to, rouse
fātum, -ī, n., fate; death; fatō, 696, in
the course of fate
faux, cis, f., jaw, pl., throat
fax, facis, f., torch
fēlix, -īcis, adj., fortunate
fēmina, -ae, f., woman
fēmineus, -a, -um, adj., of a woman
fera, -ae, f., wild beast, game
ferālis, -e, adj., of death, funereal
feriō, -īre, perf. and sup. supplied
from **percutiō,** namely, **percussī,**
percussum; strike
ferō, ferre, tulī, lātum, bear, bring,
bear off, report; pass., am borne
along, move, grope
ferox, -ōcis, adj., fierce, high-spirited
ferrum, -ī, n., iron; steel
fertilis, -e, adj., fertile
ferus, -a, -um, adj., savage, wild

ferveō, -vēre and -vere, -vuī and -buī,
  be hot, busy
fessus, -a, -um, adj., *weary*
festīnō, -āre, -āvī, -ātum, trans. and
  intr., *hasten*
festus, -a, -um, adj., *festive*
fibula, -ae, f., *brooch, pin*
fictum, -ī, n., *falsehood*
fidēs, -eī, f., *faith, belief, fidelity, loyalty*
fīgō, -ere, fixī, fixum, *fix, pierce;*
  fasten, hang up
fingō, -ere, finxī, fictum, *form, shape,*
  invent, devise, imagine, shape, 148
fīnis, -is, m. and f., *end, border;* pl.
  borders, territory
flāmen, -inis, n., *blast, wind*
flamma, -ae, f., *flame, flame of love*
flātus, -ūs, m., *breath, blast*
flāveō, -ēre, *be yellow, golden;* flavens,
  golden
flāvus, -a, -um, adj., *yellow, golden*
flectō, flectere, flexī, flexum, *bend,*
  move
flētus, -ūs, m., *weeping;* in fletum, 463,
  wailingly
flōreō, -ēre, -uī, *bloom, flourish*
flos, -ōris, m., *flower*
fluctuō, -āre, -āvī, -ātum, *rise in*
  waves, surge
fluctus, -ūs, m., *wave, billow*
fluentum, -ī, n., *stream*
flūmen, -inis, n., *river*
fluō, -ere, fluxī, fluxum, *flow*
fluvialis, -e, adj., *of a stream*
fluvius, -iī, m., *stream, river*
foedō, -āre, -āvī, -ātum, *disfigure*
foedus, -a, -um, adj., *foul, disfigured*
foedus, -eris, n., *treaty; bond, alliance*
fons, -tis, m., *spring, water*
[for], fātur, fārī, fatus, *speak, say*
forma, -ae, f., *figure, shape*
formīca, -ae, f., *ant*

forsan, adv., *perhaps* (shortened for
  forsitan, =fors, sit, an)
fortis, -e, adj., *brave, stalwart*
fortūna, -ae, f., *fortune*
forus, -ī, m., *deck*
foveō, fovēre, fōvī, fōtum, *keep warm,*
  cherish, cling to, take to the heart,
  218
frāter, -tris, m., *brother*
frāternus, -a, -um, adj., *of a brother, by*
  a brother
fraudō, -āre, -āvī, -ātum, *rob*
fraus, -dis, f., *deceit, guile*
fremō, -ere, -uī, -itum, *shout, ring,*
  668. fremens, 229, *clamorous*
frēnum, -ī, n., *bridle*
frētus, -a, -um, adj., *relying,* with abl.,
  relying on
frīgidus, -a, -um, adj., *cold*
frondeō, -ēre, *have leaves, be leafy;*
  frondentes remos, 399, *oars with*
  leaves still on
frons, -dis, f., *leaf*
frons, -tis, f., *brow, forehead*
fruor, -ī, fructus and fruitus sum, *with*
  abl., *reap fruit, enjoy*
frustrā, adv., *in vain*
fuga, -ae, f., *flight*
fugiō, -ere, fūgī, fugitum, *flee; fly*
  from, avoid, escape
fulciō, -cire, -sī, tum, *prop, support*
fulgeō, -gēre, -sī, *shine, glitter*
fulmen, -inis, n., *lightning*
fulmineus, -a, -um, adj., *lightning-like,*
  flashing
fulvus, -a, -um, adj., *tawny yellow*
fundāmentum, -ī, n., *foundation*
fundō, -āre, -āvī, -ātum, *found*
fundō, -ere, fūdī, fūsum, *pour, pour*
  forth, overthrow
fūnereus, -a, -um, adj., *belonging to*
  death, funereal

fūnis, -is, m., *rope, cable*
fūnus, -eris, n., *funeral, death*
furia, -ae, f., *fury, demon*
furibundus, -a, -um, adj., *wild,
    maddened*
furō, -ere, -uī, *be wild, frenzied, act
    like a madman;* **furens,** *frenzied, in
    madness*
furor, -ōris, m., *madness, passion*
furtīvus, -a, -um, adj., *secret,
    clandestine*
furtum, -ī, n., *stealth, theft, deception*
futūrum, -ī, n., *the future* (**futūrus,** fut.
    part. of **sum**)
futūrus, -a, -um, fut. part. of **sum** as
    adj., *future, coming, to come*
G
Gaetūlus, -a, -um, adj., *Gaetulian. The
    Gaetuli were an African people
    who lived south of the Mauri and
    Numidians,* 40, 326
Garamantis, -idis, f., adj., *belonging to
    the Garamantes, people of Libya,*
    198
gaudeō, gaudēre, gāvīsus, *rejoice*
gelu, -ūs, n., *cold, frost*
geminus, -a, -um, adj., *twin, twofold,
    double*
gemitus, -ūs, m., *groaning, groan*
gemō, gemere, gemuī, gemitum, *groan*
gena, -ae, f., *cheek*
genetrix, -trīcis, f., *mother*
genitor, -ōris, m., *father*
gens, -tis, f., *family, clan, race*
genus, -eris, n., *race, stock, kind*
germāna, -ae, f., *sister*
germānus, -ī, m., *brother*
gignō, gignere, genuī, genitum, *beget*
glaciēs, -ēī, f., *ice*
gladius, -ī, m., *sword*
glomerō, -āre, -āvī, -ātum, *make into a
    ball, mass*

glōria, -ae, f., *glory*
gradior, -ī, gressus sum, *walk*
gradus, -ūs, m., *step*
Grāius, -a, -um, gen. pl. **Graium,** adj.,
    Greek
grāmen, -inis, n., *grass*
grandis, -e, adj., *large*
grandō, -inis, f., *hail*
grātia, -ae, f., *favor, gratitude*
grātor, arī, atus, *wish joy*
gravidus, -a, -um, adj., *pregnant*
gravis, -e, adj., *heavy, grievous*
gremium, -iī, n., *lap, bosom*
Grynēus, -a, -um, adj. *of Grynium,
    town on coast of Aeolis, with a
    celebrated temple and oracle of
    Apollo,* 345
H
habeō, -ēre, -uī, -itum, *have, hold, keep*
haereō, -ēre, -haesī, -haesum, with
    dat., *stick, remain, cleave to;* **hic
    terminus haeret,** 614, *this is the
    fixed goal*
hālitus, -ūs, m., *breath*
Hammon, -ōnis, m., African god
    assimilated to Jupiter, 198
haud, adv., *not*
hauriō, -rīre, -sī, -stum, *draw, drink,
    drain the cup of; drink in, of words,*
    359
Hecatē, -ēs, f., *Hecate,* a night-
    worshipped power of the
    underworld, identified with Diana
    as the moon-goddess, 511, 609
hēia, interj., *Ho!*
herba, -ae, f., *blade of grass, grass;* pl.
    grass, herbage, herbs
hērēs, -ēdis, m., *heir*
hērōs, -ōis, m., *hero*
Hesperia, -ae, f., *the western land, Italy,*
    355
Hesperides, -um, f. pl., daughters of

Atlas and Hesperia, who lived in a garden, guarded by a dragon, in which the golden apples grew, 484
heu, interj., *alas!*
hībernus, -a, -um, adj., *wintry* (**hiems**)
hic, haec, hōc, dem. pron., *this* near the speaker
hīc, adv., *here; at this time* or *place; hereupon, then; of this,* for **de hac re,** 237
hiems, hiēmis, f., *winter; storm, winter tempest*
hinc, adv., *hence, from here, from this place, next;* **hinc...hinc (illinc),** *on this side...on that side*
homō, -inis, m., *man, human being*
honor, -ōris, m., *honor, glory*
hōra, -ae, f., *hour; season*
horreō, -ēre, *be rough, shudder at;* **horrens,** *bristling, rough, trembling;* **horrendus,** *to be shuddered at, horrible*
horridus, -a, -um, adj., *rough, bristling, awful*
horrifīcō, -āre, -āvī, -ātum, *horrify*
horror, -ōris, m., *shivering; shudder, terror, dread*
hospes, -tis, m. and f., *guest*
hospitium, -iī, n., *hospitality*
hostis, -is, m. and f., *stranger; enemy, foe*
hūc, adv., *hither;* **huc...illuc (atque huc),** *this way and that*
humilis, -e, adj., *low, lowly*
hymenaeus, -ī, m., *bridal song, wedding;* personified as the marriage god, 127
Hyrcānus, -a, -um, adj., *belonging to Hyrcania,* country bordering on the Caspian Sea, 367
I
Iarbas, -ae, m., suitor of Dido, 36, etc.

iaspis, -idis, f., *jasper*
īdem, eadem, idem, pron., *the same, he too,* etc. (**is,** suffix **-dem**)
ideō, adv., *therefore, for that*
igitur, adv., *therefore, in that case*
ignārus, -a, -um, adj., *ignorant;* with gen., *ignorant of*
igneus, -a, -um, adj., *fiery*
ignis, -is, m., *fire, flame*
ignōtus, -a, -um, adj., *unknown*
īlex, -icis, f., *holm-oak*
Īliacus, -a, -um, adj., *of Ilium, Trojan*
ille, illa, illud, demonst. pron., *that* remote from the speaker, *he;* **hoc illud fuit,** 675, *was this what he meant?*
illinc, adv., *from that place* or *side, thence*
illuc, adv., *to that place, thither*
imāgō, -inis, f., *likeness, phantom, vision*
imber, -bris, m., *rain*
immānis, -e, adj., *enormous, huge*
immemor, -oris, adj., *forgetful; regardless of,* with gen.
immisceō, -miscēre, -miscuī, -mixtum or **mistum,** *mingle in*
immittō, -ere, -mīsī, -missum, *send on* or *in; let loose on*
immōtus, -a, -um, adj., *unmoved, unshaken*
impellō, -ere, -pulī, -pulsum, *drive onward, dash in; shake*
imperium, -iī, n., *command; empire, rule*
impius, -a, -um, adj., *neglectful of duty, godless, unholy*
impleō, -plēre, -plēvī, -plētum, *fill*
implicō, -are, -uī, -itum, *entwine, fasten up*
implōrō, -āre, -āvī, -ātum, *implore*
impōnō, -ere, -posuī, -positum, *set on,*

set to

imprecor, -ārī, -ātus, *pray for something against a person*

imprimō, -primere, -pressī, -pressum, *press on, impress*

improbus, -a, -um, adj., *wicked, relentless*

īmus, -a, -um, adj., used as superl. of **inferus,** *lowest*

in, prep. with abl., *in, on;* with acc., *into, to, for*

inānis, -e, adj., *empty, useless*

incautus, -a, -um, adj., *not careful, off his (her) guard, heedless, unawares*

incēdō, -cedere, -cendī, -censum, *set on fire, kindle*

inceptum, -ī, n., *undertaking, purpose*

incertus, -a, -um, adj., *uncertain*

incīdō, -cidere, -cīdī, cīsum, *cut*

incipiō, -ere, cēpī, ceptum, *begin*

inclūdō, -cludere, -clusī, clusum, *shut in*

incomitatus, -a, -um, adj., *solitary*

incubō, -cubare, -cubuī, -cubitum, *recline on*

incumbō, -cumbere, -cubuī, -cubitum, *rest on, lay weight on, lie down on, apply oneself to*

indāgō, -inis, f., *encircling, circle of nets*

indignus, -a, -um, adv., *unworthy, undeserved*

indulgeō, -gēre, -sī, -tum, *give play, indulge*

iners, -tis, adj., *slothful, spiritless*

inexpertus, -a, -um, adj., *untried*

infabricatus, -a, -um, adj., *unformed, rough*

infandus, -a, -um, adj., *unspeakable, horrible, accursed*

infectus, -a, -um, adj., *not-done, fictitious*

infēlix, -īcis, adj., *unsuccessful,*

unhappy

infensus, -a, -um, adj., *hostile, angry*

inferō, -ferre, -tulī, -lātum, *carry;* pass., *advance, proceed*

infigō, -figere, -fixī, -fixum, *fix in, on*

inflammō, -āre, -āvī, -ātum, *set on fire, kindle, enflame*

inflectō, -ere, flexī, flexum, *bend*

infrēnus, -a, -um, adj., *unbridled*

infundō, -fundere, -fūdī, -fūsum, *pour on, in;* **nix infusa,** 250, *a mantle of snow*

ingeminō, -āre, -āvī, -ātum, *redouble*

ingemō, -gemere, -gemuī, *groan, sigh, sigh at*

ingens, -tis, adj., *huge, monstrous*

ingredior, -ī, -gressus sum, *advance; march on, stalk along; begin*

inhiō, -āre, -āvī, -ātum, *gape, pore over*

inhospitus, -a, -um, adj., *inhospitable*

inhumātus, -a, -um, adj., *unburied*

iniciō, -icere, -iēcī, -iectum, *fling, cast on*

inimīcus, -a, -um, adj., *hostile*

inīquus, -a, -um, adj., *uneven, unfair, unjust*

iniūria, -ae, f., *wrong, injury, guilt*

inlūdō, -dere, -sī, -sum, *make sport, mock; mock at,* with dat.

innectō, -nectere, -nexuī, -nexum, *weave together, string*

inops, -opis, adj., *powerless*

inrīdeō, -ridēre, -rīsī, -rīsum, *laugh at, mock*

inrītō, -āre, -āvī, -ātum, *vex, exasperate*

inrumpō, -rumpere, -rūpī, -ruptum, *burst into, through*

insānia, -ae, f., *madness*

insequor, -ī, secūtus sum, *follow on*

insignis, -e, adj., *conspicious*

insomnis, -e, adj., *sleepless*

insomnium, -ī, n., *dream*
instaurō, -āre, -āvī, -ātum, *renew;*
inst. diem donis, 63, *begins the day with similar gifts*
instimulō, -āre, -āvī, -ātum, *goad, spur on, urge*
instō, -stare, -stitī, -stātum, *press on, be urgent, lie near*
insuperābilis, -e, adj., *invincible*
intendō, -ere, -dī, -sum and **-tum,** *stretch out; stretch on, cover,* 506
inter, prep. with acc., *between, among*
intereā, adv., *meanwhile*
interfundō, -fundere, -fūdī, -fūsum, *pour between;* **interfusa,** 644, *stained*
interior, -ius, adj., *inner* (comparative fr. obsolete **interus,** cf. **inter;** superl. **intimus**)
interpres, -etis, m. and f., *intermediary, agent; medium, messenger*
interrumpō, -rumpere, -rūpī, -ruptum, *break off, interrupt*
intrō, -āre, -āvī, -ātum, *enter*
intus, adv., *within*
inultus, -a, -um, adj., *unavenged*
invādō, -ere, vāsī, vāsum, *attack, accost*
inveniō, -īre, -vēnī, -ventum, *come upon, discover*
invideō, -vidēre, -vīdī, -vīsum, *begrudge, be jealous of*
invidia, -ae, f., *ill will, grudge, ground for jealousy,* 350
invīsō, -vīsere, -vīsī, -vīsum, *visit*
invīsus, -a, -um, adj., *hated*
invius, -a, -um, *pathless, impassable*
ipse, -a, -um, pron., *self; him-, her-, itself, very*
īra, -ae, f., *anger, wrath*
Īris, -idis, f., *Iris,* rainbow-messenger of gods, 694, 700

is, ea, id, demonstr. pron., *that;* with reference to second person, *that of yours*
ita, adv., *so*
Ītalia, -ae, f., *Italy*
Ītalus, -a, -um, adj., *Italian,* 106, etc.
iter, itineris, n., *journey, way*
iterum, adv., *a second time, again*
Iūlus, -ī., m., *son of Aeneas;* also called Ascanius, 140, 274, 616
iactō, -āre, -āvī, -ātum, *toss about* (freq. of **iacio**)
iam, adv., *already, by now, now, soon;* **iam...iam,** *at one time...at another time*
iamdūdum, adv., *long since, this long while*
iubar, -aris, n., *ray; dawn*
iubeō, -ēre, iussī, iussum, *bid, order*
iugālis, -e, adj., *marital, of wedlock*
iugum, -ī, n., *yoke, mountain-ridge, hill ridge*
iungō, -ere, -nxī, -nctum, *unite, join, yoke,* **foedera i.,** *enter into agreements;* **agmina i.,** 142
Iūnō, -ōnis, f., daughter of Saturn, wife of Jupiter, 45, etc.
Iūppiter, Iovis, m., the greatest of the gods, *Jupiter,* 91 etc. **Iup. Stygius,** 638
iūrō, -āre, -āvī, -ātum, *swear*
ius, iūris, n., *right*
iussum, -ī, n., *command* (**iubeo**)
iustus, -a, -um, adj., *just*
iuventa, -ae, f., *youth*
iuventūs, -ūtis, f., *youth, the young men,* esp. of military age
iuvō, -āre, iūvī, iūtum, *help, please;* **iuvat,** impersonal, *it delights, it is a joy to*
iuxtā, adv. and prep. with acc., *close at hand; near to*

L

labefaciō, -facere, -fēcī, factum, *make to totter* or *stagger*

labō, -āre, -āvī, -ātum, *waver*

labor, -ōris, m., *toil, work, suffering*

lābor, -bī, -psus sum, *glide, slip; fall down, fall to earth*

lac, lactis, n., *milk*

lacrima, -ae, f., *tear*

lacus, -ūs, m., *lake*

laena, -ae, f., *mantle, cloak,* 262

laetus, -a, -um, adj., *glad, joyful*

lāmentum, -ī, n., *lamentation*

lampas, -adis, f., *torch, lamp*

Lāomedonteus, -a, -um, adj., *of Laeomedon,* founder of Troy, who cheated the gods, 542

lapsus, -ūs, m., *gliding; gliding motion; smooth course*

lātē, adv. *far and wide, at large*

lateō, -ēre, -uī, -ītum, *lie hid, lurk*

latex, -icis, m., *water*

Latium, -ī, n., *Latium,* 432

latus, -eris, n., *side, flank*

lātus, -a, -um, adj., *broad*

laus, -dis, f., *praise, honor*

Lāvīnius, -a, -um, adj., *belonging to the city Lavinium,* 236

lectus, -ī, m., *couch*

lēgifer, -era,- erum, adj., *law-bringing, founder of law,* epithet of Ceres, the introduction of settled law following on that of agriculture, 58 (**lex, fero**)

legō, -ere, lēgī, lēctum, *gather, choose, collect; catch;* 658, **lectus,** adj, *choice*

Lēnaeus, -a, -um, adj., *of Bacchus,* as god of the winepress, 207

lēniō, -īre, -īvi, -ītum, *soothe, alleviate*

leō, -ōnis, m., *lion*

lētālis, -e, adj., *deadly*

lētum, -ī, n., *death*

levō, -āre, -āvī, -ātum, *make light, lighten, alleviate, relieve; lift,* 690

lex, lēgis, f., *law,* pl., *conditions, terms; jurisdiction,* 213

lībō, -āre, -āvī, -ātum, *sip, pour out as a libation*

Libya, -ae, f., *Libya,* often used of much of North Africa, 36, etc.

Libycus, -a, -um, adj., *of Libya*

licet, -ere, -uit, impers., *it is lawful, one may*

limbus, -ī, m., *stripe, border*

līmen, -inis, n., *threshold, doorway*

lingua, -ae, f., *tongue*

linquō, -ere, līquī, lictum, *leave, abandon*

liquidus, -a, -um, adj., *liquid, clear*

litō, -āre, -āvī, -ātum, *perform sacrifice with favorable omens, sacrifice successfully,* 50

lītus, -oris, n., *shore, coast*

locō, -āre, -āvī, -ātum, *place, lay foundations*

locus, -ī, m. plur. **loci** and **loca,** *place, room, region*

longus, -a, -um, adj., *long; tedious*

loquor, -ī, locūtus sum, *speak, say*

luctor, -arī, -atus, *wrestle, struggle*

lūdō, -ere, -sī, -sum, *play*

lūmen, -inis, n., *light; eye*

lūna, -ae, f., *moon*

lustrō, -āre, -āvī, -ātum, *survey, traverse*

lustrum, -ī, n., *lair*

lux, -ūcis, f., *light; day*

luxus, -ūs, m., *luxury*

Lyaeus, -ī, m., *Bacchus,* as the looser from cares, 58

Lycia, -ae, f., *Lycia,* a territory of Asia Minor, 143, 346

Lycius, -a, -um, adj., *Lycian,* epithet

of Apollo, who was worshipped at Patara, in Lycia, 346, etc.

lympha, -ae, f., *water*

M

māchina, -ae, f., *structure, mechanism, crane,* 89

mactō, -āre, -āvī, -ātum, *slay in sacrifice*

macula, -ae, f., *spot, stain*

madeō, -ēre, -uī, *be wet*

Maeonius, -a, -um, adj., *Maeonian, Lydian, Asiatic*

maereō, -ēre, -uī, *mourn*

maestus, -a, -um, adj., *sorrowful, grieving*

māgālia, -ium, n. pl, *huts, low buildings on the outskirts of Carthage,* a Punic word, 259

magicus, -a, -um, adj., *magic*

magis, adv., *more*

magnus, -a, -um, adj., comp. **maior,** sup. **maximus,** *great, mighty, august*

male, adv., *ill, badly; scarce,* often almost *not,* e.g., **male sana,** 8

mālō, malle, maluī, *prefer*

malum, -ī, n., *evil*

mandātum, -ī, n., *command*

mandō, -āre, -āvī, -ātum, *entrust, commit, command*

mandō, -ēre, -dī, -sum, *champ*

maneō, -ēre, mansī, mansum, *remain; await*

mānēs, -ium, m. pl., *the souls of the dead,* 34, etc.

manīca, -ae, f., *sleeve*

manifestus, -a, -um, *palpable, unmistakable*

manus, -ūs, f., *hand, power, troop*

mare, -is, n., *sea*

marītus, -ī, m., *husband*

marmor, -oris, n., *marble*

marmoreus, -a, -um, adj., *of marble*

Mars, -tis, m., god of War

Martius, -a, -um, adj., *of Mars, martial*

Massylus, -a, -um, adj., *belonging to Mauretania, Massylian*

maximus, see **magnus**

mēcum, i.e., **cum me,** *with me*

medītor, -ārī, -ā tus, *think of, plan*

medius, -a, -um, adj., *middle, midst of;* as subst. **medio caelī,** 184, *in the space between...*

medulla, -ae, f., *marrow*

mel, mellis, n., *honey*

melior, -us, adj., used as comp. of **bonus;** *better*

membrum, -ī, n., *limb*

mēmet, strengthened form of **me (ego)**

meminī, -esse, defect., *be mindful of, remember,* with gen.

memor, -oris, adj., *having memory, thoughtful, mindful of,* with gen.

memorābilis, -e, adj., *worth recording, memorable*

memorō, -āre, -āvī, -ātum, *relate, speak of, mention*

mēne, me (from **ego**) with interrog. suffix, **-ne**

mens, -tis, f., *mind*

mensa, -ae, f., *table*

mentum, -ī, n., *chin*

Mercurius, -ī, m., *Mercury,* the messenger god, 222, 558

mereō, -ēre, -uī, -itum and **mereor, -ērī, -itus,** *deserve;* **meritus,** *deserved, due*

metō, metere, messuī, messum, *reap, cut*

metuō, -uere, -uī, -ūtum, *fear*

meus, -a, -um, adj., *my*

migrō, -āre, -āvī, -ātum, *move, shift abode*

mille, sing. indecl. adj. **pl. millia** or

mīlis, decl. subst., *thousand*
mina, -ae, f., *threat*
mīrābilis, -e, adj., *wondrous*
mīrus, -a, -um, adj., *wonderful, wondrous*
misceō, -ēre, -uī, mistum and mixtum, *mingle, confound,* 160
miser, -era, -erum, adj., *wretched*
miserābilis, -e, adj., *pitiable, piteous*
misereor, -ērī, -itus, *feel pity,* obj. in gen.
miseror, -ārī, -ātus sum, *pity*
mitra, -ae, f., *cap, turban,* 216
mittō, -ere, mīsī, missum, *send*
Mnestheūs, -eī and -eos, m., a Trojan, companion of Aeneas, 288
mōbilitās, -tis, f., *quick movement*
modo, adv., *only*
modus, -ī, m., *manner, limit*
moenia, -ium, n. pl., *walls, city buildings, the town,* 74
mola, -ae, f., *meal;* mola salsa, mixture of bruised grain and salt used in sacrifices
mōlior, -īrī, -ītus sum, *do* or *make with toil, labor at, task oneself to do; toil to prepare,* 309
mollis, -e, adj., *soft, yielding*
moneō, -ere, -uī, -itum, *advise, advise of, warn*
monimentum, -ī, n., *reminder, record*
monitum, -ī, n., *words of warning*
monitus, -ūs, m., *warning*
mons, -tis, m., *mountain*
monstrō, -āre, -āvī, -ātum, *show*
monstrum, -ī, n., *omen, prodigy, monster, portent*
mōra, -ae, f., *delay*
morior, -ī, mortuus sum, *die*
moror, -ārī, -ātus sum, *delay, pause*
mors, -tis, f., *death*
mortālis, -e, adj., *belonging to death; mortal*
mōs, mōris, m., *manner, custom;* pl., *character;* more, *after manner of,* with gen.; de more, *according to custom, duly*
moveō, -ēre, mōvī, mōtum, *move, influence*
mox, adv., *soon*
mūgiō, -īre, -īvi or -iī, -ītum, *bellow, roar*
multiplex, -plicis, adj., *manifold, varied*
multus, -a, -um, *much, many;* predicatively, multus recursat, 3, *comes back often*
mūnus, -eris, n., *gift, offering*
mūrex, -icis, m., *purple-dye*
murmur, -uris, n., *murmur, noise*
mūrus, -ī, m., *wall, rampart*
mūtābilis, -e, adj., *changeable*
mūtō, -āre, -āvī, -ātum, *change*
N
nam, namque, conj., *for*
narrō, -āre, -āvī, -ātum, *relate*
nascor, -ī, nātus sum, *be born;* nascens, 515, *new born;* nate dea, 560, *goddess-born*
natō, -āre, -āvī, -ātum, *float*
nātus, -ī, m., *child, son*
nauta, -ae, m., *sailor*
nāvāle, -is, n., *dockyard,* pl. in same sense
nāvīgō, -āre, -āvī, -ātum, *sail*
nāvis, -is, f., *ship*
-ne, enclitic interrog. particle
nē, adv. with imper., *not do, not;* conj. with subj., *lest, that...not*
nec, see neque
necdum, adv., *nor yet, and not yet*
necesse, adj., used only in neut. *necessary*
nectō, nectere, nexuī, nexum, *weave,*

fetter, bind
nefandus, -a, -um, adj., *unutterable, shocking, abominable*
nefās, n. indecl., *that which is contrary to divine law, sin, crime*
negō, -āre, -āvī, -ātum, *deny, refuse*
nēmō, -inem, pron., *no one*
nemus, -oris, n., *grove, wood*
nepos, -pōtis, m., *grandson; descendant*
neque or **nec,** conj., *and not, nor;* **neque...neque,** *neither...nor;* **neque enim,** *for indeed...not;* **nec non,** *nor not, i.e., and also, moreover*
nēquīquam, adv., *in vain*
nesciō, -īre, -īvī and **-iī, -itum,** *not know, be in ignorance of*
nescius, -a, -um, adj., *ignorant*
niger, -gra, -grum, adj., *black*
nigrans, -tis, part. of **nigro,** as adj., *black*
nigrescō, -grescere, -gruī, *grow black*
nihil or **nil,** indecl. n., *nothing;* as adv., *in no way*
nimbus, -ī, m., *storm cloud*
nimium, adv., *too much, too*
nītor, nītī, nixus and **nisus,** *rest upon, strive, work*
niveus, -a, -um, adj., *snowy*
nix, nivis, f., *snow*
nocturnus, -a, -um, adj., *by night, of night*
nōdō, -āre, -āvī, -ātum, *knot;* **nodantur in aurum,** 138, *are fastened into a knot with a golden pin*
Nomas, -adis, m., *Nomad,* or *Wanderer,* hence a *Numidian,* 320, etc.
nōmen, -inis, n., *name, fame*
nōn, adv., *not*

nondum, adv., *not yet*
nōris, for **noveris,** see **nosco**
noscō, noscere, nōvī, nōtum, *learn,* perf., *know,* **nōtus,** *well-known, familiar*
noster, -tra, -trum, adj., *our*
nōvō, -āre, -āvī, -ātum, *make new, renew, change, alter*
novus, -a, -um, adj., *new, novel, startling, strange;* superl. **novissimus,** 650, last
nox, noctis, f., *night*
nūbēs, -is, f., *cloud*
nūbilus, -a, -um, adj., *cloudy,* n. pl. as subst., *clouds*
nullus, -a, -um, adj., *not any, no, none*
num, interrogative expecting answer "no"
nūmen, -inis, n., *divinity, divine presence, will,* or *regard; wrathful regard,* 611
Numīdae, -arum, m. pl., *Numidians,* 41
numquam, adv., *never*
nunc, adv., *now*
nuntia, -ae, f., *messenger*
nuntius, -a, m., *messenger*
nusquam, adv., *nowhere*
nūtō, -āre, -āvī, -ātum, *nod*
nūtrix, -īcis, f., *nurse*
nympha, -ae, f., *nymph*
O
ō, interj., *oh!*
obiciō, -ere, -iēcī, -iectum, *throw in the way; expose*
obītus, -ūs, m., *death;* pl., *death struggles,* 694
oblīviscor, -ī, oblītus sum, *be forgetful;* with gen., *forget*
obmūtescō, -tescere, -tuī, *be struck dumb, stand speechless*
obnītor, -nītī, -nixus, *push against, use*

strong effort

oborior, -īrī, -ortus sum, *rise up* or *in front of*

obscēnus, -a, -um, adj., *filthy, disgusting, revolting, foul*

obscūrus, -a, -um, adj., *dark, dim*

obstō, -stare, -stitī, -statum, *stand in the way*

obstruō, -struere, -struxī, -structum, *block, stop*

occupō, -āre, -āvī, -ātum, *seize, fill*

ōceanus, -ī, m., *the ocean, thought by ancients to flow around the land mass of the known world, and closest to them at the Atlantic Ocean*

ōcius, comp. adv., *swiftly*

oculus, -ī, m., *eye*

ōdī, -isse, defective, *hate*

odium, -ī, n., *hatred*

odōrus, -a, -um, adj., *scented, keen scented*

offerō, offerre, obtulī, oblātum, *present*

ōlim, adv., *once, at one time, one day*

olle, old form of **ille**

Olympus, -ī, m., mountain on which the gods dwelt, *the heavens,* 268, 694

ōmen, -inis, n., *omen, sign*

omnīnō, adv., *altogether*

omnipotens, -tis, adj., *all-powerful*

omnis, -e, adj., *all, every, whole*

onerō, -āre, -āvī, -ātum, *burden, load*

opācus, -a, -um, adj., *dark*

operiō, -perire, -peruī, -pertum, *cover*

ops, opis, f., *aid,* pl., *resources, power, wealth*

optimus, -a, -um, adj., *best,* used as superl. of **bonus;** 291, *kindest of friends*

optō, -āre, -āvī, -ātum, *wish, pray for*

opus, -eris, n., *work, task*

ōra, -ae, f., *coast, shore*

orbis, -is, m., *circle, round, world,* 119, etc.

Orcus, -ī, m., *Orcus,* the Underworld, 242, 699

Orestēs, -is, m., son of Agamemnon and Clytaemnestra, 471

orgia, -ōrum, n. pl., *mysterious religious rites*

Orīōn, -ōnis, m., a celebrated hunter changed into a constellation, the rising and setting of which is accompanied by storms, 52 (see n. for prosody)

ornus, -ī, f., *ash-tree*

ōrō, -āre, -āvī, -ātum, *pray, crave*

ortus, -ūs, m., *rising*

ōs, ōris, n., *mouth, face, lips*

os, ossis, n., *bone;* pl., *frame,* 101

ostendō, -ere, -tendī, -tentum, *show*

ostentō, -āre, -āvī, -ātum, *keep showing, display*

ostrum, -ī, n., *purple*

ōtium, -ī, n., *leisure, idle hours*

ovīle, -is, n., *sheepfold*

ovō, -āre, -āvī, -ātum, *exult, triumph*

P

paciscor, -ciscī, pactus, *make compact;* perf. part. in pass. sense, *established, firm,* 99

pallens, -entis, adj., *pale*

pallor, -ōris, m., *pallor*

papāver, -eris, n., *poppy*

par, paris, adj., *equal;* of wings, 252, *equally poised*

parens, -ntis, m. or f., *parent*

pāreō, -ēre, -uī, -itum, with dat., *obey*

Paris, -idis, m., *Paris,* son of Priam, seducer of Helen, 215

pariter, adv., *equally, alike*

parō, -āre, -āvī, -ātum, *make ready,*

prepare; **parātus,** *ready; built ready to dwell in,* 75
pars, -tis, f., *part, direction;* **pars... pars,** 405, *some...others*
parvūlus, -a, -um, adj., dimin., *tiny*
parvus, -a, -um, adj., *small*
passim, adv., *everywhere, in all directions*
pastor, -ōris, m., *shepherd* (**pasco**)
pāteō, patēre, -uī, *lie open;* **patens,** *open*
pater, -tris, m., *father;* **Pater,** *the Father,* i.e. Jupiter, 25
patera, -ae, f., *open saucer-like goblet used in sacrifice* (**păteo**)
patior, patī, passus sum, *suffer; endure*
patria, -ae, f., *fatherland, native land*
patrius, -a, -um, adj., *belonging to a father or fatherland*
paucus, -a, -um, adj., *small;* pl., *few;* **paucis,** 116, *in few words*
paulum, adv., *a little; somewhat*
pax, pācis, f., *peace; leave,* 56
pectus, -oris, n., *heart, breast*
pecus, -oris, n., *cattle,* collect., *game,* 158
pecus, -udis, f., *single beast; lamb,* 120; pl. *flocks,* 692
pelagus, -ī, n., *sea*
penātēs, -ium, m., *gods of the household,* 21, 598
pendeō, -ēre, pependī, *hang, be suspended*
penetrālis, -e, adj., *innermost*
penna, -ae, f., *wing*
Penthēūs, -eī and **-eos,** king of Thebes, 469
per, prep. with acc., *through, over;* in asseverations, *by;* **per aras,** 56, *from altar to altar*
peragō, -ere, -ēgī, -actum, *go through with, accomplish, finish*

perāgrō, -āre, -āvī, -ātum, *roam through, scour*
percūtiō, -cutēre, -cussī, -cussum, *strike deeply, smite*
perdō, -dere, -didī, -ditum, *lose*
pereō, -īre, -īvi or- **iī, -itum,** *pass through* or *away; perish*
perrerō, -āre, -āvī, -ātum, *wander over, peruse, survey*
perferō, -ferre, -tulī, -lātum, *bear to the end, endure*
perficiō, -ere, -fēcī, -fectum, *finish, accomplish*
perfidus, -a, -um, adj., *treacherous, disloyal*
Pergama, -ōrum, n. pl., *the citadel of Troy,* 344, etc.
pergō, pergere, perrexī, perrectum, *move forwards, go on*
perhibeō, -hibēre, -hibuī, -hibitum, *relate*
perīcūlum or **perīclum, -ī,** n., *danger, peril*
periūrium, -ī, n., *falsehood, oathbreaking*
permittō, -mittere, -mīsī, -missum, *commit*
pernix, -īcis, adj., *swift*
perpetuus, -a, -um, adj., *lasting, all through, continuous*
persentiō, -sentire, -sensī, -sensum, *perceive clearly, feel deeply*
pertaedet, -taesum est, impers. with acc. of pers., gen. of thing, *be sick, thoroughly weary of*
pēs, pedis, m., *foot*
pestis, -is, f., *plague, disease, destruction*
petō, -ere, -īvi or **-iī, -itum,** *seek;* **me fraude petebas,** 675, *were you seeking to deceive me?*
pharetra, -ae, f., *quiver*

Phoebēus, -a, -um, adj., *belonging to Phoebus,* i.e. Apollo, 6

Phoebus, -a, -um, adj., lit, *the radiant one,* name of Apollo, as god of sunlight, 58

Phoenissa, -ae, fem. adj., *Phoenician, Carthaginian*

Phrygius, -a, -um, adj., *Trojan, Asiatic, Phrygian*

Phryx, -ygis, m., *a Phrygian, Trojan*

piāculum, -ī, n., *expiatory rite or sacrifice*

piget, -ēre, -uit, impers. with acc. and inf., **me piget,** *I am disinclined, I find no pleasure*

pingō, pingere, pinxī, pictum, *paint embroider; tattoo,* 146; **pictus,** 525, of birds, *bright-plumaged, many-colored*

pinguis, -e, adj., *fat, rich, fertile*

pinifer, -era, -erum, adj., *pinebearing*

pinna, -ae, f., *wing*

piscōsus, -a, -um, adj., *full of fish*

pius, -a, -um, adj., *dutiful* to gods, country, parents, etc., *good; pious*

placeō, -ēre, -uī, -itum, *be pleasing,* perf. part. pass. **placitus,** *pleasing,* 38

placidus, -a, -um, adj., *calm, kindly, peaceful, gracious*

plaga, -ae, f., *net,* 131

plangor, -ōris, m., *beating of the breast, loud mourning*

planta, -ae, f., *sole of the foot, foot*

plūma, -ae, f., *feather*

plūrimus, -a, -um, adj., used as superl. of **multus,** *most*

poena, -ae, f., *penalty*

Poenus, -a, -um, adj., *Carthaginian*

polus, -ī, m., *sky*

pōnō, -ere, posuī, positum, *place, build, lay;* pass. *lie there,* 681

populō, -āre, -āvī, -ātum, *plunder, carry off, loot*

populus, -ī, m., *people, nation*

porta, -ae, f., *gate*

portō, -āre, -āvī, -ātum, *carry, bring*

portus, -ūs, m., *harbor, port*

poscō, -ere, poposcī, *demand; ask eagerly for,* with double acc.

possum, posse, potuī, irreg., *be able, can;* **si quid possunt,** 382, *if they have any power*

post, prep. with acc. and adv., *after, behind*

posterus, -a, -um, adj., *following, next; of the following day,* 6

postquam, conj., *after that*

potestās, -ātis, f., *power*

potior, -us, adj., comp. of **potis;** *preferable;* neut. **potius,** used as adv., *rather*

potior, -īrī, -ītus sum, with abl., *master, gain possession of*

praeceps, -itis, adj., *head foremost, headlong, with haste*

praecipitō, -āre, -āvī, -ātum, *go headlong, fall headlong, hasten*

praeclārus, -a, -um, adj., *renowned*

praeda, -ae, f., *booty, war prize, prey*

praedictum, -ī, n., *prophecy*

praemium, -ī, n., *reward*

praeripiō, -ripere, -ripuī, -reptum, *seize first or before another*

praesentiō, -sentire, -sensī, -sensum, *perceive first, scent*

praetendō, -tendere, -tendī, -tentum, *extend, hold out before, use as screen*

praetereā, adv., *moreover, besides*

praetereō, -ire, -iī, -ītum, *pass*

praetexō, -texere, -texuī, -textum, *veil*

prāvum, -ī, n., *wrong*

prāvus, -a, -um, adj., *distorted, wrong,*

false

precor, -ārī, -ātus, sum, *pray, beseech, pray for*

premō, -ere, pressī, pressum, *press, weigh down, hide, confine*

pretium, -ī, n., *price*

[prex], precis, f., defect., *prayer*

Priamus, -ī, m., *Priam,* king of Troy at the time of the Trojan war, 343

prīmum, adv., *first;* **ut primum,** *when first, as soon as*

prīmus, -a, -um, superl. adj., *first*

principium, -iī, n., *beginning;* **principio** as adv., *first*

prior, -us, comp. adj., *former;* **prius,** adv., *sooner, before*

prō, prep. with abl., *for, on behalf of, in accordance with*

prō!, interj., *oh! ah!*

probō, -āre, -āvī, -ātum, *approve*

prōcēdō, -ere, -cessī, -cessum, *advance*

procul, adv., *at a distance; afar off*

prōcus, -ī, m., *suitor*

prōdō, -dere, -didī, -ditum, *send forth; carry forward,* 231; *begin, abandon, betray*

proficīscor, -ī, profectus sum, *set forth, issue*

[profor], -ārī, -ātus sum, *speak forth*

profundus, -a, -um, adj., *deep, boundless*

prōgignō, -gignere, -genuī, -genitum, *give birth to*

prōgredior, -ī, -gressus sum, *advance*

prōlēs, -is, f., *offspring*

prōmereor, -ērī, -ītus, *render service*

prōmittō, -mittere, -mīsī, -missum, *promise, engage*

prōnubus, -a, -um, adj., *forwarding marriage,* epithet of Juno, patron-power of wedlock, 166

properō, -āre, -āvī, -ātum, *hasten,*

hurry; impers. pass. **properarī,** 416, *that there is hastening*

proprius, -a, -um, adj., *one's own*

propter, prep. with acc., *on account of*

prōpugnāgulum, -ī, n., *rampant*

Prōserpina, -ae, f., *Proserpine,* wife of Pluto, 698

prospiciō, -spicere, -spexī, -spectum, *look out and see*

prōtinus, adv., *forthwith; in due course,* 196

proximus, -a, -um, adj., used as superl. of **propior,** *nearest*

pūbens, -tis, adj., *full of sap, juicy*

pudor, -oris, m., *shame, modesty*

puer, -erī, m., *boy*

pugna, -ae, f., *battle*

pugnō, -āre, -āvī, -ātum, *fight*

pugnus, -ī, m., *fist*

pulcher, -chra, -chrum, adj., *fair, beautiful*

pulsō, -āre, -āvī, -ātum, *strike, beat*

pulverulentus, -a, -um, adj., *dusty*

Pūnicus, -a, -um, adj., *Phoenician, Carthaginian*

puppis, -is, f., *stern* of a boat; hence *ship*

purpureus, -a, -um, adj., *purple-colored, scarlet, bright*

Pygmalion, -ōnis, m., brother of Dido, 325

pyra, -ae, f., *funeral pyre*

Q

quaerō, -ere, -sīvī, -sītum, *search for, seek, procure*

quālis, -e, adj., *of what sort, such, as, like*

quam, adv., *how; than;* **ante...quam,** *sooner than before;* **quam primum,** *as quickly as possible*

quamquam, conj., *although*

quandō, adv. and conj., *when, since*

quantus, -a, -um, adj., *how great, as great as;* neut. used as adv., **quantum...tantum, 445,** *as high... so deep*

quassō, -āre, -āvī, -ātum, *shake, batter*

quater, adv., *four times*

-que, enclitic conj., *and;* **que...et (que),** *both...and*

quercus, -ūs, f., *oak*

querella, -ae, f., *complaint*

queror, querī, questus, *complain*

questus, -ūs, m., *complaint*

quī, quae, quod, relative pron., *who, which, what*

quī, quae, quod, interrog. adj. pron., *who, what?*

quia, conj., *because*

quīcumque, quaecumque, quodcumque, relative pron., *whoever, whatever*

quid, conj., *why*

quiēs, -ētis, f., *rest*

quiescō, -ere, -ēvī, -ētum, incept., *become quiet, rest*

quiētus, -a, -um, adj., *at rest*

quīn, conj. and adv., *why not? nay more*

quippe, conj. and adv., *doubtless,* ironical

quis, quae, quid, interrog. pron., *who? what?*

quis, quā, quid, indef. pron., *any one, anything*

quisquam, quaequam, quicquam, indef. pron., or subst., *any one or thing at all,* in neg. and interrog. sentences

quisquis, quicquid, indef. pron., *whoever, whatever*

quō, adv., *whither, to what end, in order that*

quondam, adv., *at one time, once, of old, formerly*

quoniam, adv., *since*

quoque, conj., *also*

quot, num. adj., indecl., *how many*

quotiēs, or **quotiens,** adv., *as often as*

R

rabiēs, -eī, f., *rage*

radius, -ī, m., *ray*

rādix, -īcis, f., *root*

rāmus, -ī, m., *bough*

rapidus, -a, -um, adj., *swift*

rapiō, rapere, rapuī, raptum, *seize, rape, hurry*

raptum, -ī, n., *plunder*

rārus, -a, -um, adj., *at intervals; having wide spaces between, wide-meshed,* 131

ratiō, -ōnis, f., *way of thinking, method*

ratis, -is, f., *ship*

recēdō, -ere, -cessī, -cessum, *withdraw, recede, depart, pass away*

recidīvus, -a, -um, adj., *revived, renewed*

recingō, -cingere, -cinxī, -cinctum, *ungirdle*

recipiō, -ere, -cēpī, -ceptum, *receive, recover;* **poenas recepi a, 656,** *I have punished*

reclūdō, -ere, -sī, -sum, *unclose, open, bare, unsheath*

recursō, -āre, -āvī, -ātum, *come running back; course back,* 3

reddō, -ere, -didī, -ditum, *give back; restore*

redeō, -īre, -iī, -itum, *go back, return*

redūcō, -dūcere, -duxī, ductum, *bring back, restore*

refellō, -fellere, -fellī, *contradict, disprove*

referō, -ferre, -rettulī, relātum, *carry back, recall, reproduce, reply, carry off, win*

regīna, -ae, f., *queen*
regiō, -ōnis, f., *region*
rēgius, -a, -um, adj., *royal, imperial*
regnātor, -ōris, m., *ruler*
regnum, -ī, n., *kingdom, domain, empire*; pl. in same sense
regō, -ere, rexī, rectum, *rule, guide, direct*
relinquō, -ere, -līquī, -lictum, *leave behind, abandon*
rēliquiae, -ārum, f. pl., *relics, remnants*
rēmex, -igis, m., *rower*
remittō, -mittere, -mīsī, -missum, *send back, return*
rēmus, -ī, m., *oar*
reor, rērī, ratus, *think*
rēpellō, repellere, reppulī, repulsum, *repel, reject*
reperiō, reperire, repperī, repertum, *discover, find*
repleō, -ēre, -ēvī, -ētum, *fill full*
repōnō, -ere, -posuī, -positum, *replace, deposit, lay*
requiēs, -ētis, acc. sometimes **requiem**, f., *repose, rest*
rēs, reī, f., *any object of thought, thing, affair, business, exploit, circumstance, case*; pl. *fortunes;*
reservō, -āre, -āvī, -ātum, *keep back, reserve*
resignō, -āre, -āvī, -ātum, (1) *unseal, open;* (2) *seal up, close, 244*
resistō, -sistere, -stitī, *stand still, stop, resist*
resolvō, -solvere, -solvī, -solūtum, *loosen, relax*
resonō, -āre, -āvī, *resound*
respiciō, -ere, -spexī, -spectum, *look back for; regard*
restō, -stare, -stitī, *remain*
resurgō, -surgere, -surrexī, -surrectum, *rise again*

rēte, -is, n., *net*
retegō, -tegere, -texī, -tectum, *uncover*
retināculum, -ī, n., *cable, hawser*
retrō, adv., *backwards*
revellō, -vellere, -vellī, -vulsum, *tear off, away, up; pluck*
revinciō, -vincere, -vinxī, -vinctum, *bind, wreathe*
revīsō, -ere, -sī, -sum, *revisit*
revocō, -āre, -āvī, -ātum, *call back, recall*
revolvō, -volvere, -volvī, -volūtum, *roll back*
rex, rēgis, m., *king*
rīdeō, -dēre, -sī, -sum, *laugh*
rigeō, -ēre, *be stiff*
rīte, adv., *duly*
rōbur, -oris, n., *oak, timber*
rogus, -ī, m., *funeral pile* or *pyre*
Rōmānus, -a, -um, adj., *Roman*
roscidus, -a, -um, adj., *dewy*
rūmor, -ōris, m., *rumor*
rumpō, -ere, rūpī, ruptum, *break, burst, let burst*
ruō, -ere, ruī, rutum, *rush; rush onwards, hurry along, fall*
rursus, adv., *again*
rūs, rūris, n., *field*
S
sacer, -cra, -crum, adj., *consecrated, sacred;* **sacra,** *holy things, mysteries, rites, emblems, image, etc.*
sacerdos, -ōtis, m. and f., *priest, priestess*
sacrō, -āre, -āvī, -ātum, *consecrate*
sacrum, -ī, n., *sacrifice,* see **sacer**
saepe, adv., *often*
saeviō, -ire, -iī, -itum, *be cruel, vent wrath, rage, storm*
saevus, -a, -um, adj., *fierce, cruel*
sagitta, -ae, f., *arrow*

saltem, adv., *at least*

saltus, -ūs, m., *glade*

sanctus, -a, -um, adj., *sacred, holy*

sanguineus, -a, -um, adj., *bloody,
bloodshot*

sanguis, -inis, *blood*

sānus, -a, -um, adj., *sound, healthy,* in
body or mind

Sāturnius, -a, -um, adj., *belonging to or
child of Saturn,* 92, 372

sātus, see **sero**

saucius, -a, -um, adj., *wounded*

saxum, -ī, n., *rock, stone*

scaena, -ae, f., *scene, stage*

sceptrum, -ī, n., *royal scepter,* generally
in pl.

scīlicet, adv., *you must know, doubtless,*
ironical (**scire, licet**)

scopulus, -ī, m., *projecting rock*

sē or sēsē, suī, sibī, reflex. pron., 3rd
pers. sing. and pl., *himself, herself,
itself,* etc.

secō, -āre, -uī, sectum, *cut, cleave
through*

sēcrētus, -a, -um, adj., *withdrawn,
separate, secret, in secret* (part. of
secerno, *separate*)

sēcum, for **cum sē,** *with himself,* etc.

secundus, -a, -um, adj., *following;
favorable*

secus, adv., *otherwise*

sed, conj., *but*

sedeō, sedēre, sēdī, sessum, *sit;* of
immovable purpose, *is a fixed
resolve,* 15

sēdēs, -is, f., *seat, abode, palace*

sēdūcō, -dūcere, -duxī, -ductum,
withdraw, divide, part

segnis, -e, adj., *slow, ungraceful*

sēmianimis, -e, adj., *half-dead*

sēmita, -ae, f., *path*

sēmivir, -virī, adj., *half-man,
womanish*

semper, adv., *always*

senex, senis, adj., *old,* subst., *old man*

sensus, -ūs, m., *feeling*

sententia, -ae, f., *opinion, resolve*

sentiō, -īre, sensī, sensum, *think, feel,
perceive*

sepeliō, -īre, -īvi or -iī, sepultum, *bury*

sepulchrum, -ī, n., *tomb*

sequor, -ī, secūtus sum, *follow*

serēnō, -āre, -āvī, -ātum, *lighten;* **spem
fronte serenat,** *shows the calm of
hope upon her brow*

Serestus, -ī, m., *a Trojan, companion of
Aeneas,* 288

Sergestus, -ī, m., *a Trojan, companion
of Aeneas,* 288

sermō, -ōnis, m., *talking, words*

serō, serere, sēvī, satum, *sow;* **satus,**
son of, with abl.

serpens, -tis, m., *serpent*

sertum, -ī, n., *garland*

serviō, -īre, -īvī and -iī, -itum, *be slave,
subject*

servō, -āre, -āvī, -ātum, *guard, keep*

sēsē, see **sē**

seu=sive

sī, conj., *if; to see if,* 85

sīc, adv., *so, thus*

siccō, -āre, -āvī, -ātum, *dry, staunch*

Sīdonius, -a, -um, adj., *Sidonian,
Phoenician*

sīdus, -eris, n., *star, constellation;
season of year,* 309; **sidera dextra,**
578, *fair weather*

signum, -ī, n., *sign, token*

sileō, -ēre, -uī, *be silent;* **silens,** *silent*

silva, -ae, f., *forest*

similis, -e, adj., *like*

simul, adv., *at the same time;* = **simul
atque** or **ac,** *as soon as*

simulō, -āre, -āvī, -ātum, *pretend,*

feign

sine, prep. with abl., *without*

sinō, sinere, sīvī, situm, *permit*

sinus, -ūs, m., *fold of garment, bosom*

sistō, -ere, stitī, statum, *make to stand, stay; fetch,* 634

sitis, -is, f., *thirst, drought*

sīve or seu, conj., *or if;* sive or seu…sive or seu, *whether…or; either if…or if*

sociō, -āre, -āvī, -ātum, *unite*

sōcius, -iī, m., *companion, comrade*

sōl, sōlis, m., *sun*

sollicitō, -āre, -āvī, -ātum, *disquiet*

sōlor, -ārī, -ātus, *console*

solum, -ī, n., *ground*

sōlus, -a, -um, adj., *alone*

solvō, -ere, -vī, solūtum, *loose, unloose, release, set free, relax, break down*

somnus, -ī, m., *sleep, slumber*

sonipēs, -pedis, adj., *sounding with the feet;* subst., *horse,* 135

sonō, -āre, -uī, -ītum, *sound*

sopor, -ōris, m., *slumber*

sopōrifer, -era, -erum, adj., *sleep-giving, drowsy*

soror, -ōris, f., *sister*

sors, -tis, f., *lot,* pl., *oracle*

spargō, -ere, -sī, -sum, *scatter, sprinkle, strew*

spatior, -ārī, -ātus, *pace, walk about*

spatium, -ī, n., *course, space, time*

speciēs, -eī, f., *appearance, form*

specula, -ae, f., *watch-tower, look-out*

spēlunca, -ae, f., *cave*

spernō, spernere, sprēvī, sprētum, *reject, scorn*

spērō, -āre, -āvī, -ātum, *expect, hope*

spēs, -eī, f., *hope, expectation*

spīritus, -ūs, m., *breath, life*

spīrō, -āre, -āvī, -ātum, *breathe*

spolium, -ī, n., *spoil, war prize*

sponte, f., abl. fr. obs. spons: *of free*

will, willingly

spūma, -ae, f., *foam*

stabilis, -e, adj., *lasting, steady*

statuō, -uere, -uī, -ūtum, *make to stand, set, found*

stella, -ae, f., *star*

stellātus, -a, -um, adj., *starred*

stimulō, -āre, -āvī, -ātum, *spur, goad*

stīpes, -itis, m., *trunk, stem*

stīpō, -āre, -āvī, -ātum, *press together; throng around, attend*

stirps, -pis, f., *stock of a tree; lineage, stock, race*

stō, stāre, stetī, stātum, *stand, stand firm, abide*

strātum, -ī, n., *bed or couch covering, bed or couch*

strīdō or strīdeō, -ere or -ēre, -dī, *hiss; gurgle,* 689

strīdor, -ōris, m., *noise, roar, groaning, whizzing*

stringō, stringere, strinxī, strictum, *touch lightly, draw one thing lightly against another, unsheath*

struō, -ere, struxī, structum, *heap up, build, plan*

studium, -ī, n., *eager desire, zest, zeal*

Stygius, -a, -um, adj., *belonging to the Styx,* the underworld river, *Stygian*

suādeō, -ēre, suasī, suasum, *persuade, invite to*

sub, prep. with acc. or abl., *under, down to, down among, up to; at a crisis,* 460

subeō, -īre, -īvī or -iī, -itum, *undergo, lift* a burden, 599

subitus, -a, -um, adj., *sudden*

sublīmis, -e, adj., *uplifted, towering*

submittō, -ere, -mīsī, -missum, *lower, submit*

subnectō, -nectere, -nexuī, -nexum, *tie beneath*

subnixus, -a, -um, adj., *resting on*

suboles, -is, f., *offspring*

subrīgō, see surgo

subter, adv., *underneath*

succēdō, -ere, -cessī, -cessum, *enter*

succumbō, -cumbere, -cubuī,
-cubitum, *fall prostrate, yield*

sum, esse, fuī, irreg., *be*

summa, -ae, f., *sum total*

summus, -a, -um, adj. used as superl.
of superus; *highest, topmost, lofty*

sūmō, sūmere, sumpsī, sumptum,
take, employ

super, adv. and prep. with acc. or abl.,
*above, over; on the top of, on behalf
of*

superbus, -a, -um, adj., *haughty, proud*

superinpōnō, -pōnere, -posuī,
-positum, *lay above*

superus, -a, -um, adj., *upper, above;*
superī, *gods*

supīnus, -a, -um, adj., *on the back;
upturned,* of hands in prayer, 205

supplex, -icis, adj., *bending the knees,
suppliant*

supplicium, -ī, n., *punishment*

supra, prep. with acc., *above*

surgo or subrigo or surrigō, -ere,
surrexī, surrectum, *erect, prick up
ear; rise, grow up*

suspiciō, -ere, -spexī, -spectum,
*undertake, take up, support; bear
children*

suspensus, -a, -um, perf. part. pass.
of suspendo as adj., *fluttering,
agitated*

suspiciō, -spicere, -spexī, -spectum,
*look at from underneath, suspect,
mislike*

suus, -a, -um, possess. adj., *his-, her-,
its-, their own;* suī, *his friends,* etc.

Sychaeus, -ī, m., first husband of Dido,

20, etc.; as adj. 552

Syrtis, -is, f., *Syrtis,* sand-bank on N.
Coast of Africa, 41

T

taceō, -ēre, -uī, -itum, *be silent*

tacitus, -a, -um, adj., *silent*

taeda, -ae, f., *torch, marriage-torch*

taedet, -ēre, -uit, or taesum, impers.
with acc. and gen., *it tires of,
wearies to*

tālāria, -ium, n. pl., *ankle-wings,
winged sandals* of Mercury, 239

tālis, -e, adj., *such*

tamen, adv., *nevertheless, in spite of all,
yet*

tandem, adv., *at last, at length*

tangō, -ere, tetigī, tactum, *touch,
reach, meddle with*

tantus, -a, -um, adj., *so great;* tantum,
adv., *so much, not less,* 150; *only*

Tartara, -ōrum, n. pl., *infernal regions,
underworld,* 243, 446

tectum, -ī, n., *roof, shelter, house,
palace* (tego)

tēcum, i.e., cum te, *with you*

tegō, -ere, texī, tectum, *cover, conceal*

tēla, -ae, f., *web,* of woven garment

tellus, -ūris, f., *earth, land;* personified,
166

tēlum, -ī, n., *missile, weapon, dart*

templum, -ī, n., *temple*

temptō, -āre, -āvī, -ātum, *try, make
trial of*

tempus, -oris, n., *time;* pl., *temples* of
the head

tenax, -ācis, adj., *tenacious,* with gen.,
tenacious of

tendō, -ere, tetendī, tensum and
tentum, *stretch, extend*

teneō, -ēre, -uī, -tum, *hold, grasp; hold
on course; master,* 90; *haunt,* 527

tenuis, -e, adj., *thin, fine*

ter, num. adv., *thrice*

tergeminus, -a, -um, adj., *triple*

terminus, -ī, m., *boundary, goal*

terō, terere, trīvī, tritum, *wear; spend time*

terra, -ae, f., *land;* pl., *the lands, the Earth;* personified, 178

terreō, -ēre, -uī, -itum, *alarm*

terribilis, -e, adj., *terrifying*

terrificō, -āre, -āvī, -ātum, *scare*

testor, -ārī, -ātus sum, *invoke, summon as a witness, swear by*

Teucer or Teucrus, -crī, m., ancient king of Troy, son-in-law of Dardanus

Teucrī, -ōrum and -um, m. pl., *Trojans*

thalamus, -ī, m., *marriage-bed, chamber, marriage*

Thēbae, -ārum, f., pl., *Thebes,* capital of Boeotia in Greece

Thyīas (disyllable), -adis, f., *Thyiad, Bacchante,* 302

tigris, -is and -idis, acc. tigrim, f., *tigress*

timeō, -ēre, -uī, *fear*

timor, -ōris, m., *fear, cowardice*

Tītan, -ānis, m., *Titan,* esp., *the Titan, the sun,* son of Hyperion and Thea, 119

Tīthōnus, -ī, m., husband of Aurora, 585

tonitru, -ūs, n., *thunder*

tonō, -āre, -uī, -itum, *thunder*

torqueō, -ere, torsī, tortum, *twist, turn, hurl, sway*

torus, -ī, m., *couch*

tot, num. adj. indecl., *so many*

totidem, num. adj. indecl., *just so many*

totiens, adv., *so many times*

tōtus, -a, -um, adj., *the whole*

trabs, -is, f., *trunk* of a tree; *beam, ship*

tractābilis, -e, adj., *capable of being worked by the hand, manageable, pliant;* by metaph. of the sky, non tr., *impracticable, forbidding,* 53; of a man, *unyielding* (traho)

trādō, -dere, -didī, -ditum, *surrender, submit*

trahō, -ere, traxī, tractum, *draw, drag, trail*

trānō, -āre, -āvī, -ātum, *float, swim across*

transmittō, -ere, -mīsī, -missum, *send across, traverse*

transtrum, -ī, n., *cross-bench*

tremō, -ere, -uī, *tremble, quiver;* tremens, *trembling*

trepidō, -āre, -āvī, -ātum, *be alarmed, hurry; be astir,* 121

trepidus, -a, -um, adj., *trembling, excited*

trēs, tria, num. adj., *three*

trietēricus, -a, -um, adj., *recurring every three years, triennial*

tristis, -e, adj., *sad, gloomy*

triumphus, -ī, m., *triumphal procession, triumph*

trivium, -ī, n., *junction of three roads, crossroads*

Troia, -ae, f., *Troy*

Troiānus, -a, -um, adj., *Trojan*

Trōs, -ōis, m., *a Trojan*

trūdō, -dere, -sī, -sum, *push*

tū, tuī, etc., second pers. pron. *you*

tuba, -ae, f., *trumpet*

tueor, -ērī, -itus, *look at, eye*

tum, adv., *then*

tundō, tundere, tutudī, tunsum, *beat heavily; assail,* 448

turbidus, -a, -um, adj., *stormy, wild, angry*

turbō, -āre, -āvī, -ātum, *disturb, set in an uproar*

tūricremus, -a, -um, adj., *incense-*

burning, 453
turpis, -e, adj., *base, disgraceful*
turris, -is, f., *tower*
tūtus, -a, -um, adj., *protected, safe*
tuus, -a, -um, possess. adj., *your*
tyrannus, -ī, m., *monarch*
Tyrius, -a, -um, *Tyrian*
Tyrus or **Tyros, -ī,** f., *Tyre,* 36, 43, 670
U
ūber, -eris, n., *teat, udder*
ubī, adv., *when, where*
ulciscor, -ī, ultus sum, *avenge*
ullus, -a, -um, adj., *any*
ultimus, -a, -um, superl. adj., *last, farthest, utmost;* comp. **ulterior**
ultor, -ōris, m., *avenger*
ultrix, -īcis, f., adj., *avenging*
ultrō, adv., *beyond* what would naturally be expected, *unasked, voluntarily, unchallenged, first, even, actually*
ululātus, -ūs, m., *loud crying,* esp. of women, *howling* of animals
ululō, -āre, -āvī, -ātum, *howl, wail; shout* of festive cries, 168; perf. p. pass. **ululata,** 609, *whose name is yelled*
umbra, -ae, f., *shade, ghost, phantom*
ūmeō, -ēre, *be wet*
umerus, -ī, m., *shoulder*
ūmidus, -a, -um, adj., *wet, damp*
umquam, adv., *ever, at any time*
ūnā, adv., *together, at once*
ūnanimus, -a, -um, adj., *one-souled, sympathizing*
unda, -ae, f., *wave, water*
undique, adv., *from all sides*
undōsus, -a, -um, adj., *full of waves, billowy*
unguis, -is, m., *nail*
unguō, unguere, unxī, unctum, *smear, caulk*

ūnus, -a, -um, adj., *one, alone*
urbs, -bis, f., *city*
ūrō, ūrere, ussī, ustum, *burn*
ūsus, -ūs, m., *use, service*
ut, conj., *as, when;* **ut prīmum,** *as soon as*
uterque, utraque, utrumque, pron., *each* of two
uxōrius, -a, -um, adj., *uxorious, controlled by a wife*
V
vacca, -ae, f., *cow*
vacuus, -a, -um, adj., *empty*
vādō, -ere, *go*
vāgīna, -ae, f., *sheath*
vagor, -ārī, -ātus, *roam, wander*
valeō, -ēre, -uī, -itum, *be strong,* with inf., *be able to, can*
validus, -a, -um, adj., *strong*
vallis, -is, f., *valley*
vānus, -a, -um, adj., *empty, ungrounded*
varius, -a, -um, adj., *varying, changeable*
vātēs, -is, m. and f., *prophet, prophetess; bard, seer*
-ve, enclitic conj., *or*
vel, adv. and conj., *or, even;* **vel...vel,** *either...or*
vellus, -eris, n., *fleece*
vēlox, -ōcis, adj., *swift*
vēlum, -ī, n., *sail*
velut or **velutī,** conj. and adv., *as, as if*
vēna, -ae, f., *vein,* pl., *life blood,* 2
vēnābulum, -ī, n., *hunting-spear*
venēnum, -ī, n., *poison*
vēnia, -ae, f., *indulgence, pardon*
veniō, -īre, vēnī, ventum, *come,* impers. **ventum est,** *they had come,* 151
vēnor, -arī, -ātus, *hunt*
ventus, -ī, m., *wind*
Venus, -eris, f., *Venus,* mother of

Aeneas, goddess of love, 33, etc.

verbum, -ī, n., *word*

vereor, -ērī, -itus, *fear*

vērō, adv., *truly; in truth,* ironical

verrō, -ere, -ī, versum, *sweep; sweep over*

versō, -āre, -āvī, -ātum, *turn and turn, revolve*

vertex, -icis, m., *the turning thing; head, crest, summit*

vertō, -ere, -tī, -sum, *turn*

vērum, adv., *truly, but yet, but*

vērum, -ī, n., *truth*

vestīgium, -ī, n., *footstep, trace*

vestis, -is, f., *garment, robe*

vetus, -eris, adj., *old*

vexō, -āre, -āvī, -ātum, *harass*

via, -ae, f., *path, course, way;* pl. *journeyings*

vicissim, adv., *by turns, in turn*

videō, vidēre, vīdī, vīsum, *see;* pass. **videor,** *I seem*

vigeō, -ēre, *grow vigorous, flourish*

vigil, -ilis, adj., *wakeful, watchful, undying*

vigilō, -āre, -āvī, -ātum, *wake, watch*

vincō, vincere, vīcī, victum, *conquer*

vinculum or **vinclum, -ī,** n., *chain; bands* of sandals, 518

vindicō, -āre, -āvī, -ātum, *claim as free, rescue*

vīnum, -ī, n., *wine*

violō, -āre, -āvī, -ātum, *outrage*

vir, virī, gen. pl., **virum,** m., *man, hero, husband*

virga, -ae, f., *rod, wand*

virgō, -inis, f., *maiden*

virtūs, -ūtis, f., *manliness, valor*

vīs, vim, vī, f., *force; number;* pl. **vīrēs, -ium,** *strength*

vīsum, -ī, n., *sight, appearance*

vīsus, -ūs, m., *sight*

vīta, -ae, f., *life*

vitta, -ae, f., *fillet, headband* used by priests and for religious decorations

vivō, -ere, vixī, victum, *live*

vix, adv., *scarcely, with difficulty*

vocō, -āre, -āvī, -ātum, *call, call on, summon, invoke, name*

volātilis, -e, adj., *flying*

vulnus or **volnus, -eris,** n., *wound*

volō, -āre, -āvī, -ātum, *fly*

volō, velle, -uī, *wish, be willing, consent*

voltus, -ūs, m., *face, look*

volucris, -is, f., *bird*

voluntās, -ātis, f., *will, sanction*

volūtō, -āre, -āvī, -ātum, *keep rolling, revolve*

volvō, -ere, -vī, volūtum, *roll, revolve;* pass., *roll,* intrans.

vōtum, -ī, n., *vow, prayer*

vox, vōcis, f., *voice, words*

X

Xanthus, -ī, m., *river in Lycia,* 143

Z

Zephyrus ī, m., *west wind, breeze,* 223, 562

Index

This index lists grammatical, metrical, and stylistic items mentioned in the commentary; numbers refer to lines in the Latin text and the corresponding commentary notes.

ablative absolute 45-6, 128
ablative, of cause 42-4, of comparison 31, 174, of place 2, 28-9, 35-8, 42-4, 489, instrumental 2, of origin/place from which 35-8, 42-4, of quality/description 11, of separation 479, of specification 35-8, 40-1, of time or duration of time 32
accusative, adverbial 65, cognate 468, cognate used adverbially 395, double, after a verb of asking 50, of place to which 106, of respect 65
address of self by name 596-9
adjective, compound 135, diminutive 328, neuter used as substantive 188-90, proleptic 22
adverb, modifying adjective 8
alliteration 28-9, 81, 135, 160, 216-17, 390, 460-7, Appendix B
ambiguity, temporary syntactical 19, 124
anaphora 369-70, 548, Appendix B
anastrophe of preposition 320-1
apostrophe 27, 65, 408, 412, 548, Appendix B
arsis, syllable lengthened in 64, 146, 222, Appendix A
assonance 271, 463, Appendix B
asyndeton 373, Appendix B

attraction 347-50
conditions, contrary-to-fact 15-16, 311-13, 327, with indicative of *posse* in place of subjunctive 19
consonance 390, Appendix B
dative, of agent 31, double 59, predicate 520, of purpose 59, with simple verb as if with compound 69-73, with verbs of contending 35-8
ellipse 12, 53, 60, 80, 115-16, 113, 151, 200-2, 383, 529, 540, 611, 620 Appendix B
enallage 226, 303, 385, 477, 506, 623, 683, Appendix B
enjambment 69-73, 311, 390, Appendix B
epanalepsis 24-6, 174, 248, Appendix B
etymologizing 2, 3, 271, Appendix B
explanatory clause 639-40
focalization 141, 172, 281
free indirect discourse 281
genitive of sphere in which/specification 203, 300
genitive, objective 65, 178, 272, objective with adjective 188-90, possessive 65, subjective 274
gerund 175, in genitive with adjective of knowledge 554
gerundive 290